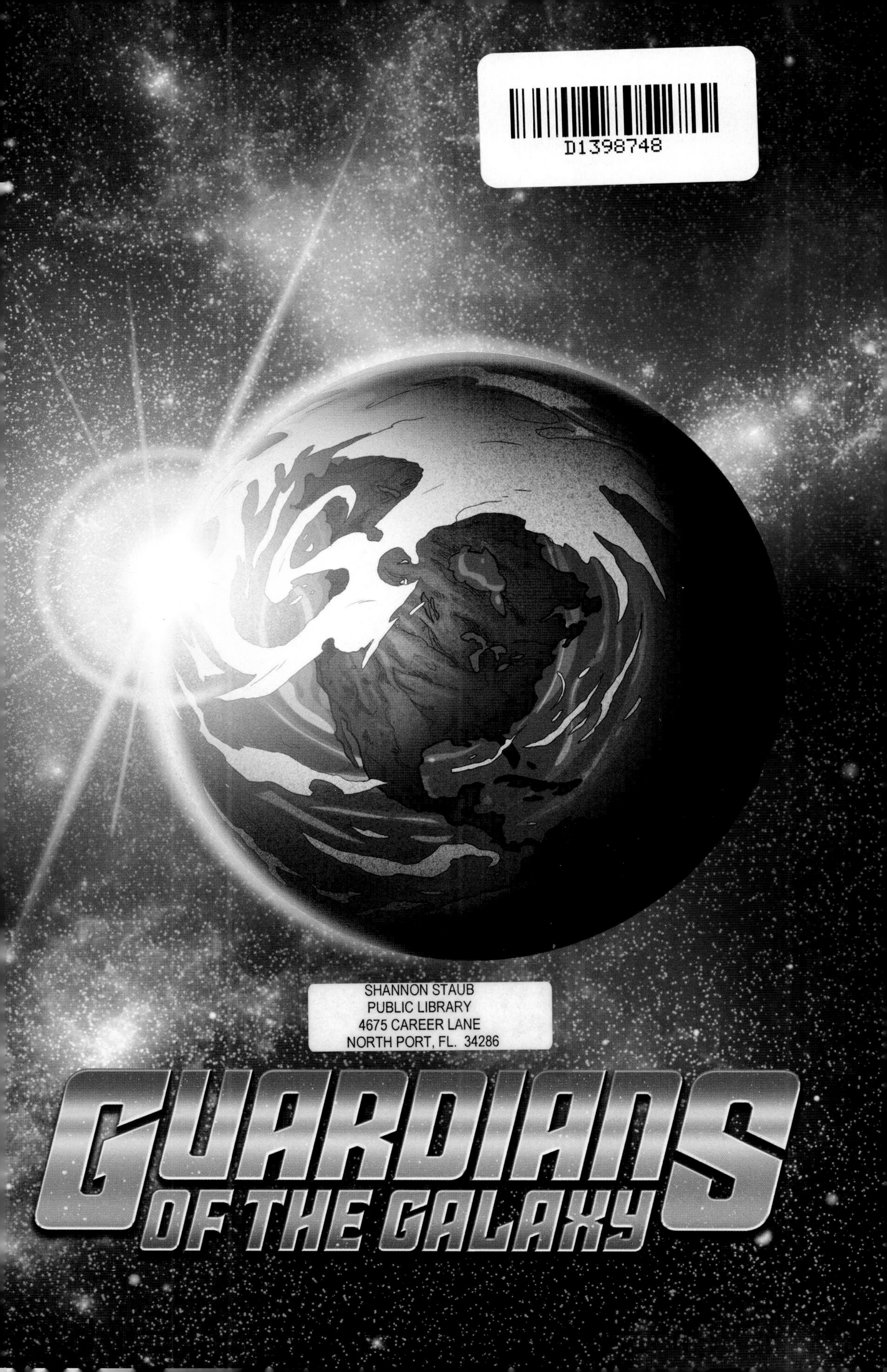
GUARDIANS
OF THE GALAXY

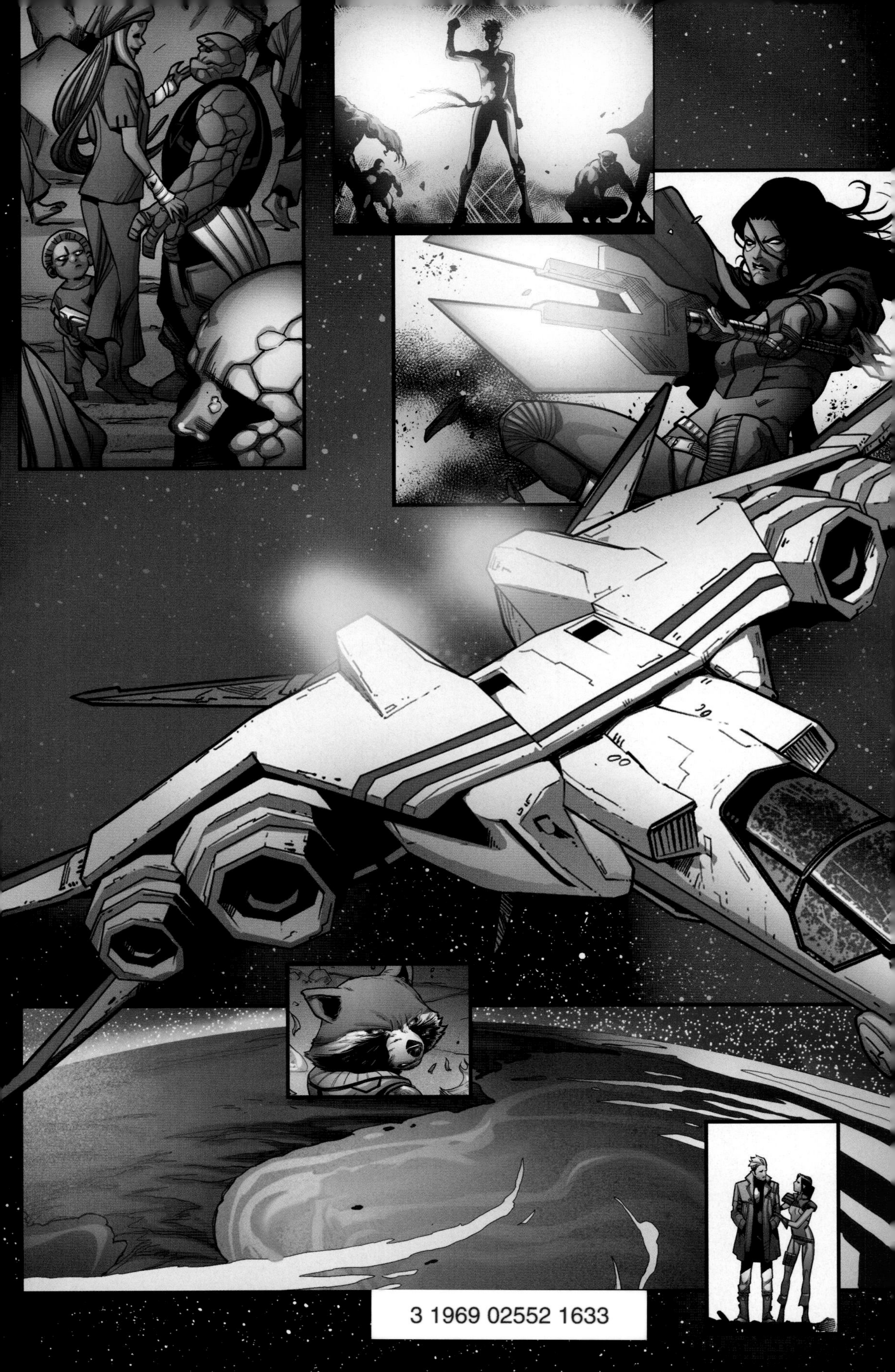

GUARDIANS OF THE GALAXY

OF THE GALAXY

CIVIL WAR II

BRIAN MICHAEL BENDIS
WRITER

VALERIO SCHITI [#11-13]
& KEVIN MAGUIRE [#14]
ARTISTS

RICHARD ISANOVE
COLOR ARTIST

VC's CORY PETIT
LETTERER

ARTHUR ADAMS & JASON KEITH [#11-13] **& KEVIN MAGUIRE** [#14] COVER ART

KATHLEEN WISNESKI
ASSISTANT EDITOR

DARREN SHAN
ASSOCIATE EDITOR

JORDAN D. WHITE
EDITOR

FREE COMIC BOOK DAY 2016

JIM CHEUNG
PENCILER

JOHN DELL
INKER

JUSTIN PONSOR
COLORIST

VC's CLAYTON COWLES
LETTERER

JIM CHEUNG &
JUSTIN PONSOR
COVER ART

ALANNA SMITH
ASSISTANT EDITOR

TOM BREVOORT
WITH **WIL MOSS**
EDITORS

COLLECTION EDITOR: *JENNIFER GRÜNWALD*
ASSISTANT EDITOR: *CAITLIN O'CONNELL*
ASSOCIATE MANAGING EDITOR: *KATERI WOODY*
EDITOR, SPECIAL PROJECTS: *MARK D. BEAZLEY*
VP PRODUCTION & SPECIAL PROJECTS: *JEFF YOUNGQUIST*
SVP PRINT, SALES & MARKETING: *DAVID GABRIEL*
BOOK DESIGNER: *JAY BOWEN*

EDITOR IN CHIEF: *AXEL ALONSO*
CHIEF CREATIVE OFFICER: *JOE QUESADA*
PRESIDENT: *DAN BUCKLEY*
EXECUTIVE PRODUCER: *ALAN FINE*

ARDIANS OF THE GALAXY: NEW GUARD VOL. 3 — CIVIL WAR II. Contains material originally published in magazine form as GUARDIANS OF THE GALAXY #11-14 and FREE COMIC BOOK DAY 2016 (CIVIL WAR II) #1. First printing 7. ISBN# 978-1-302-90302-2. Published by MARVEL WORLDWIDE, INC., a subsidiary of MARVEL ENTERTAINMENT, LLC. OFFICE OF PUBLICATION: 135 West 50th Street, New York, NY 10020. Copyright © 2017 MARVEL No similarity een of the names, characters, persons, and/or institutions in this magazine with those of any living or dead person or institution is intended, and any such similarity which may exist is purely coincidental. **Printed in the U.S.A.** DAN LEY, President, Marvel Entertainment; JOE QUESADA, Chief Creative Officer; TOM BREVOORT, SVP of Publishing; DAVID BOGART, SVP of Business Affairs & Operations, Publishing & Partnership; C.B. CEBULSKI, VP of Brand Management velopment, Asia; DAVID GABRIEL, SVP of Sales & Marketing, Publishing; JEFF YOUNGQUIST, VP of Production & Special Projects; DAN CARR, Executive Director of Publishing Technology; ALEX MORALES, Director of Publishing Operations; N CRESPI, Production Manager; STAN LEE, Chairman Emeritus. For information regarding advertising in Marvel Comics or on Marvel.com, please contact Vit DeBellis, Integrated Sales Manager, at vdebellis@marvel.com. For Marvel cription inquiries, please call 888-511-5480. **Manufactured between 7/21/2017 and 8/22/2017 by LSC COMMUNICATIONS INC., KENDALLVILLE, IN, USA.**

8 7 6 5 4 3 2 1

FREE COMIC BOOK DAY

CIVIL WAR II

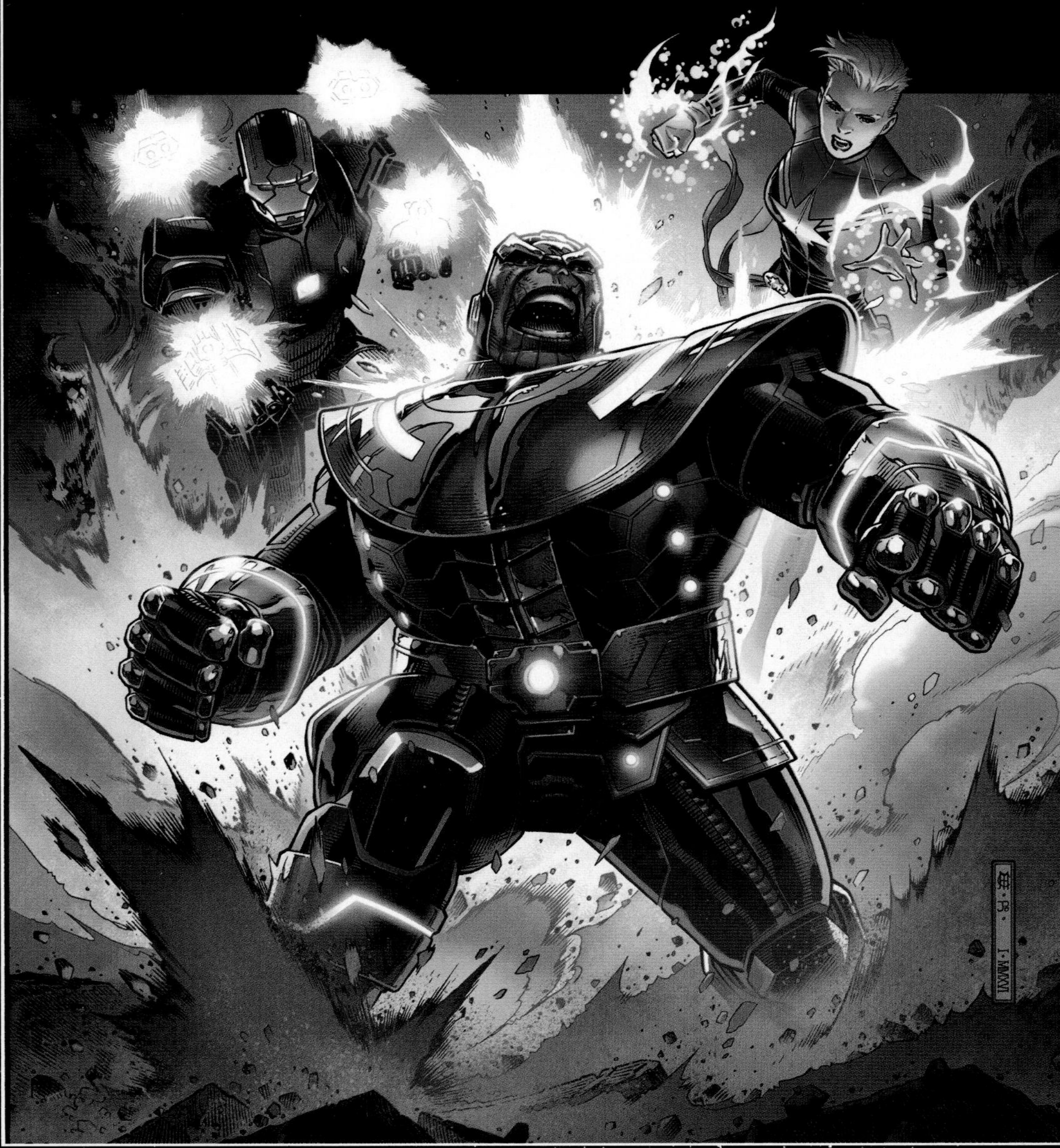

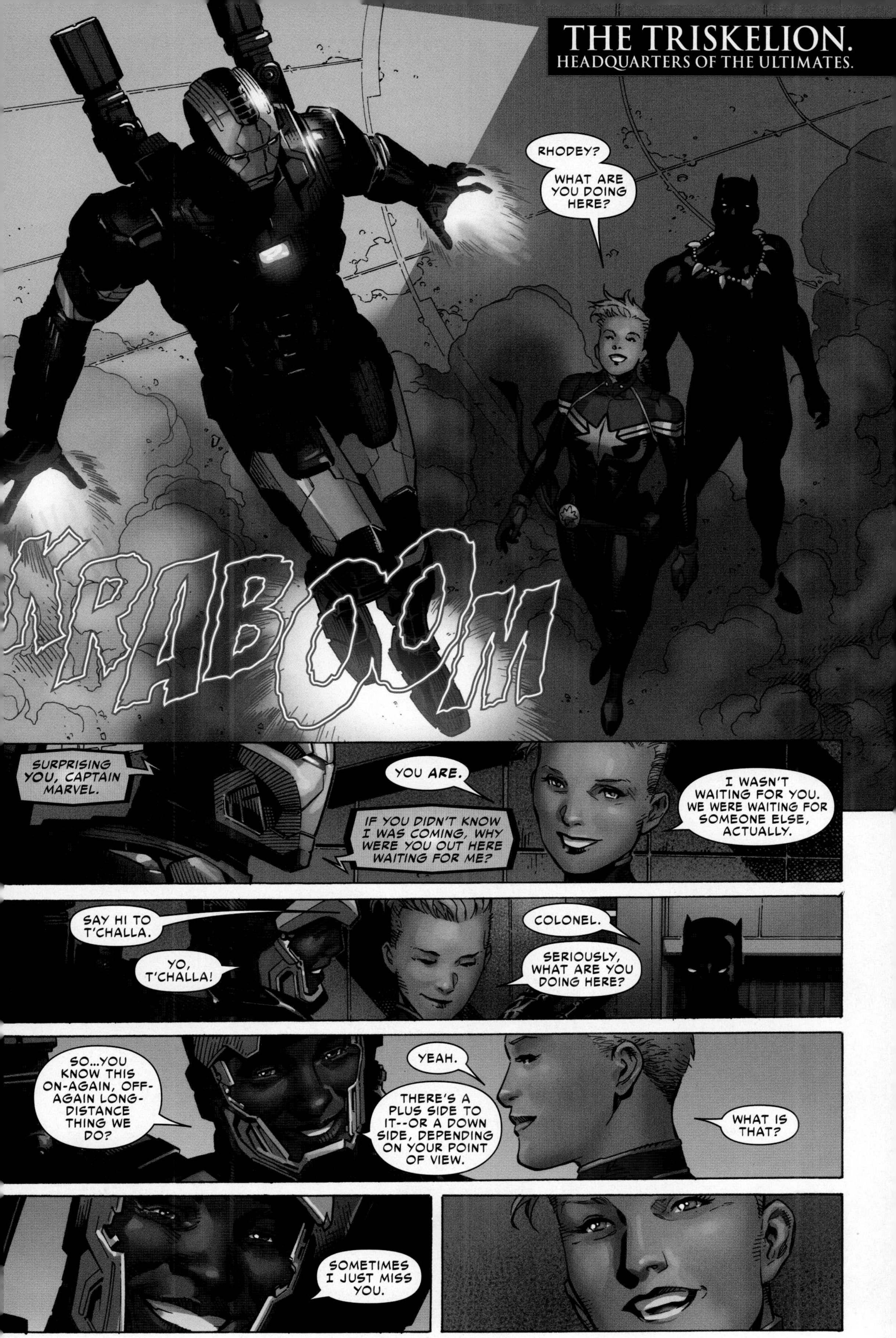
THE TRISKELION.
HEADQUARTERS OF THE ULTIMATES.
RHODEY?
WHAT ARE YOU DOING HERE?
KRABOOM
SURPRISING YOU, CAPTAIN MARVEL.
YOU ARE.
IF YOU DIDN'T KNOW I WAS COMING, WHY WERE YOU OUT HERE WAITING FOR ME?
I WASN'T WAITING FOR YOU. WE WERE WAITING FOR SOMEONE ELSE, ACTUALLY.
SAY HI TO T'CHALLA.
YO, T'CHALLA!
COLONEL.
SERIOUSLY, WHAT ARE YOU DOING HERE?
SO...YOU KNOW THIS ON-AGAIN, OFF-AGAIN LONG-DISTANCE THING WE DO?
YEAH.
THERE'S A PLUS SIDE TO IT--OR A DOWN SIDE, DEPENDING ON YOUR POINT OF VIEW.
WHAT IS THAT?
SOMETIMES I JUST MISS YOU.

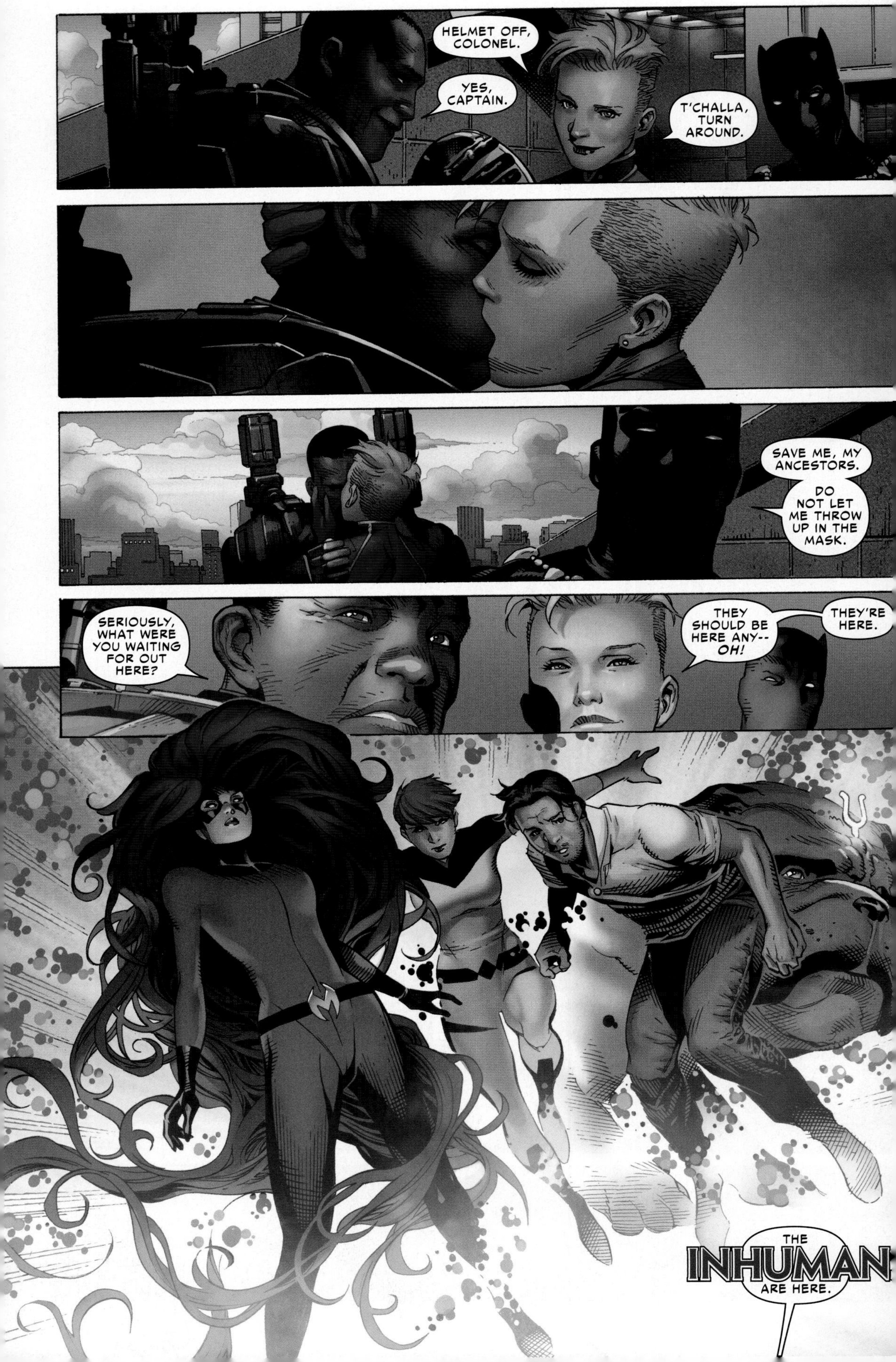
HELMET OFF, COLONEL.
YES, CAPTAIN.
T'CHALLA, TURN AROUND.
SAVE ME, MY ANCESTORS.
DO NOT LET ME THROW UP IN THE MASK.
SERIOUSLY, WHAT WERE YOU WAITING FOR OUT HERE?
THEY SHOULD BE HERE ANY-- OH!
THEY'RE HERE.
THE INHUMANS ARE HERE.

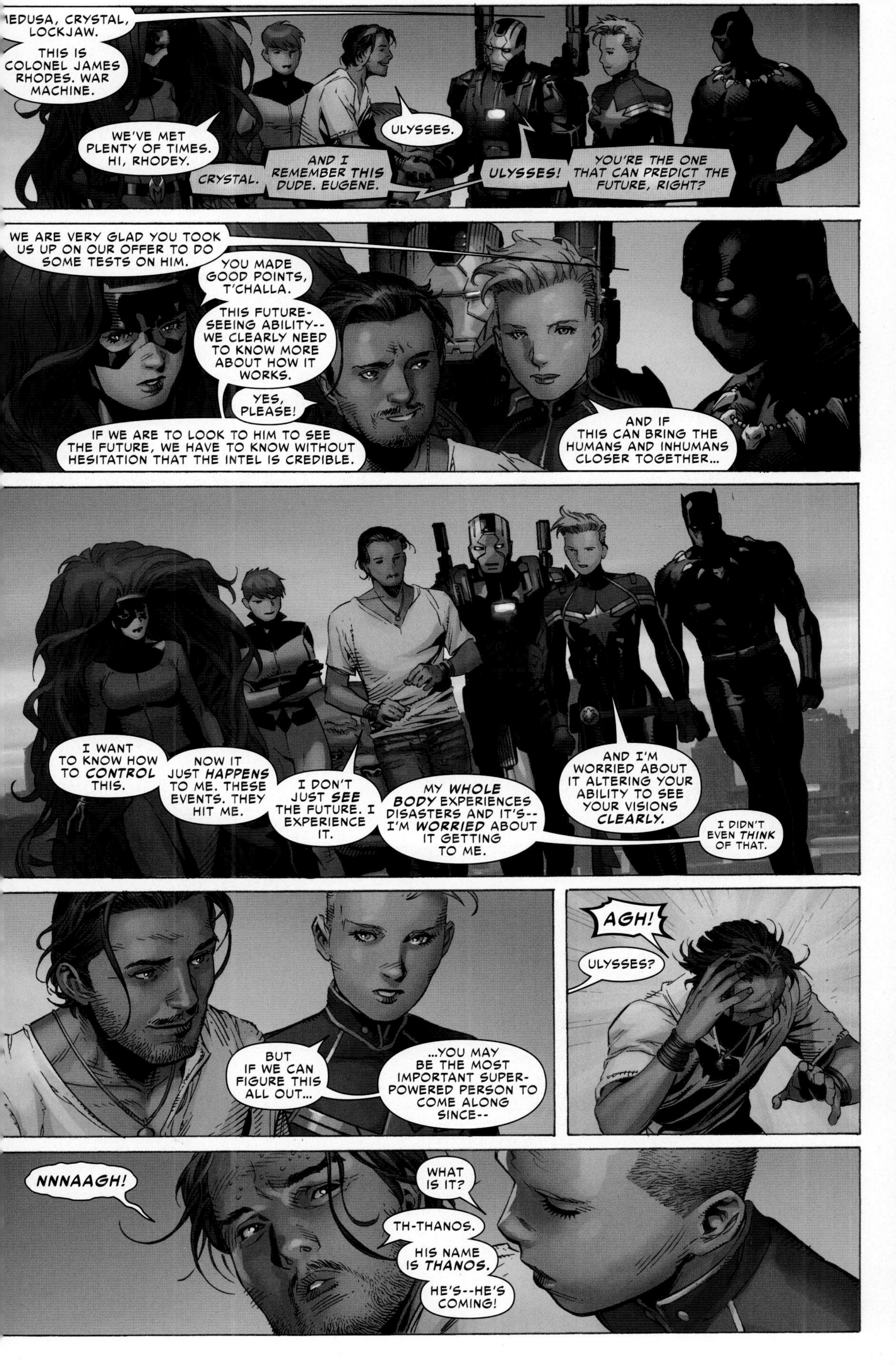
MEDUSA, CRYSTAL, LOCKJAW.
THIS IS COLONEL JAMES RHODES. WAR MACHINE.
WE'VE MET PLENTY OF TIMES. HI, RHODEY.
CRYSTAL.
AND I REMEMBER THIS DUDE. EUGENE.
ULYSSES.
ULYSSES!
YOU'RE THE ONE THAT CAN PREDICT THE FUTURE, RIGHT?
WE ARE VERY GLAD YOU TOOK US UP ON OUR OFFER TO DO SOME TESTS ON HIM.
YOU MADE GOOD POINTS, T'CHALLA.
THIS FUTURE-SEEING ABILITY-- WE CLEARLY NEED TO KNOW MORE ABOUT HOW IT WORKS.
YES, PLEASE!
IF WE ARE TO LOOK TO HIM TO SEE THE FUTURE, WE HAVE TO KNOW WITHOUT HESITATION THAT THE INTEL IS CREDIBLE.
AND IF THIS CAN BRING THE HUMANS AND INHUMANS CLOSER TOGETHER...
I WANT TO KNOW HOW TO CONTROL THIS.
NOW IT JUST HAPPENS TO ME. THESE EVENTS. THEY HIT ME.
I DON'T JUST SEE THE FUTURE. I EXPERIENCE IT.
MY WHOLE BODY EXPERIENCES DISASTERS AND IT'S-- I'M WORRIED ABOUT IT GETTING TO ME.
AND I'M WORRIED ABOUT IT ALTERING YOUR ABILITY TO SEE YOUR VISIONS CLEARLY.
I DIDN'T EVEN THINK OF THAT.
BUT IF WE CAN FIGURE THIS ALL OUT...
...YOU MAY BE THE MOST IMPORTANT SUPER-POWERED PERSON TO COME ALONG SINCE--
AGH!
ULYSSES?
NNNAAGH!
WHAT IS IT?
TH-THANOS.
HIS NAME IS THANOS.
HE'S--HE'S COMING!

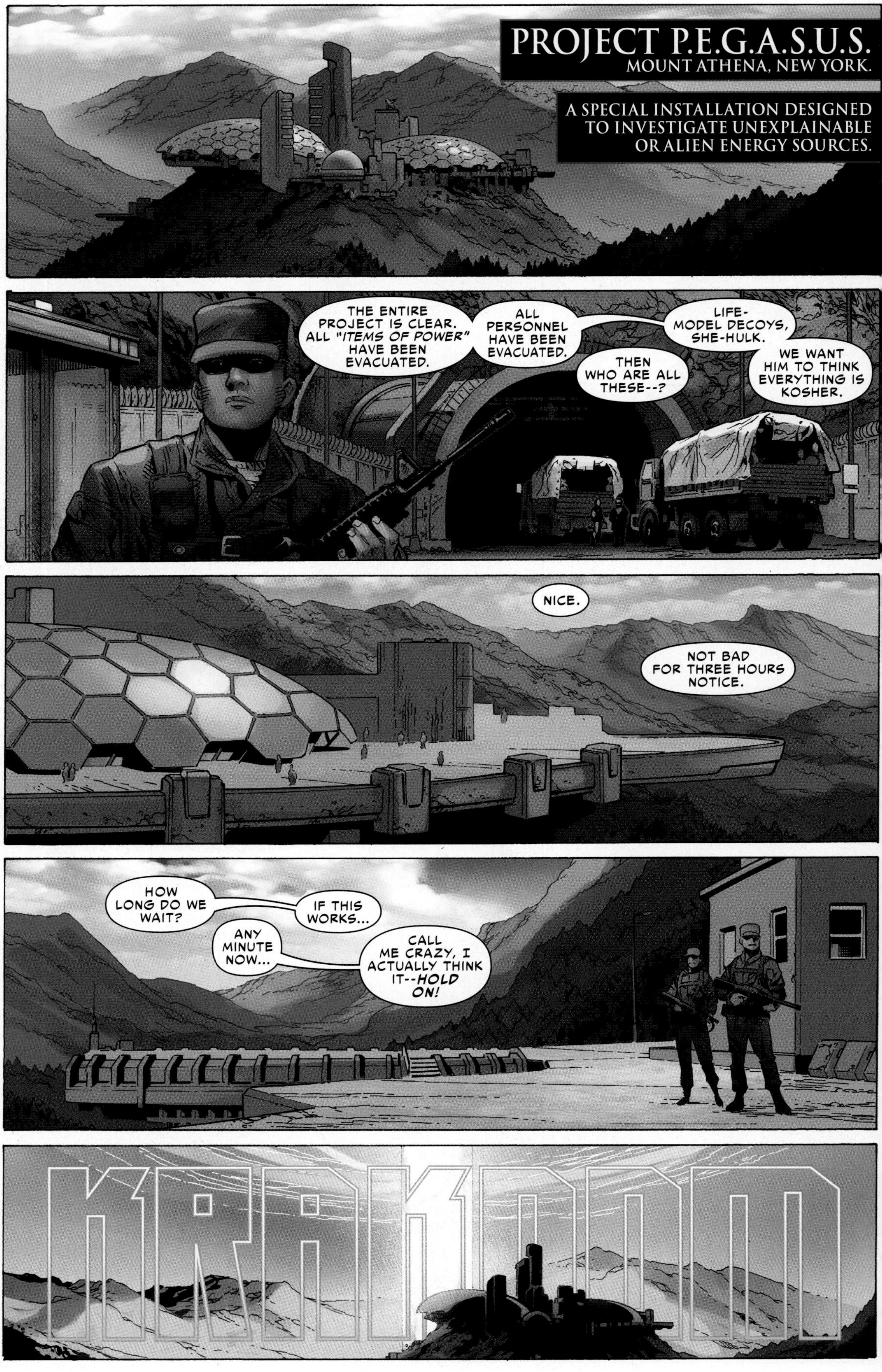
PROJECT P.E.G.A.S.U.S.
MOUNT ATHENA, NEW YORK.
A SPECIAL INSTALLATION DESIGNED TO INVESTIGATE UNEXPLAINABLE OR ALIEN ENERGY SOURCES.
THE ENTIRE PROJECT IS CLEAR. ALL "ITEMS OF POWER" HAVE BEEN EVACUATED.
ALL PERSONNEL HAVE BEEN EVACUATED.
LIFE-MODEL DECOYS, SHE-HULK.
THEN WHO ARE ALL THESE--?
WE WANT HIM TO THINK EVERYTHING IS KOSHER.
NICE.
NOT BAD FOR THREE HOURS NOTICE.
HOW LONG DO WE WAIT?
IF THIS WORKS...
ANY MINUTE NOW...
CALL ME CRAZY, I ACTUALLY THINK IT--HOLD ON!
KRAKOOM

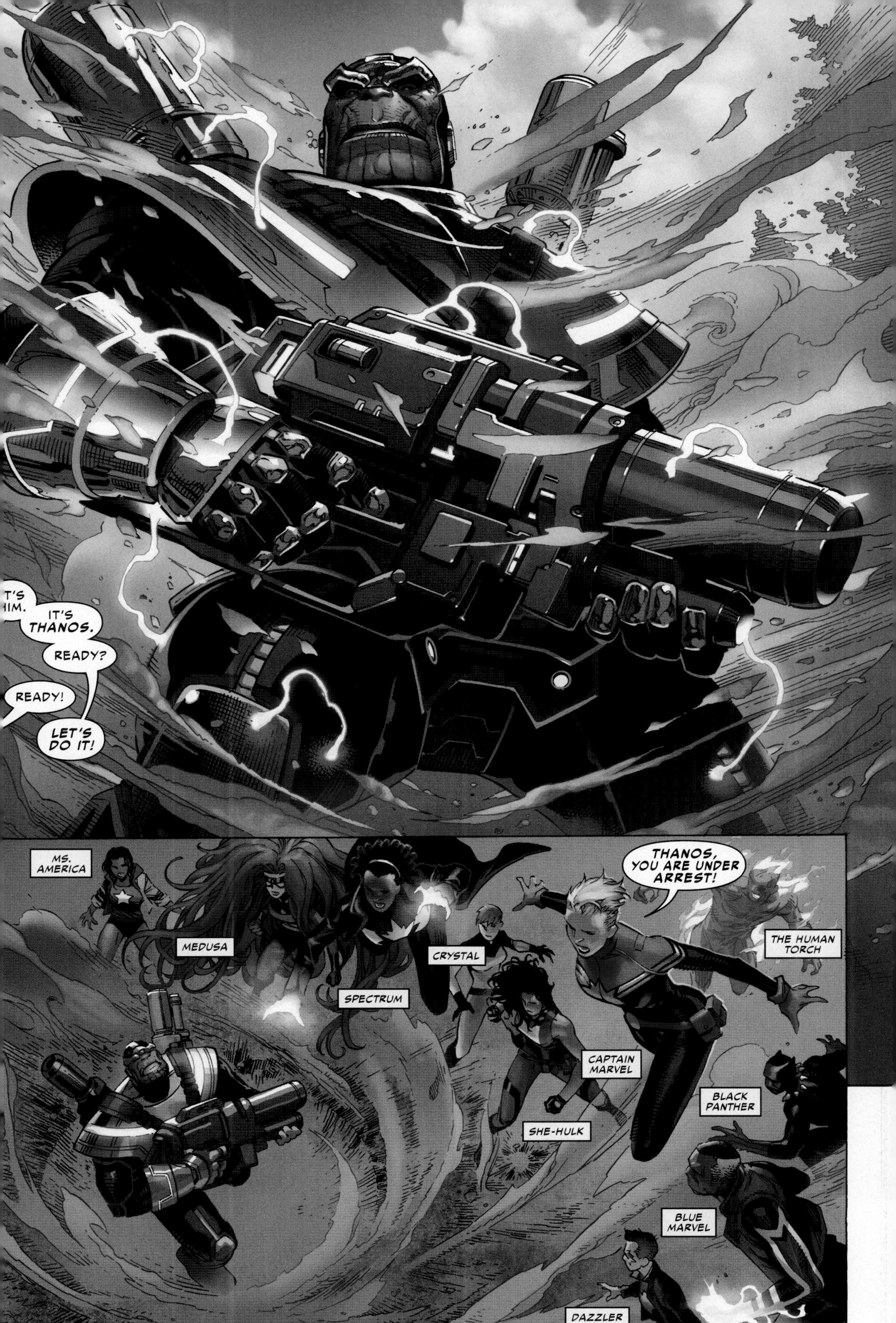
IT'S THANOS.
READY?
READY!
LET'S DO IT!
MS. AMERICA
MEDUSA
SPECTRUM
CRYSTAL
THANOS, YOU ARE UNDER ARREST!
THE HUMAN TORCH
CAPTAIN MARVEL
SHE-HULK
BLACK PANTHER
BLUE MARVEL
DAZZLER

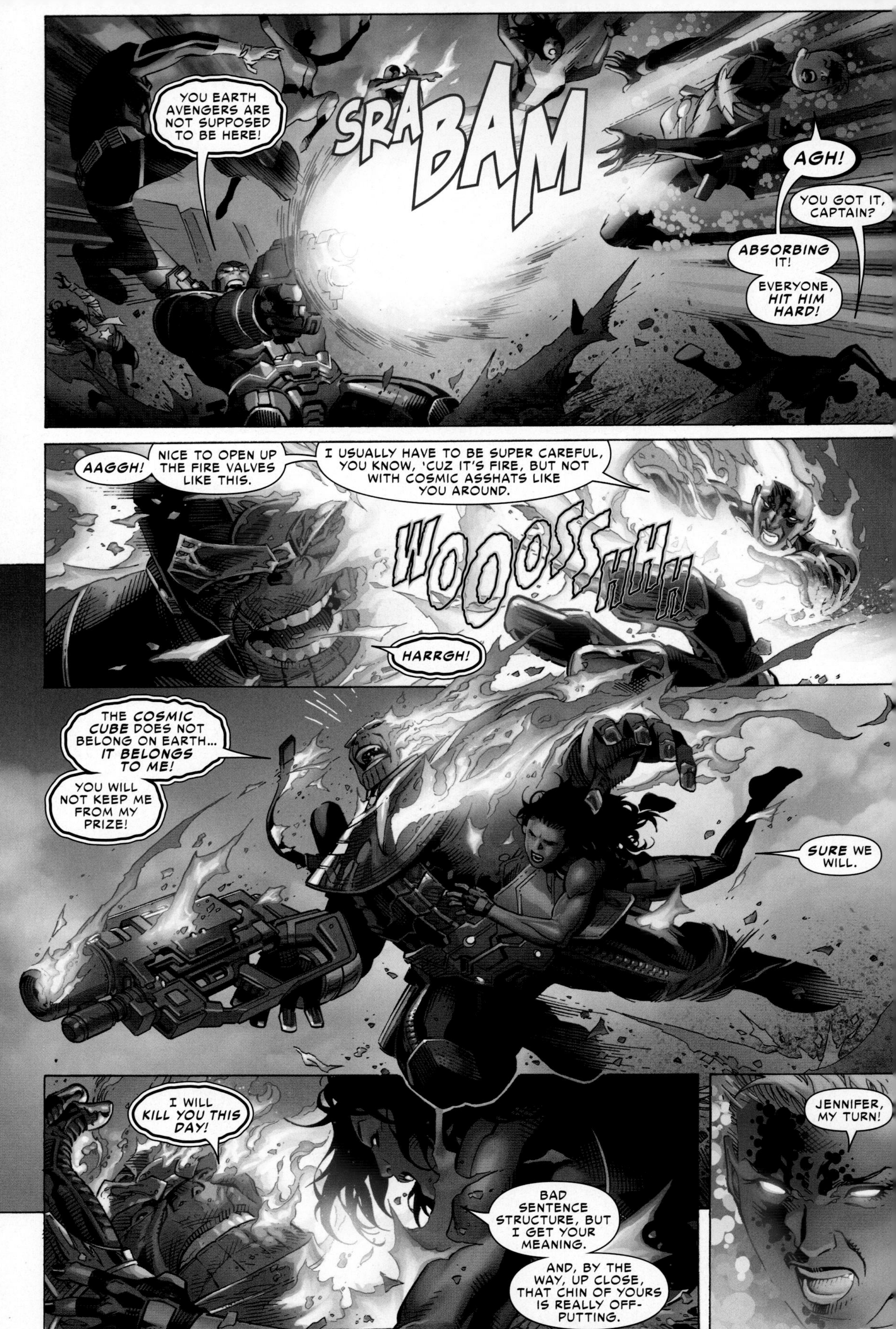

YOU EARTH AVENGERS ARE NOT SUPPOSED TO BE HERE!
SRABAM
AGH!
YOU GOT IT, CAPTAIN?
ABSORBING IT!
EVERYONE, HIT HIM HARD!
AAGGH!
NICE TO OPEN UP THE FIRE VALVES LIKE THIS.
I USUALLY HAVE TO BE SUPER CAREFUL, YOU KNOW, 'CUZ IT'S FIRE, BUT NOT WITH COSMIC ASSHATS LIKE YOU AROUND.
WOOOSSHHH
HARRGH!
THE COSMIC CUBE DOES NOT BELONG ON EARTH... IT BELONGS TO ME!
YOU WILL NOT KEEP ME FROM MY PRIZE!
SURE WE WILL.
I WILL KILL YOU THIS DAY!
BAD SENTENCE STRUCTURE, BUT I GET YOUR MEANING.
AND, BY THE WAY, UP CLOSE, THAT CHIN OF YOURS IS REALLY OFF-PUTTING.
JENNIFER, MY TURN!

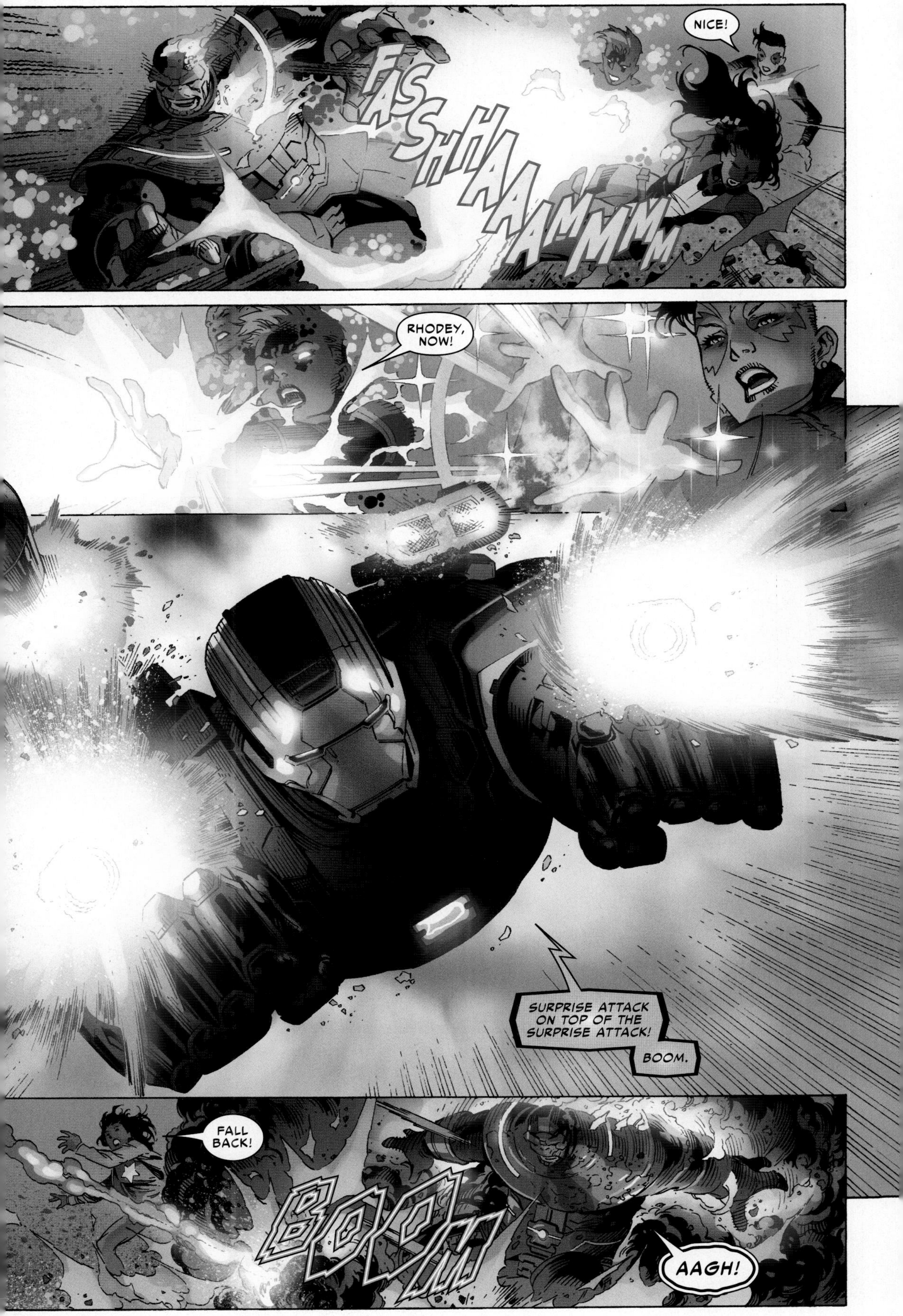
FASSHHAAAMMMM
NICE!
RHODEY, NOW!
SURPRISE ATTACK ON TOP OF THE SURPRISE ATTACK!
BOOM.
FALL BACK!
BOOM
AAGH!

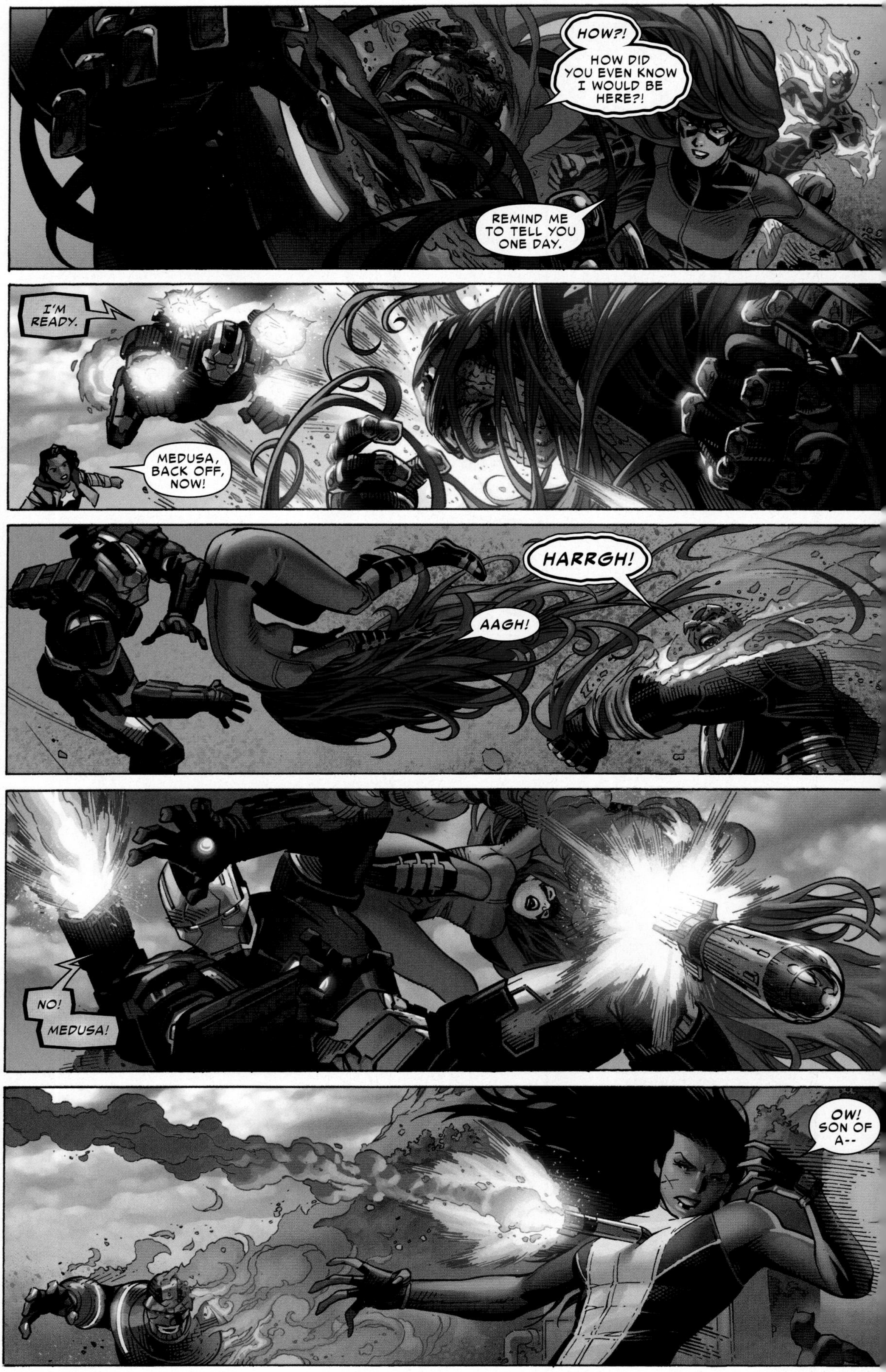
HOW?!
HOW DID YOU EVEN KNOW I WOULD BE HERE?!
REMIND ME TO TELL YOU ONE DAY.
I'M READY.
MEDUSA, BACK OFF, NOW!
HARRGH!
AAGH!
NO! MEDUSA!
OW! SON OF A--

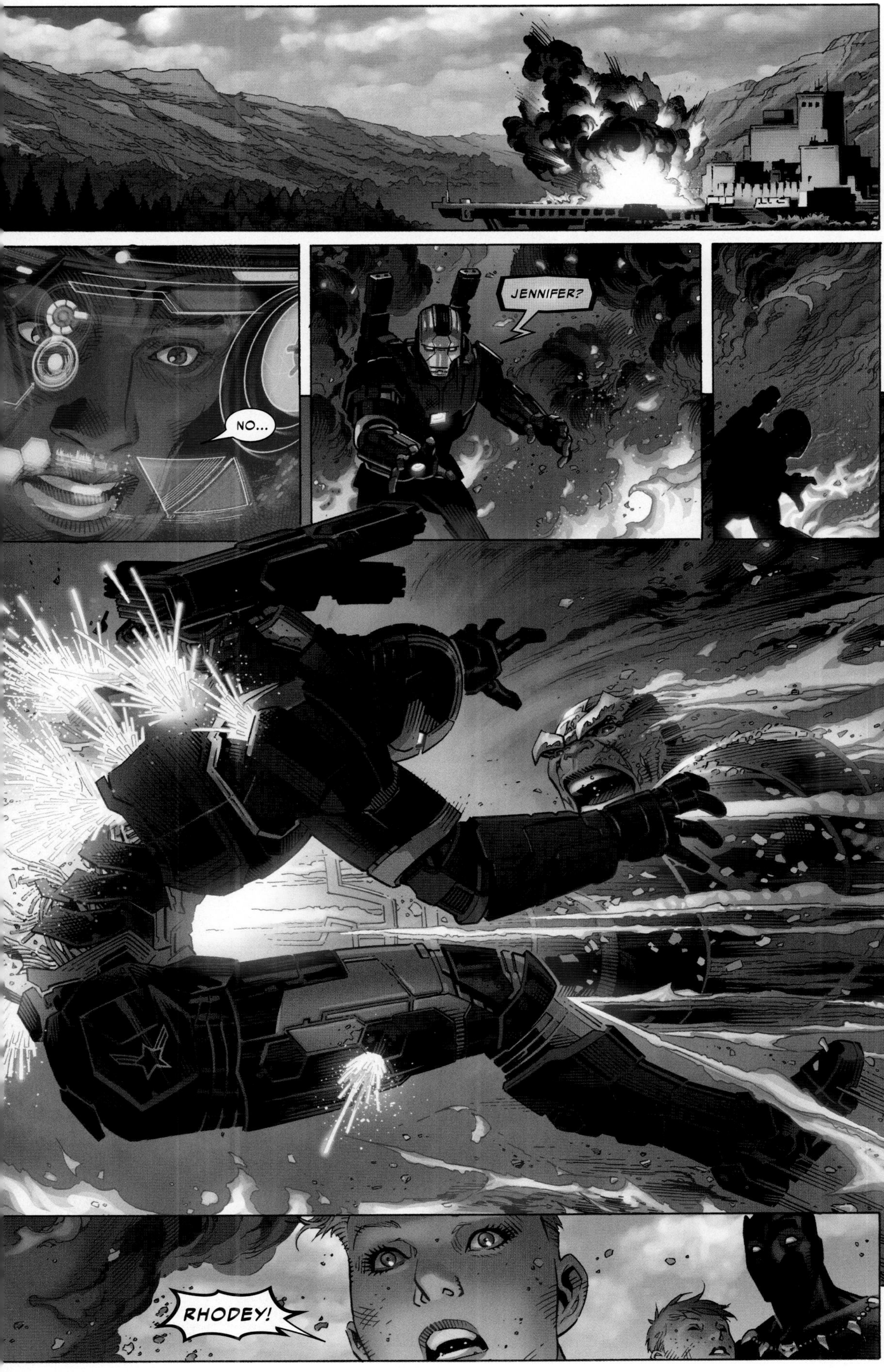
NO...
JENNIFER?
RHODEY!

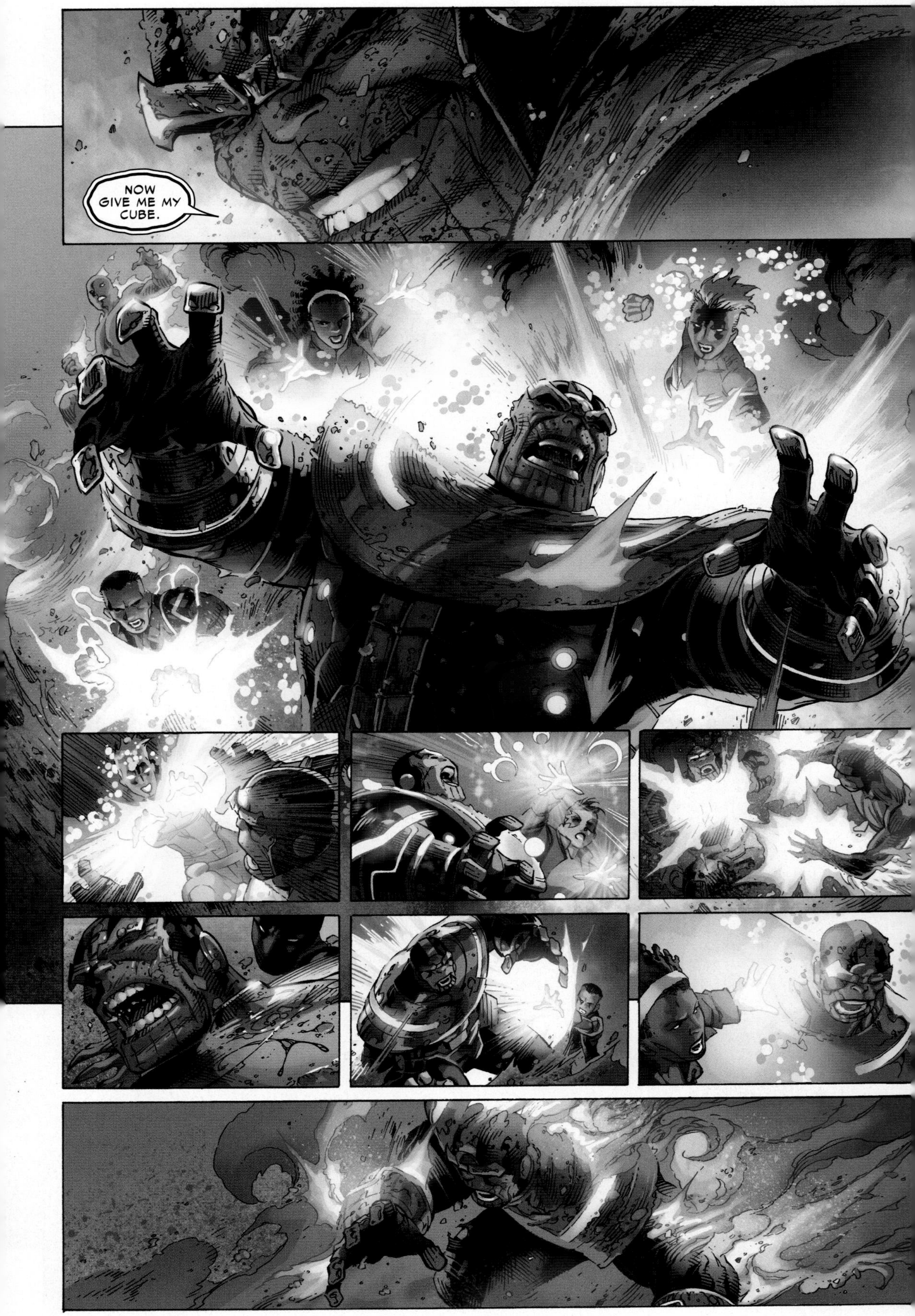
NOW GIVE ME MY CUBE.

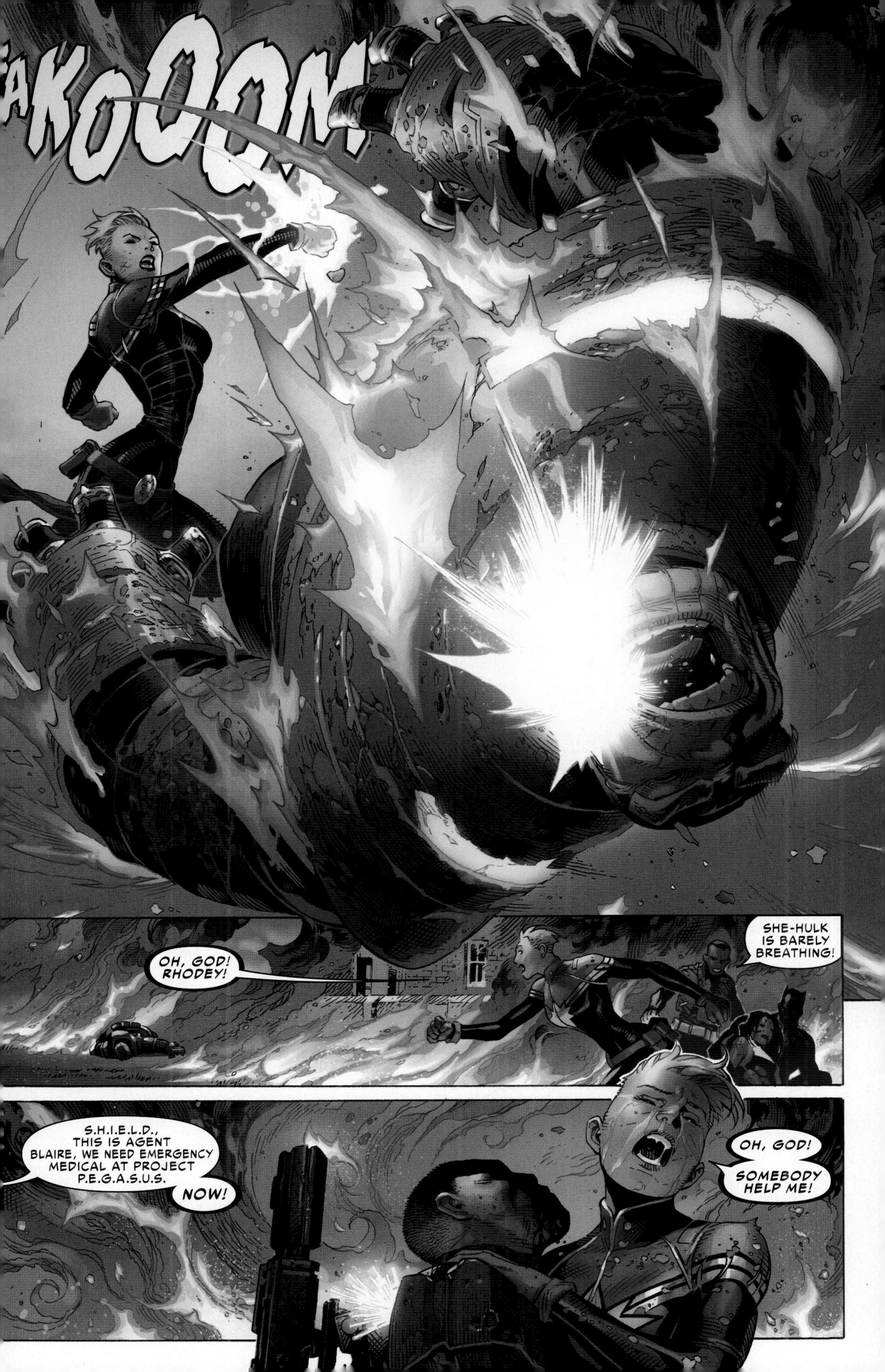

AKOOOM
OH, GOD! RHODEY!
SHE-HULK IS BARELY BREATHING!
S.H.I.E.L.D., THIS IS AGENT BLAIRE, WE NEED EMERGENCY MEDICAL AT PROJECT P.E.G.A.S.U.S.
NOW!
OH, GOD!
SOMEBODY HELP ME!

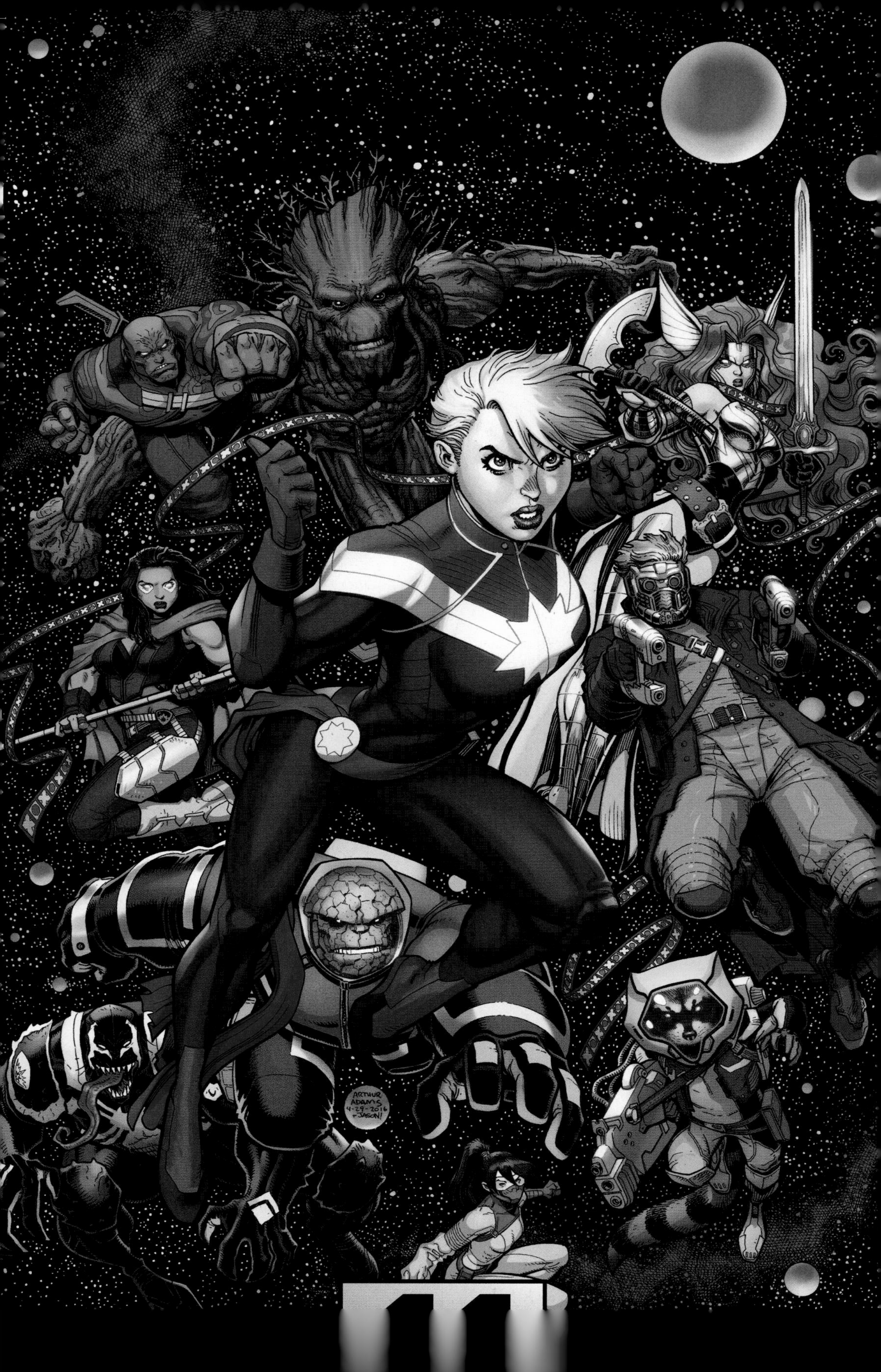
ARTHUR ADAMS 4-29-2016 T.JASON!

GUARDIANS OF THE GALAXY

THE ENTIRE GALAXY IS A MESS. WARRING EMPIRES AND COSMIC TERRORISTS PLAGUE EVERY CORNER. SOMEONE HAS TO RISE ABOVE IT ALL AND FIGHT FOR THOSE WHO HAVE NO ONE TO FIGHT FOR THEM. A GROUP OF MISFITS — **DRAX THE DESTROYER**, GAMORA, **ROCKET RACCOON, GROOT, FLASH THOMPSON**, A.K.A. **VENOM, KITTY PRYDE**, AND **BEN GRIMM**, A.K.A. **THE THING** — JOINED TOGETHER UNDER THE LEADERSHIP OF **PETER QUILL**, A.K.A. **STAR-LORD**. THEY SERVE A HIGHER CAUSE AS THE **GUARDIANS OF THE GALAXY.**

THE GUARDIANS HAVE OVERTHROWN A PRISON PLANET, RESCUING INNOCENT POLITICAL SLAVES OF THE BADOON EMPIRE. ONE WAS THEIR OLD TEAMMATE ANGELA, WHO REJOINED THE GUARDIANS JUST AS CAPTAIN MARVEL, ANOTHER OLD TEAMMATE, CALLED TO ASK THEM TO RETURN TO EARTH.

THANKS TO AN INHUMAN WHO SEEMS TO BE ABLE TO PREDICT THE FUTURE, EARTH'S HEROES PREVENTED A CATACLYSMIC EVENT. CAPTAIN MARVEL BELIEVES THAT ACTING ON HIS VISIONS SAVES LIVES, BUT THERE HAVE BEEN TERRIBLE COSTS. A NEW SUPER HERO CIVIL WAR IS IMMINENT. NOW THE GUARDIANS WILL HAVE TO MAKE A CHOICE: PROTECT THE FUTURE...OR CHANGE IT?

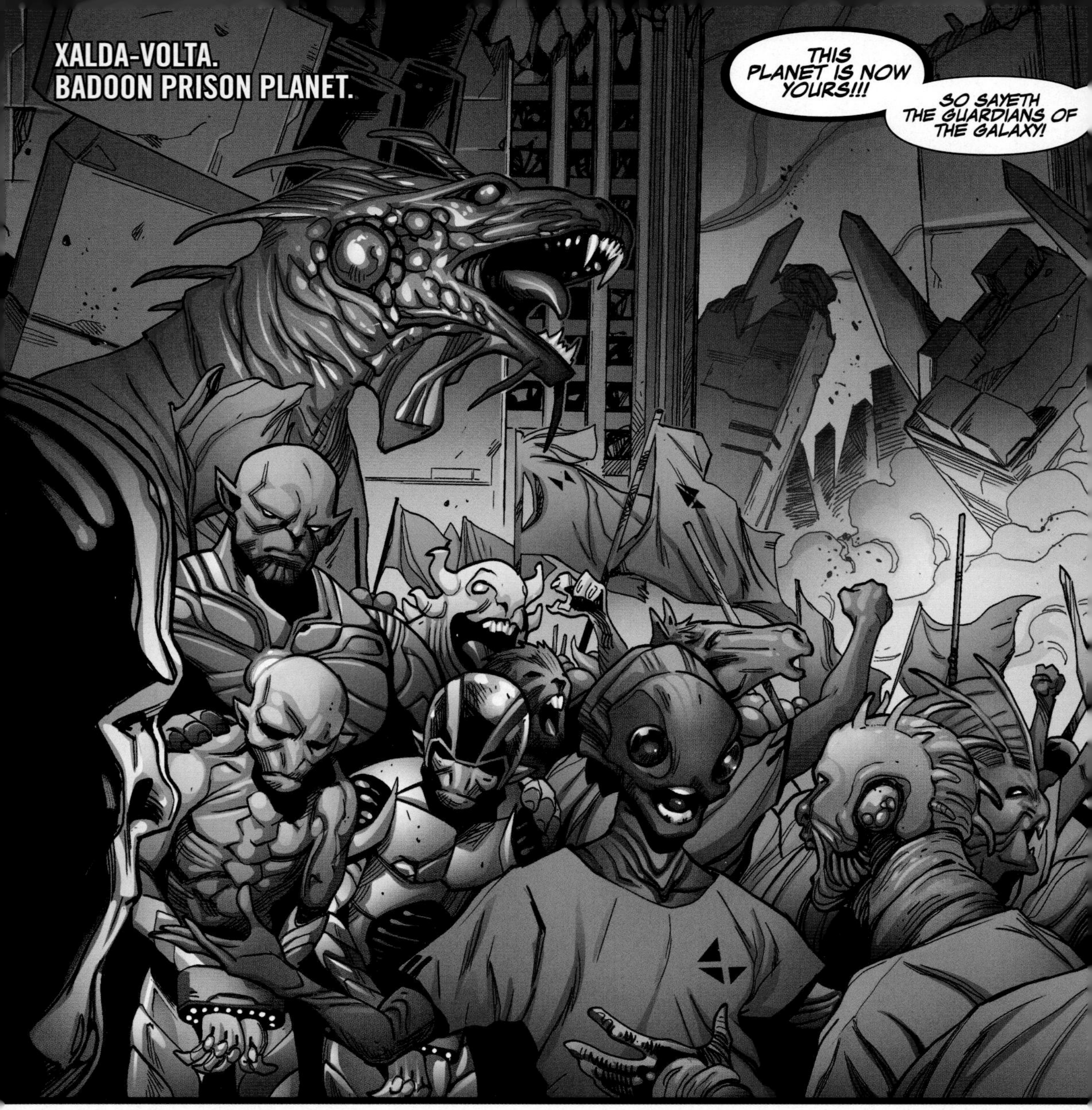
XALDA-VOLTA.
BADOON PRISON PLANET.
THIS PLANET IS NOW YOURS!!!
SO SAYETH THE GUARDIANS OF THE GALAXY!

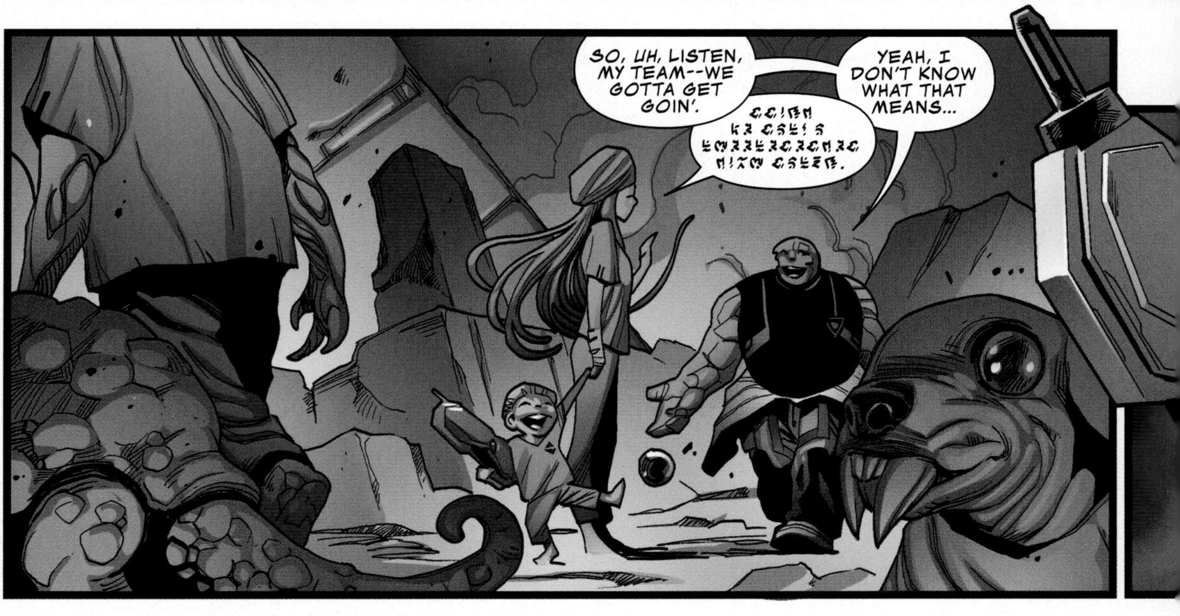
SO, UH, LISTEN, MY TEAM--WE GOTTA GET GOIN'.
YEAH, I DON'T KNOW WHAT THAT MEANS...

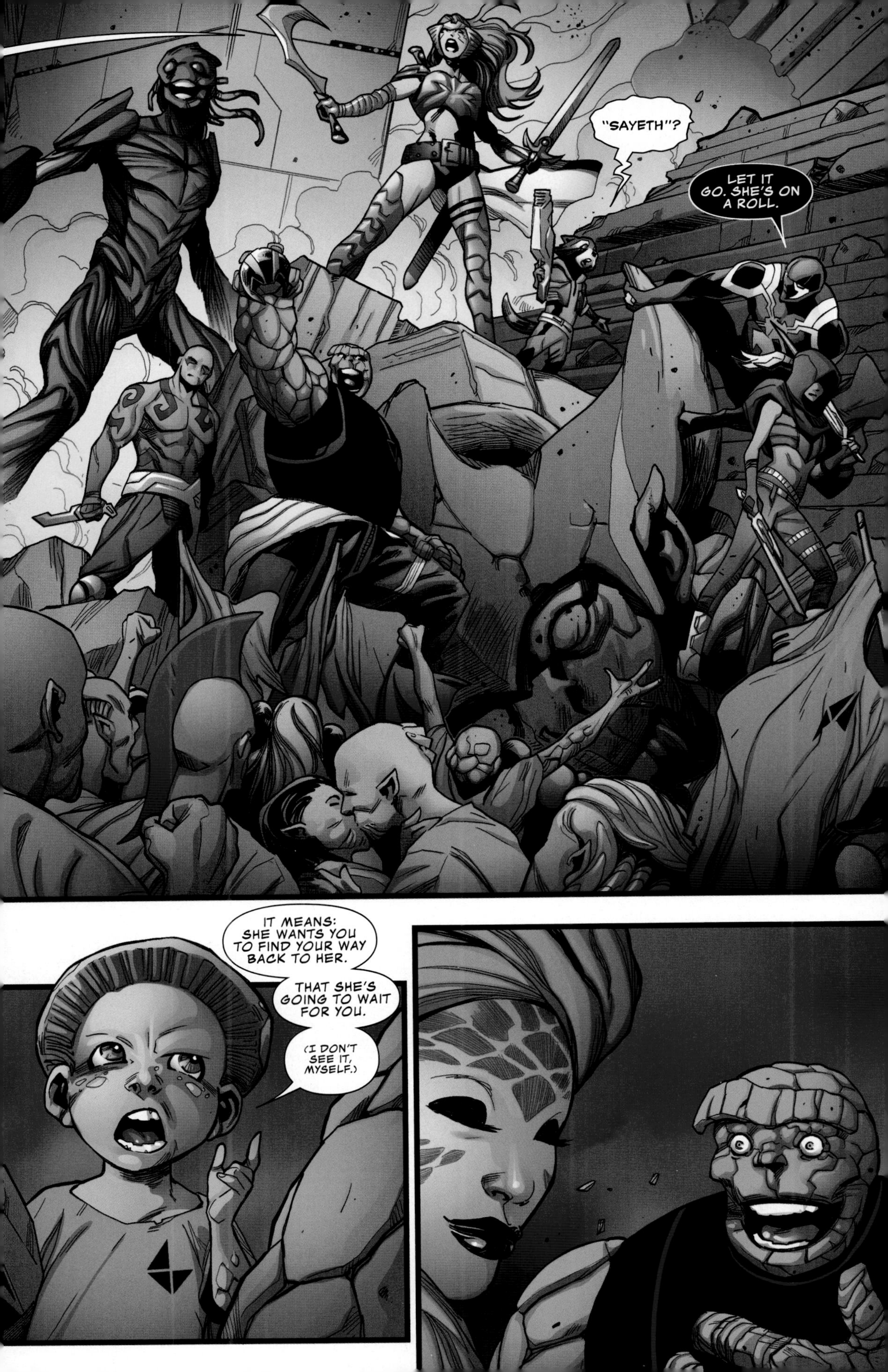
"SAYETH"?
LET IT GO. SHE'S ON A ROLL.
IT MEANS: SHE WANTS YOU TO FIND YOUR WAY BACK TO HER.
THAT SHE'S GOING TO WAIT FOR YOU.
(I DON'T SEE IT, MYSELF.)

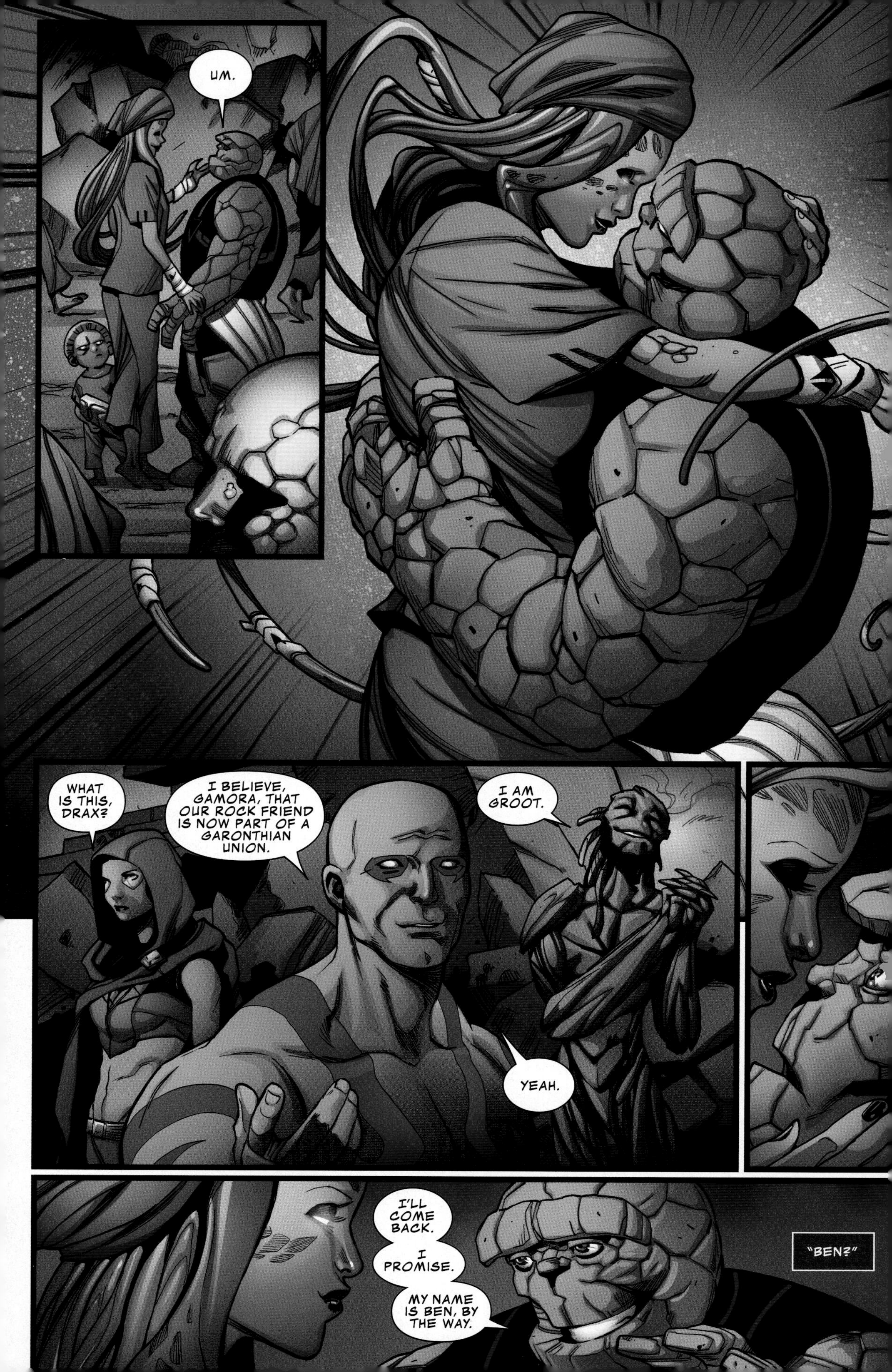
UM.
WHAT IS THIS, DRAX?
I BELIEVE, GAMORA, THAT OUR ROCK FRIEND IS NOW PART OF A GARONTHIAN UNION.
I AM GROOT.
YEAH.
I'LL COME BACK.
I PROMISE.
MY NAME IS BEN, BY THE WAY.
"BEN?"

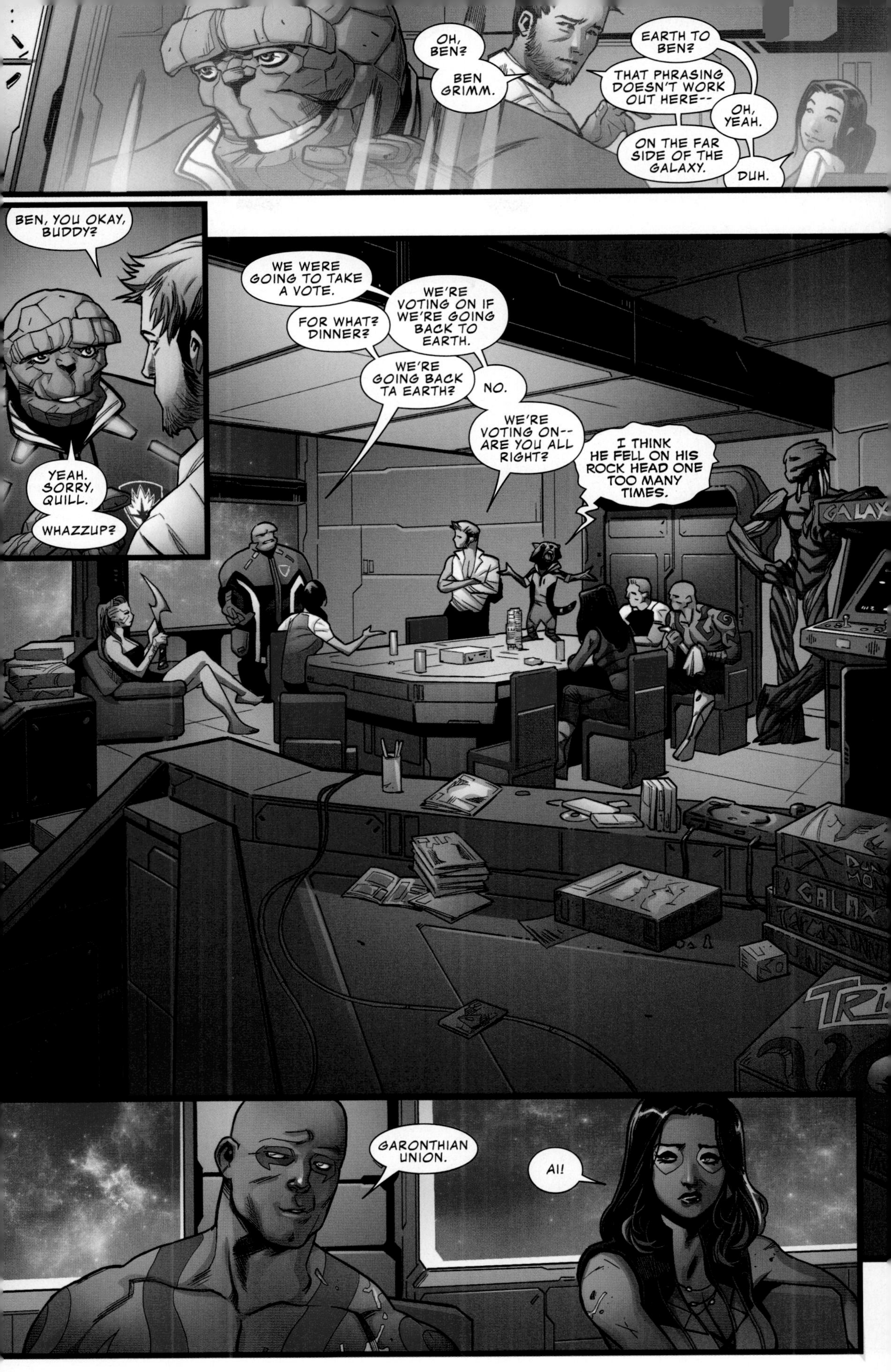
OH, BEN?
BEN GRIMM.
EARTH TO BEN?
THAT PHRASING DOESN'T WORK OUT HERE--
OH, YEAH.
ON THE FAR SIDE OF THE GALAXY.
DUH.
BEN, YOU OKAY, BUDDY?
YEAH. SORRY, QUILL.
WHAZZUP?
WE WERE GOING TO TAKE A VOTE.
FOR WHAT? DINNER?
WE'RE VOTING ON IF WE'RE GOING BACK TO EARTH.
WE'RE GOING BACK TA EARTH?
NO.
WE'RE VOTING ON-- ARE YOU ALL RIGHT?
I THINK HE FELL ON HIS ROCK HEAD ONE TOO MANY TIMES.
GARONTHIAN UNION.
AI!

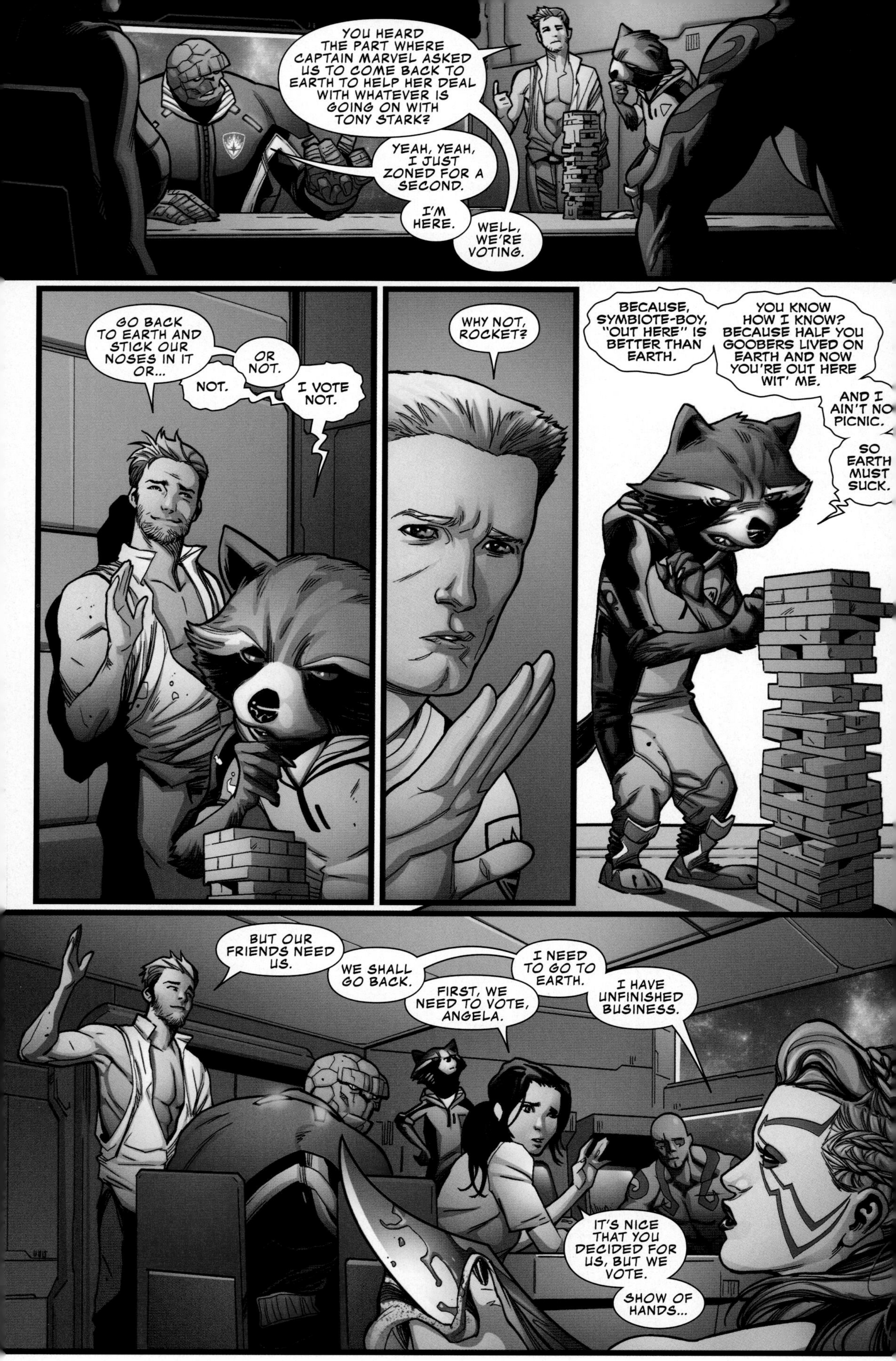
YOU HEARD THE PART WHERE CAPTAIN MARVEL ASKED US TO COME BACK TO EARTH TO HELP HER DEAL WITH WHATEVER IS GOING ON WITH TONY STARK?
YEAH, YEAH, I JUST ZONED FOR A SECOND.
I'M HERE.
WELL, WE'RE VOTING.
GO BACK TO EARTH AND STICK OUR NOSES IN IT OR...
OR NOT.
NOT.
I VOTE NOT.
WHY NOT, ROCKET?
BECAUSE, SYMBIOTE-BOY, "OUT HERE" IS BETTER THAN EARTH.
YOU KNOW HOW I KNOW? BECAUSE HALF YOU GOOBERS LIVED ON EARTH AND NOW YOU'RE OUT HERE WIT' ME.
AND I AIN'T NO PICNIC.
SO EARTH MUST SUCK.
BUT OUR FRIENDS NEED US.
WE SHALL GO BACK.
I NEED TO GO TO EARTH.
FIRST, WE NEED TO VOTE, ANGELA.
I HAVE UNFINISHED BUSINESS.
IT'S NICE THAT YOU DECIDED FOR US, BUT WE VOTE.
SHOW OF HANDS...

I VOTE YES.

I AM AMBIVALENT.

I AM GROOT.

I VOTE YES. CAROL WOULD DO IT FOR US.

I VOTE YES. (I NEED TO BUY SOME NEW UNDERWEAR.)

SO NOW IF I VOTE NO... I'M THE JERK?

YOU DON'T WANT TO GO BACK TO EARTH?

YOU NEVER DID TELL US WHY YOU LEFT EARTH AND CAME OUT HERE WITH US IN THE FIRST PLACE...

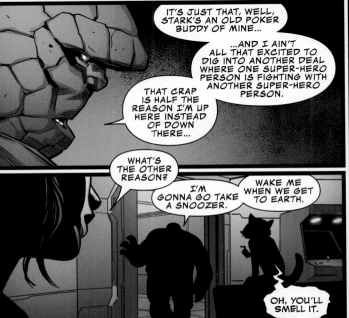

IT'S JUST THAT, WELL, STARK'S AN OLD POKER BUDDY OF MINE...

...AND I AIN'T ALL THAT EXCITED TO DIG INTO ANOTHER DEAL WHERE ONE SUPER-HERO PERSON IS FIGHTING WITH ANOTHER SUPER-HERO PERSON.

THAT CRAP IS HALF THE REASON I'M UP HERE INSTEAD OF DOWN THERE...

WHAT'S THE OTHER REASON?

I'M GONNA GO TAKE A SNOOZER.

WAKE ME WHEN WE GET TO EARTH.

OH, YOU'LL SMELL IT.

I WAS UNDER THE IMPRESSION THAT DANVERS AND TONY STARK WERE CLOSE ALLIES.

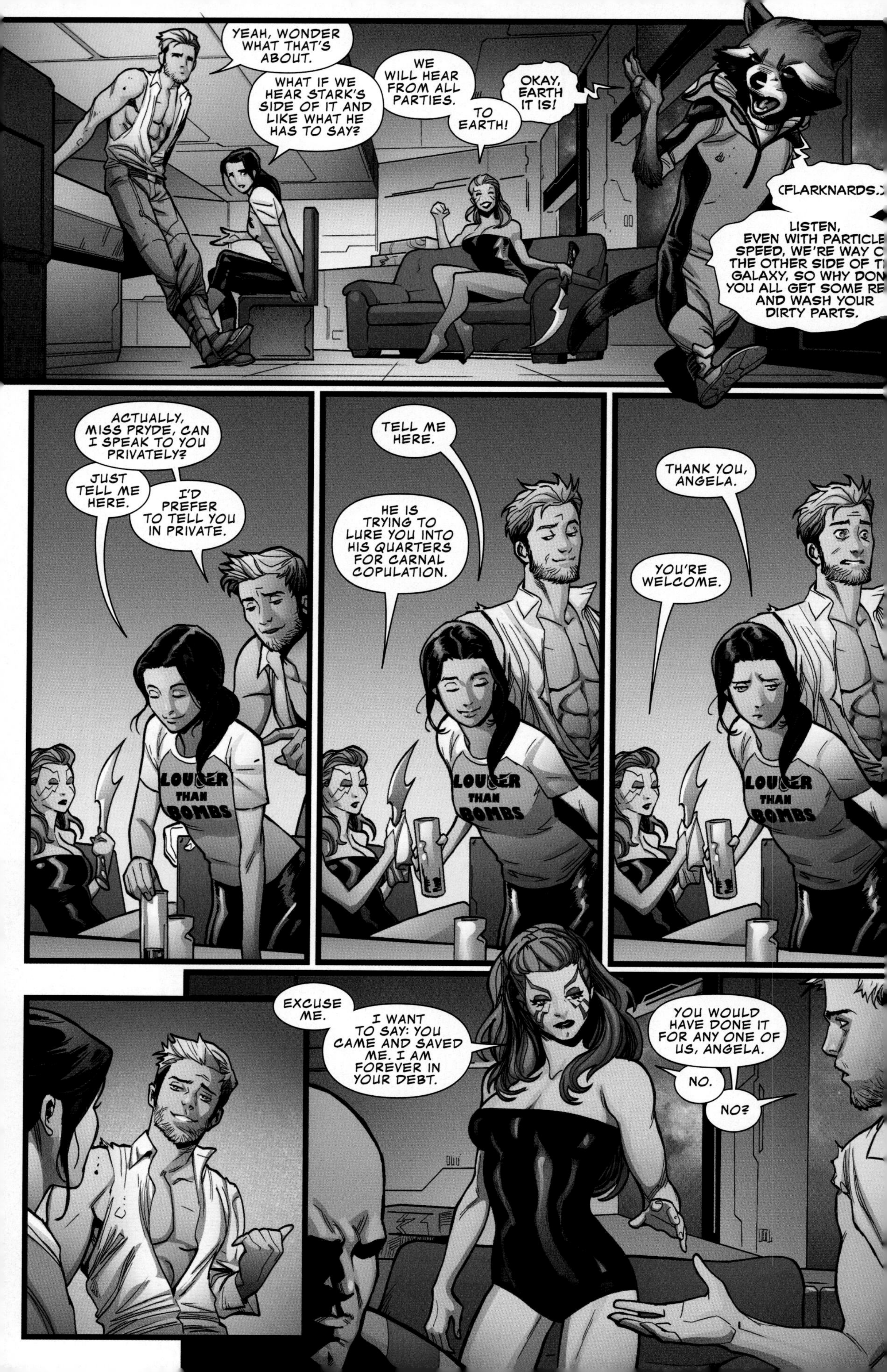
YEAH, WONDER WHAT THAT'S ABOUT.
WHAT IF WE HEAR STARK'S SIDE OF IT AND LIKE WHAT HE HAS TO SAY?
WE WILL HEAR FROM ALL PARTIES.
TO EARTH!
OKAY, EARTH IT IS!
(FLARKNARDS.)
LISTEN, EVEN WITH PARTICLE SPEED, WE'RE WAY O THE OTHER SIDE OF T GALAXY, SO WHY DON YOU ALL GET SOME RE AND WASH YOUR DIRTY PARTS.
ACTUALLY, MISS PRYDE, CAN I SPEAK TO YOU PRIVATELY?
JUST TELL ME HERE.
I'D PREFER TO TELL YOU IN PRIVATE.
TELL ME HERE.
HE IS TRYING TO LURE YOU INTO HIS QUARTERS FOR CARNAL COPULATION.
THANK YOU, ANGELA.
YOU'RE WELCOME.
EXCUSE ME.
I WANT TO SAY: YOU CAME AND SAVED ME. I AM FOREVER IN YOUR DEBT.
YOU WOULD HAVE DONE IT FOR ANY ONE OF US, ANGELA.
NO.
NO?

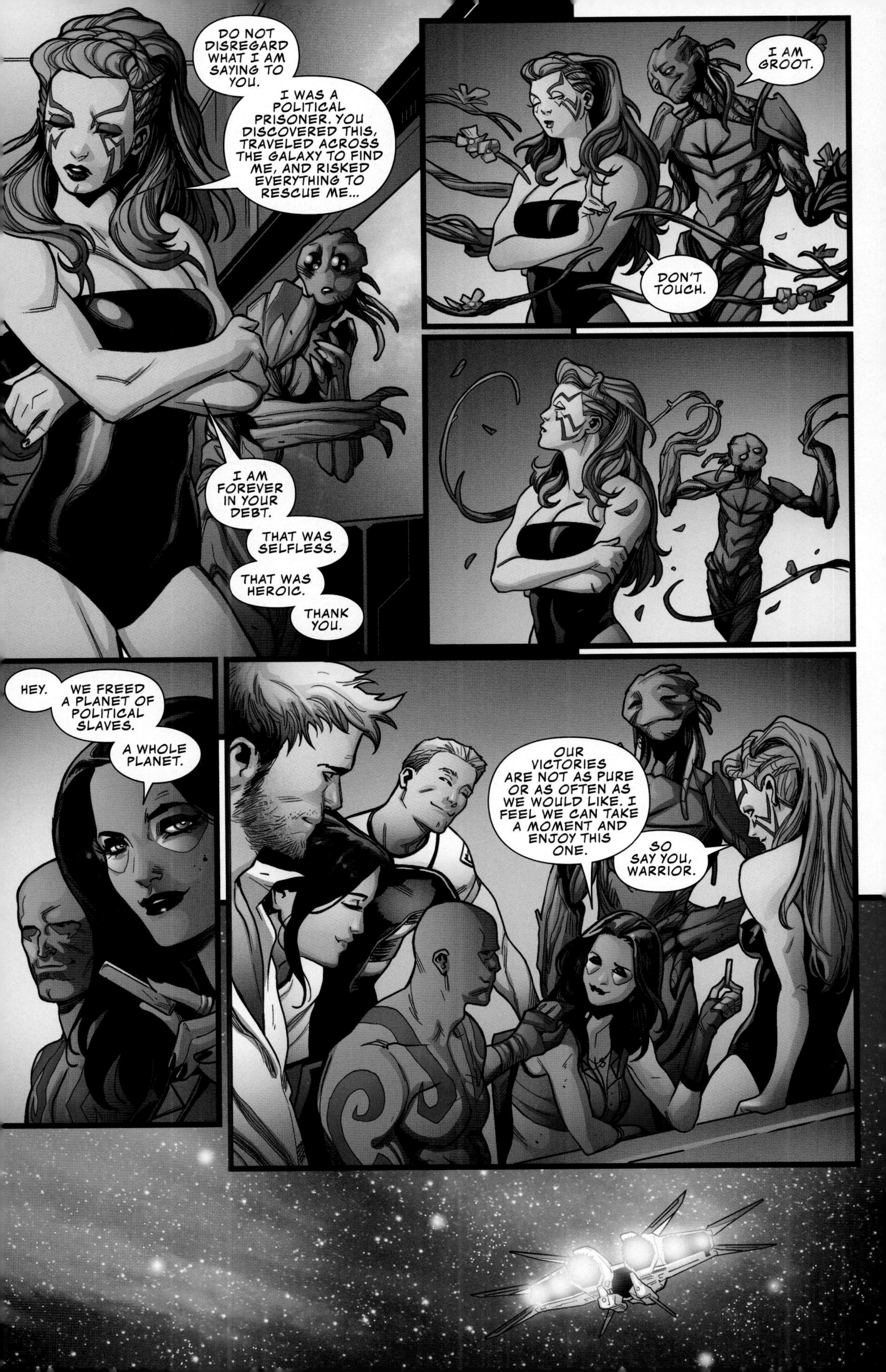
DO NOT DISREGARD WHAT I AM SAYING TO YOU.
I WAS A POLITICAL PRISONER. YOU DISCOVERED THIS, TRAVELED ACROSS THE GALAXY TO FIND ME, AND RISKED EVERYTHING TO RESCUE ME...
I AM FOREVER IN YOUR DEBT.
THAT WAS SELFLESS.
THAT WAS HEROIC.
THANK YOU.
I AM GROOT.
DON'T TOUCH.
HEY.
WE FREED A PLANET OF POLITICAL SLAVES.
A WHOLE PLANET.
OUR VICTORIES ARE NOT AS PURE OR AS OFTEN AS WE WOULD LIKE. I FEEL WE CAN TAKE A MOMENT AND ENJOY THIS ONE.
SO SAY YOU, WARRIOR.

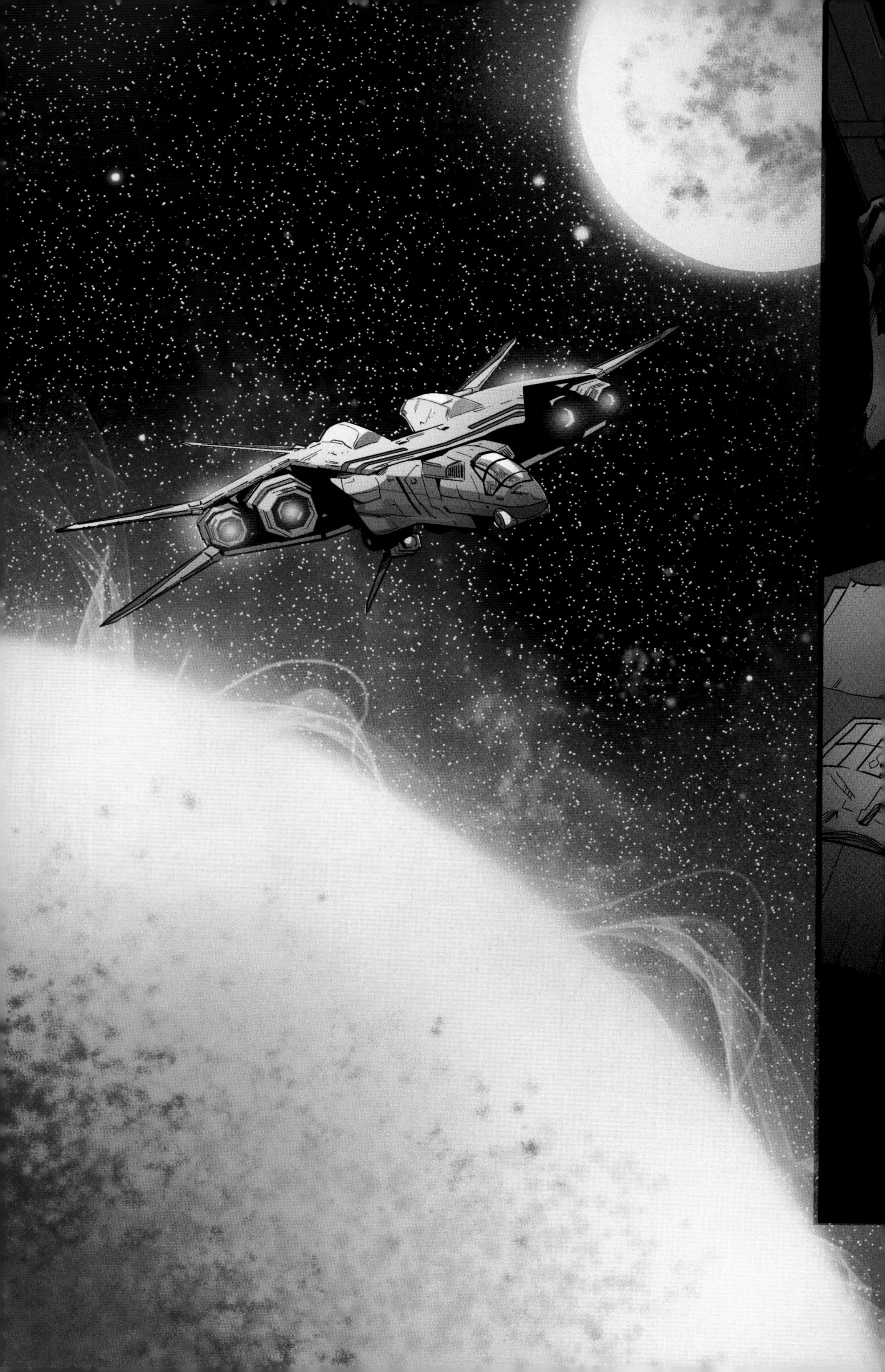

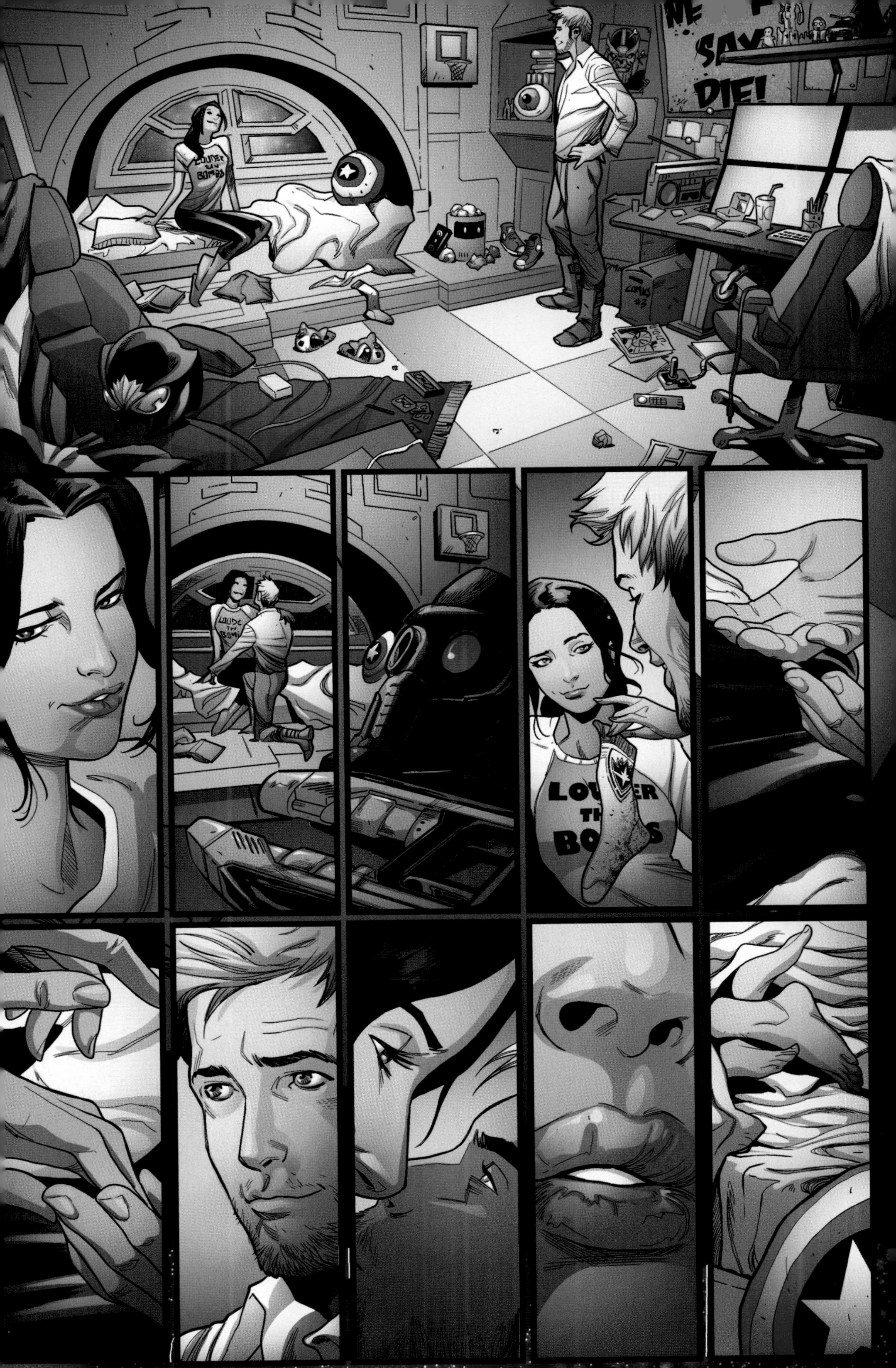
SAY DIE!
COMICS #3

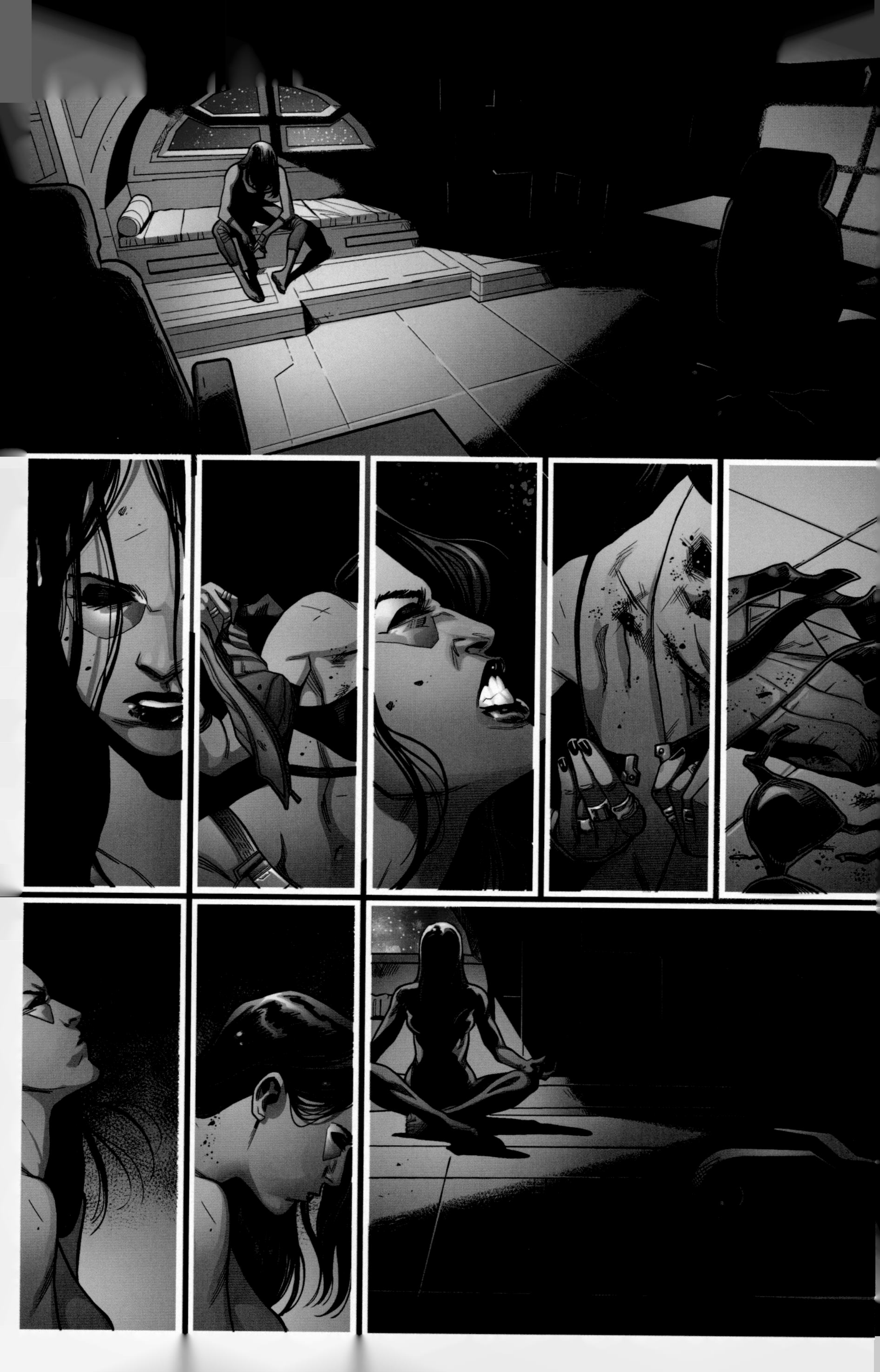

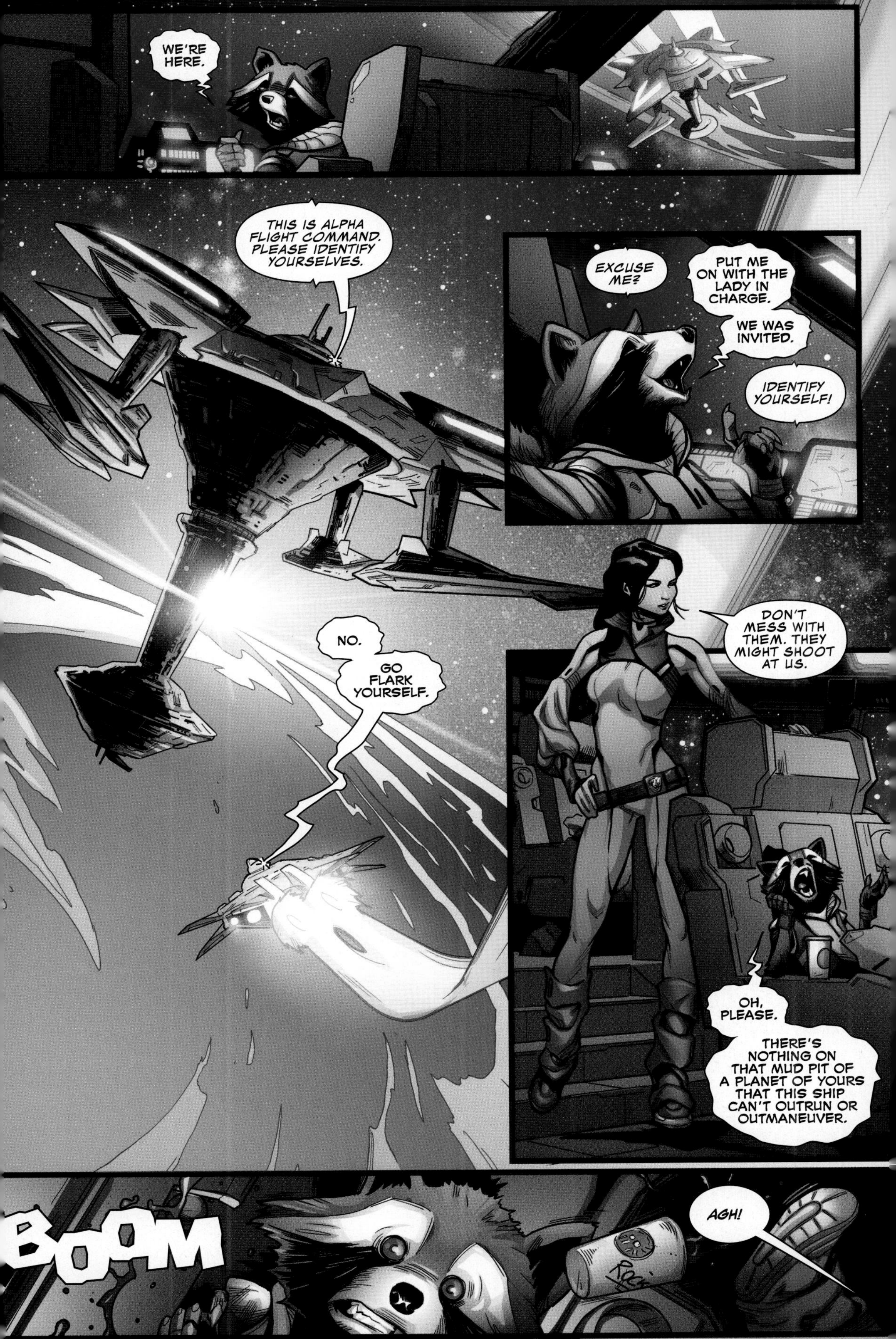
WE'RE HERE.
THIS IS ALPHA FLIGHT COMMAND. PLEASE IDENTIFY YOURSELVES.
EXCUSE ME?
PUT ME ON WITH THE LADY IN CHARGE.
WE WAS INVITED.
IDENTIFY YOURSELF!
NO.
GO FLARK YOURSELF.
DON'T MESS WITH THEM. THEY MIGHT SHOOT AT US.
OH, PLEASE.
THERE'S NOTHING ON THAT MUD PIT OF A PLANET OF YOURS THAT THIS SHIP CAN'T OUTRUN OR OUTMANEUVER.
BOOM
AGH!

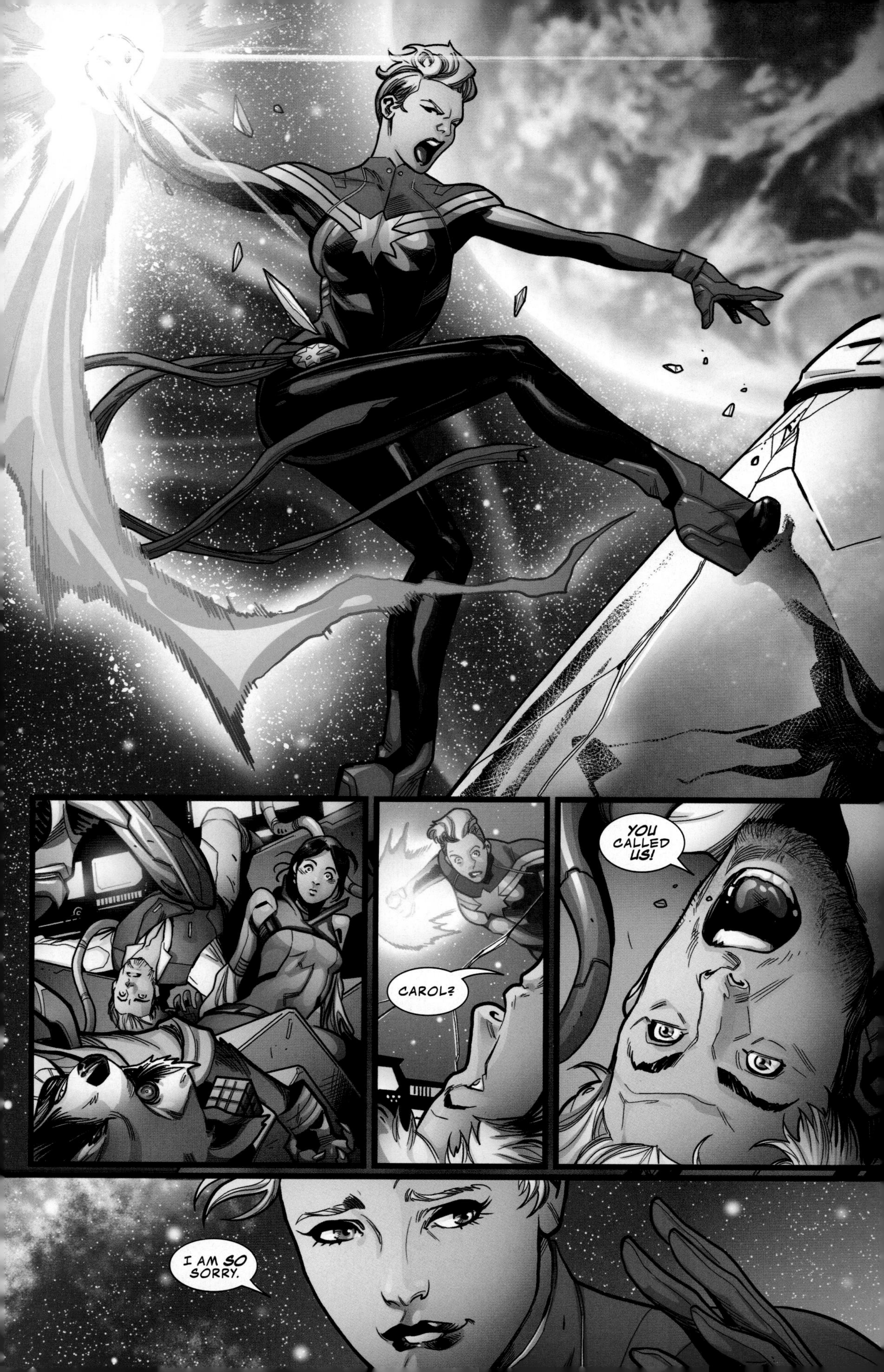
CAROL?
YOU CALLED US!
I AM SO SORRY.

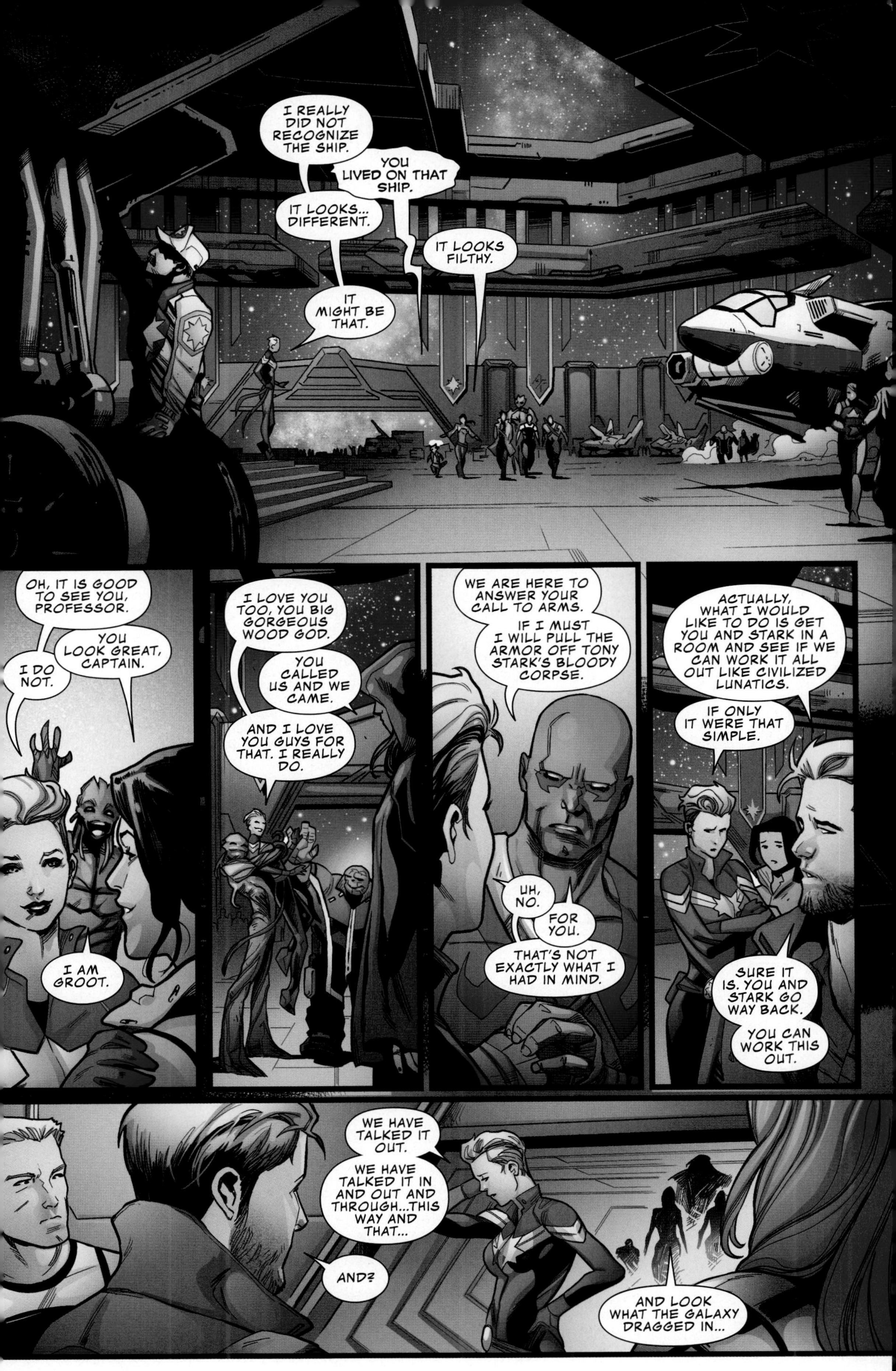
I REALLY DID NOT RECOGNIZE THE SHIP.
YOU LIVED ON THAT SHIP.
IT LOOKS... DIFFERENT.
IT LOOKS FILTHY.
IT MIGHT BE THAT.
OH, IT IS GOOD TO SEE YOU, PROFESSOR.
YOU LOOK GREAT, CAPTAIN.
I DO NOT.
I AM GROOT.
I LOVE YOU TOO, YOU BIG GORGEOUS WOOD GOD.
YOU CALLED US AND WE CAME.
AND I LOVE YOU GUYS FOR THAT. I REALLY DO.
WE ARE HERE TO ANSWER YOUR CALL TO ARMS.
IF I MUST I WILL PULL THE ARMOR OFF TONY STARK'S BLOODY CORPSE.
UH, NO.
FOR YOU.
THAT'S NOT EXACTLY WHAT I HAD IN MIND.
ACTUALLY, WHAT I WOULD LIKE TO DO IS GET YOU AND STARK IN A ROOM AND SEE IF WE CAN WORK IT ALL OUT LIKE CIVILIZED LUNATICS.
IF ONLY IT WERE THAT SIMPLE.
SURE IT IS. YOU AND STARK GO WAY BACK.
YOU CAN WORK THIS OUT.
WE HAVE TALKED IT OUT.
WE HAVE TALKED IT IN AND OUT AND THROUGH...THIS WAY AND THAT...
AND?
AND LOOK WHAT THE GALAXY DRAGGED IN...

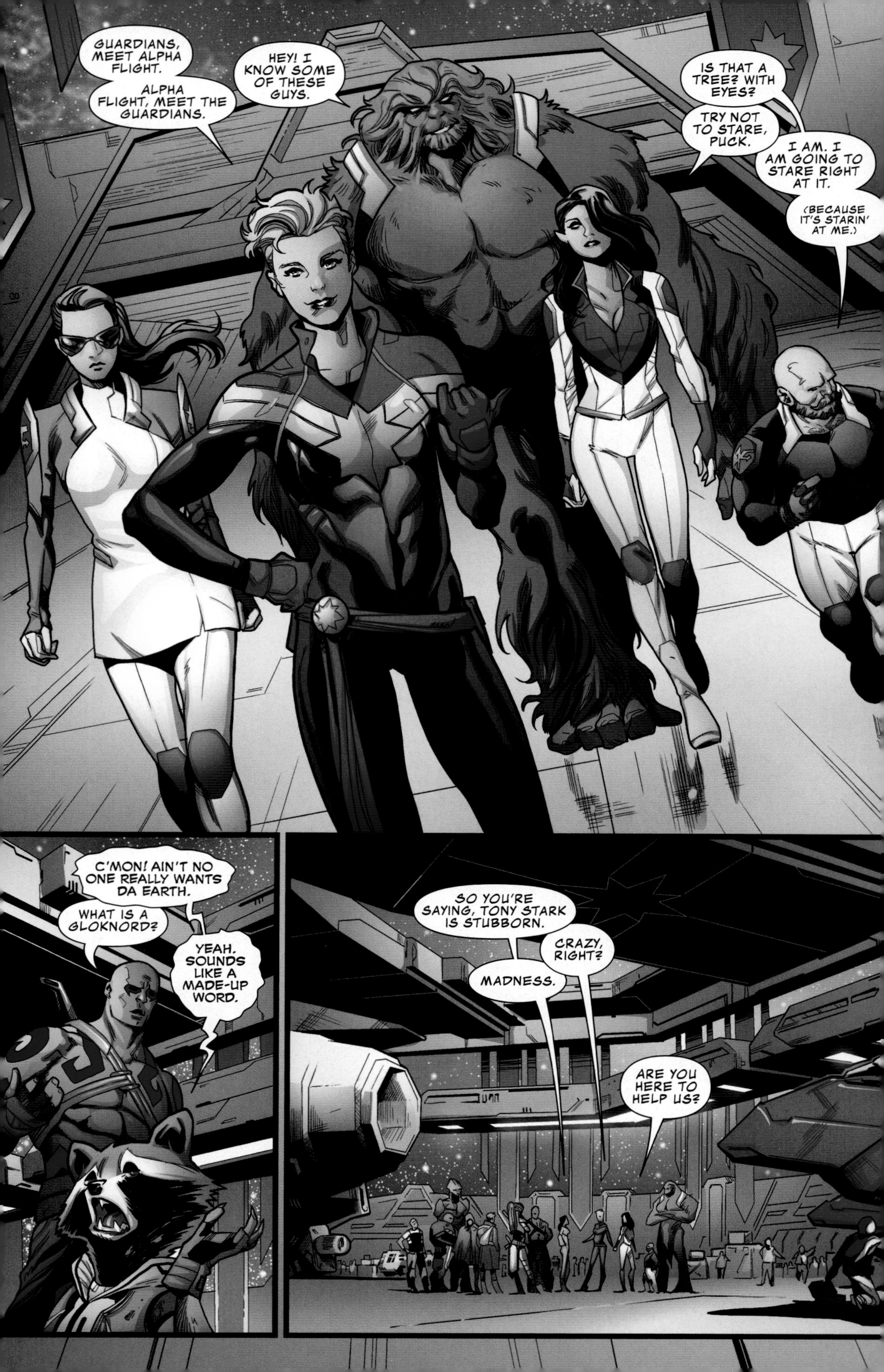
GUARDIANS, MEET ALPHA FLIGHT.
ALPHA FLIGHT, MEET THE GUARDIANS.
HEY! I KNOW SOME OF THESE GUYS.
IS THAT A TREE? WITH EYES?
TRY NOT TO STARE, PUCK.
I AM. I AM GOING TO STARE RIGHT AT IT.
(BECAUSE IT'S STARIN' AT ME.)
C'MON! AIN'T NO ONE REALLY WANTS DA EARTH.
WHAT IS A GLOKNORD?
YEAH. SOUNDS LIKE A MADE-UP WORD.
SO YOU'RE SAYING, TONY STARK IS STUBBORN.
CRAZY, RIGHT?
MADNESS.
ARE YOU HERE TO HELP US?

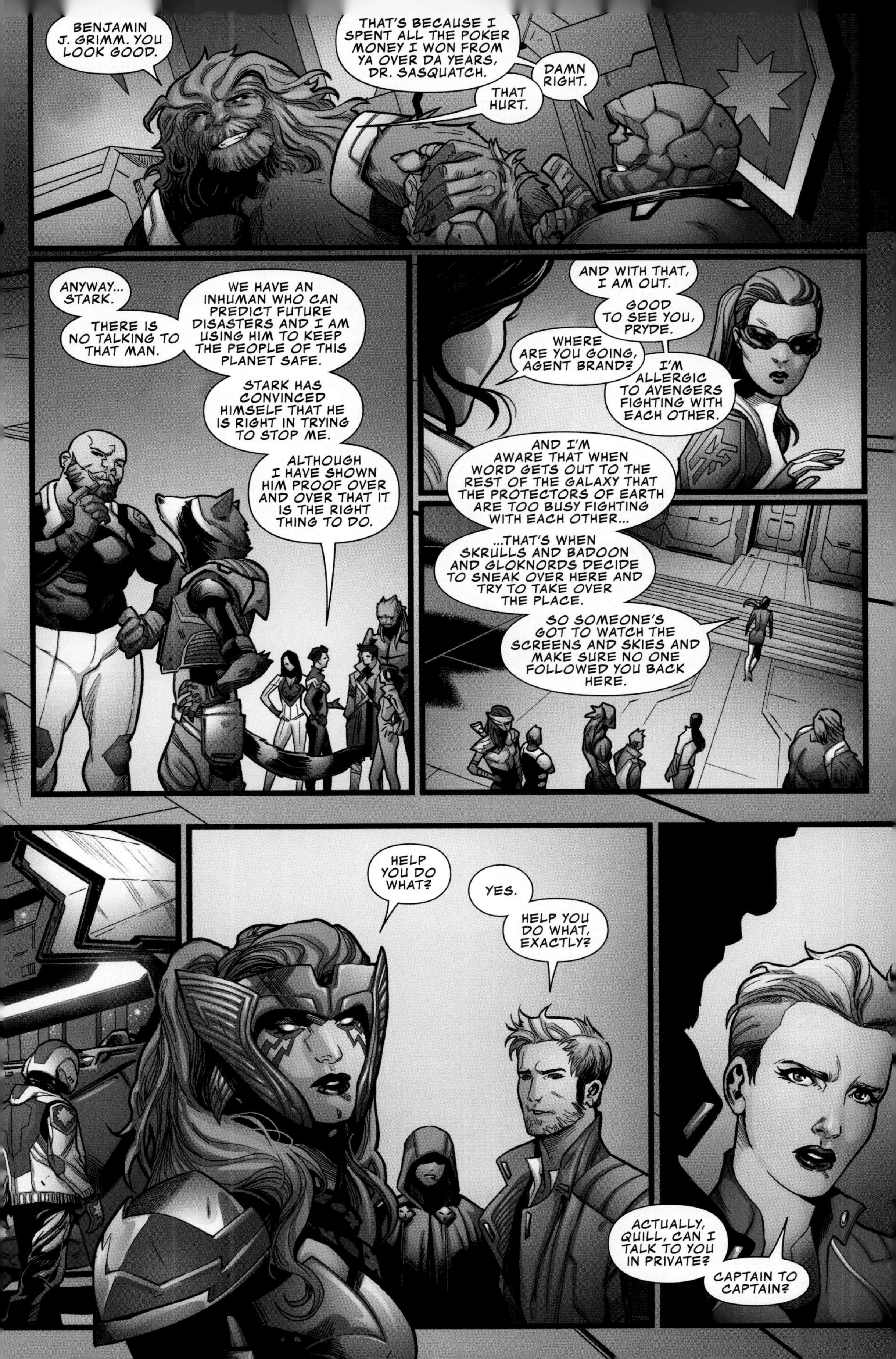
BENJAMIN J. GRIMM. YOU LOOK GOOD.
THAT'S BECAUSE I SPENT ALL THE POKER MONEY I WON FROM YA OVER DA YEARS, DR. SASQUATCH.
THAT HURT.
DAMN RIGHT.
ANYWAY... STARK.
THERE IS NO TALKING TO THAT MAN.
WE HAVE AN INHUMAN WHO CAN PREDICT FUTURE DISASTERS AND I AM USING HIM TO KEEP THE PEOPLE OF THIS PLANET SAFE.
STARK HAS CONVINCED HIMSELF THAT HE IS RIGHT IN TRYING TO STOP ME.
ALTHOUGH I HAVE SHOWN HIM PROOF OVER AND OVER THAT IT IS THE RIGHT THING TO DO.
AND WITH THAT, I AM OUT.
GOOD TO SEE YOU, PRYDE.
WHERE ARE YOU GOING, AGENT BRAND?
I'M ALLERGIC TO AVENGERS FIGHTING WITH EACH OTHER.
AND I'M AWARE THAT WHEN WORD GETS OUT TO THE REST OF THE GALAXY THAT THE PROTECTORS OF EARTH ARE TOO BUSY FIGHTING WITH EACH OTHER...
...THAT'S WHEN SKRULLS AND BADOON AND GLOKNORDS DECIDE TO SNEAK OVER HERE AND TRY TO TAKE OVER THE PLACE.
SO SOMEONE'S GOT TO WATCH THE SCREENS AND SKIES AND MAKE SURE NO ONE FOLLOWED YOU BACK HERE.
HELP YOU DO WHAT?
YES.
HELP YOU DO WHAT, EXACTLY?
ACTUALLY, QUILL, CAN I TALK TO YOU IN PRIVATE?
CAPTAIN TO CAPTAIN?

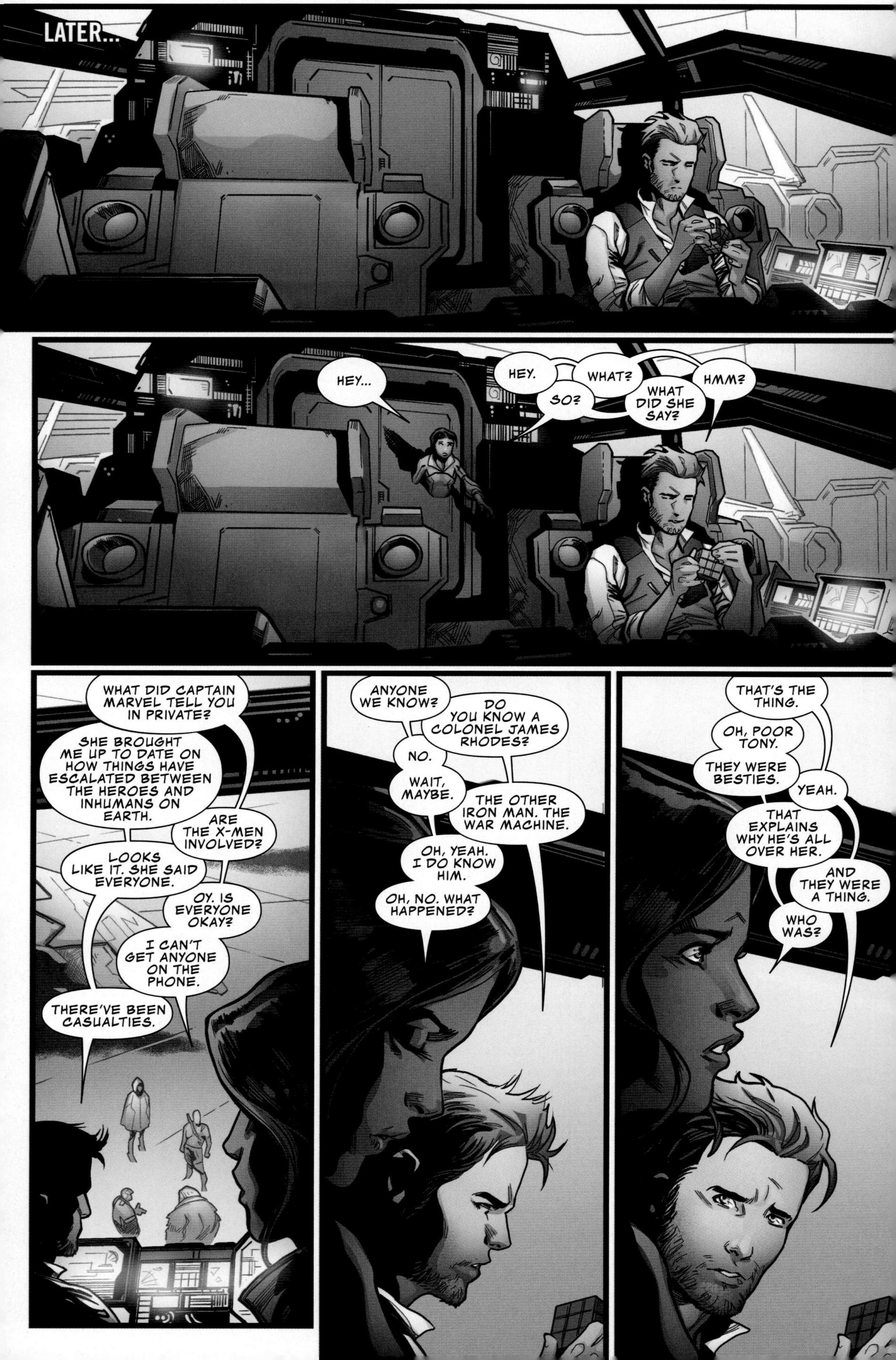
LATER...
HEY...
HEY.
WHAT?
HMM?
SO?
WHAT DID SHE SAY?
WHAT DID CAPTAIN MARVEL TELL YOU IN PRIVATE?
SHE BROUGHT ME UP TO DATE ON HOW THINGS HAVE ESCALATED BETWEEN THE HEROES AND INHUMANS ON EARTH.
ARE THE X-MEN INVOLVED?
LOOKS LIKE IT. SHE SAID EVERYONE.
OY. IS EVERYONE OKAY?
I CAN'T GET ANYONE ON THE PHONE.
THERE'VE BEEN CASUALTIES.
ANYONE WE KNOW?
DO YOU KNOW A COLONEL JAMES RHODES?
NO.
WAIT, MAYBE.
THE OTHER IRON MAN. THE WAR MACHINE.
OH, YEAH. I DO KNOW HIM.
OH, NO. WHAT HAPPENED?
THAT'S THE THING.
OH, POOR TONY.
THEY WERE BESTIES.
YEAH.
THAT EXPLAINS WHY HE'S ALL OVER HER.
AND THEY WERE A THING.
WHO WAS?

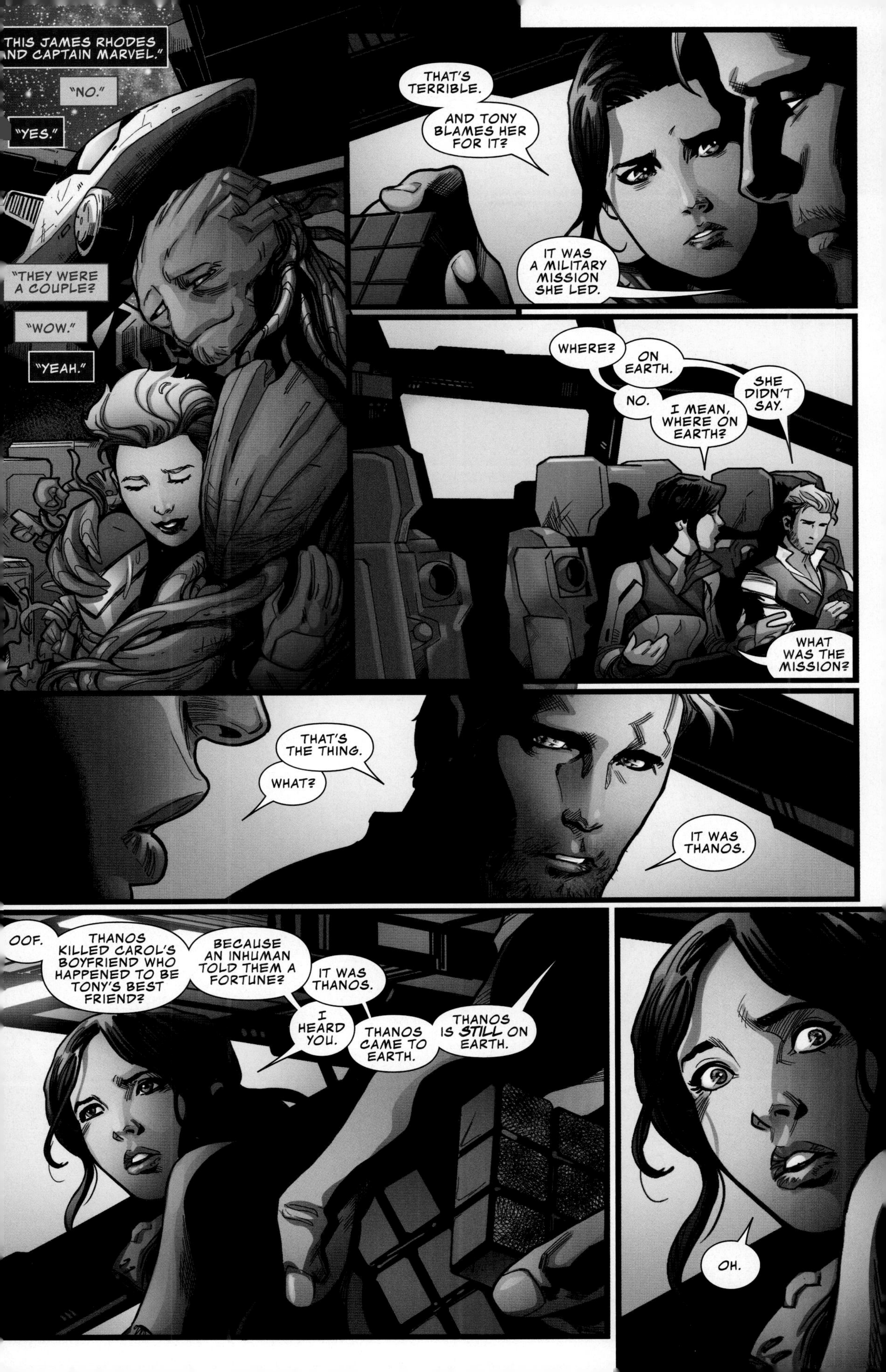

THIS JAMES RHODES AND CAPTAIN MARVEL."
"NO."
"YES."
"THEY WERE A COUPLE?
"WOW."
"YEAH."
THAT'S TERRIBLE.
AND TONY BLAMES HER FOR IT?
IT WAS A MILITARY MISSION SHE LED.
WHERE?
ON EARTH.
NO.
I MEAN, WHERE ON EARTH?
SHE DIDN'T SAY.
WHAT WAS THE MISSION?
THAT'S THE THING.
WHAT?
IT WAS THANOS.
OOF.
THANOS KILLED CAROL'S BOYFRIEND WHO HAPPENED TO BE TONY'S BEST FRIEND?
BECAUSE AN INHUMAN TOLD THEM A FORTUNE?
IT WAS THANOS.
I HEARD YOU.
THANOS CAME TO EARTH.
THANOS IS STILL ON EARTH.
OH.

THE SAME THANOS THAT DRAX AND GAMORA ARE ALWAYS TALKING ABOUT.

YES.

THE SAME THANOS THAT'S GAMORA'S ADOPTED FATHER?

I DO BELIEVE THERE IS ONLY ONE THANOS.

"THE ONE GAMORA'S BEEN SCOURING THE GALAXY FOR EVERY FREE SECOND SHE HAS."

"YES."

"WHERE IS THANOS NOW?"

"DANVERS DIDN'T SAY."

"YOU ASKED?"

SHE SAID IT WAS CLASSIFIED.

BUT THEY CAUGHT HIM? THEY HAVE HIM?

HE'S IN, HER WORDS, "PROTECTIVE CUSTODY."

WE HAVE TO TELL GAMORA.

SHE'LL BE THRILLED!

PETER, YOU HAVE TO TELL HER.

FIRST OF ALL, SHE WON'T BE THRILLED.

IT WON'T BE ENOUGH FOR HER.

YOU HAVE TO TELL HER.

YOU. HAVE. TO. TELL. HER. NOW.

LISTEN, SHE'S THE BEST FIGHTER IN THE WORLD.

SHE'S THE MOST DANGEROUS WOMAN IN THE GALAXY.

THAT'S HOW I WAS INTRODUCED TO HER.

AND THE ONLY THING SHE HASN'T BEEN ABLE TO PULL OFF WITH THE SAME PRECISION AND CONFIDENCE THAT GAVE HER THAT REPUTATION...

"...IS DEALING WITH HER FATHER.

"EVERY TIME SHE HAS GOTTEN HER HANDS AROUND THANOS' THROAT, SOMETHING HAS GONE HORRIBLY WRONG.

"HE ALWAYS GETS TO HER. HE ALWAYS GETS AWAY.

"AND MORE TIMES THAN NOT, US TRYING TO HELP HER ONLY MADE IT WORSE.

"PEOPLE--FRIENDS OF OURS--HAVE DIED TRYING TO HELP HER WITH THIS.

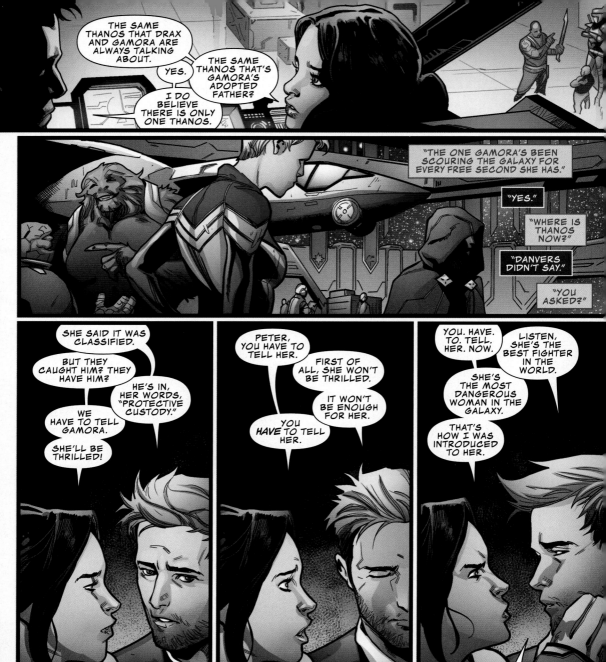

"ALL I AM SAYING IS--WHAT IF, JUST THIS ONCE, WE THOUGHT ABOUT THE CONSEQUENCES OF OUR ACTIONS...
"WHAT WOULD HAPPEN IF I TELL HER NOW?
"DON'T ANSWER. I'LL TELL YOU.
"I'M PRETTY SURE SHE WILL RIP THE EARTH APART LOOKING FOR HIM.
"AND THEN THE HEROES OF EARTH WILL DO EVERYTHING THEY CAN TO STOP HER.
"I TELL HER. SHE GOES NUTS.
"AND IN THE CHAOS...THANOS GETS AWAY.
"YET AGAIN.
AND WHATEVER HE DOES AFTER THAT WILL MEAN BLOOD ON OUR HANDS FOR LETTING IT HAPPEN..."
"BUT WHAT WILL GAMORA DO WHEN SHE FINDS OUT YOU KEPT THIS FROM HER?"
"YEAH..."

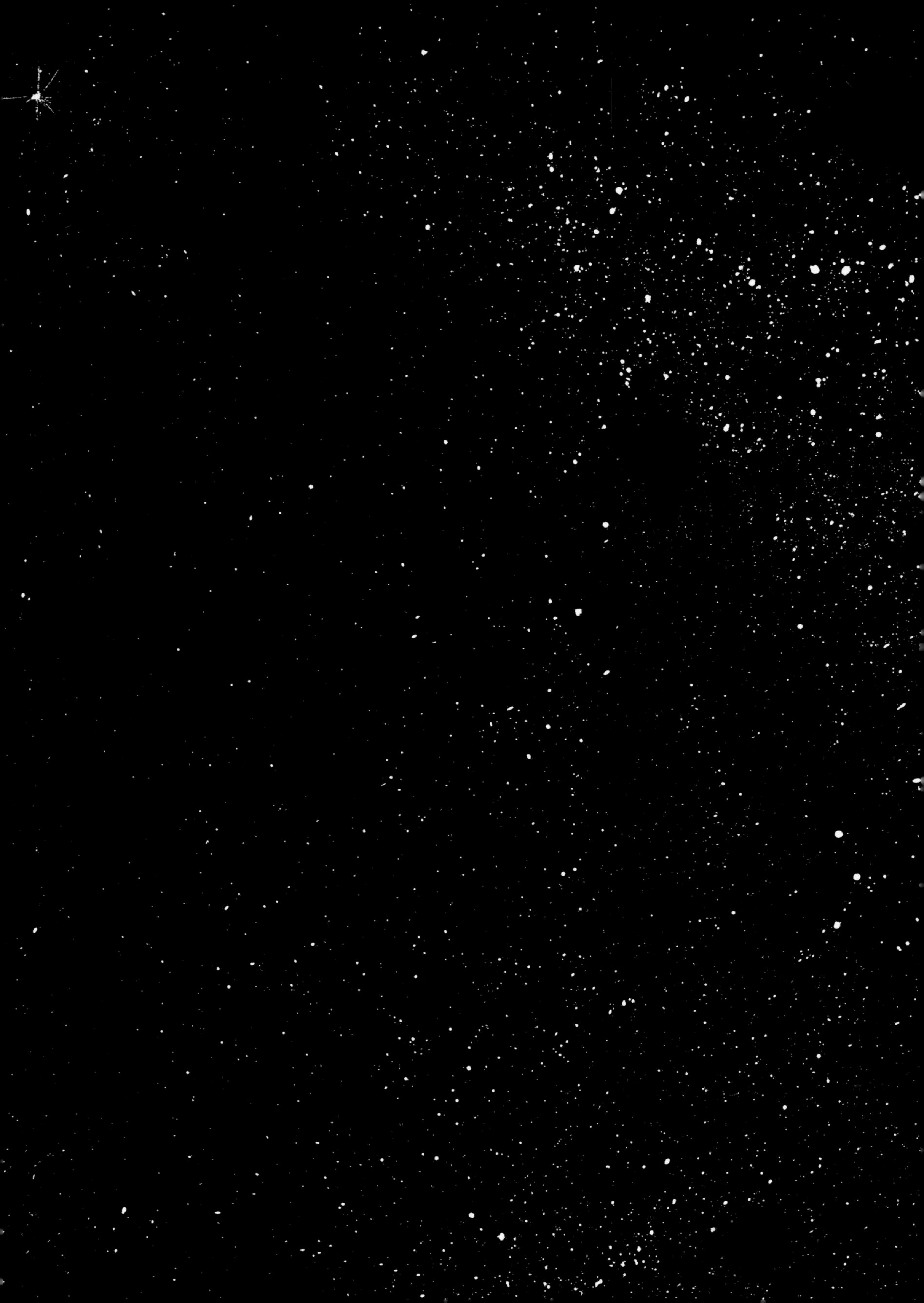

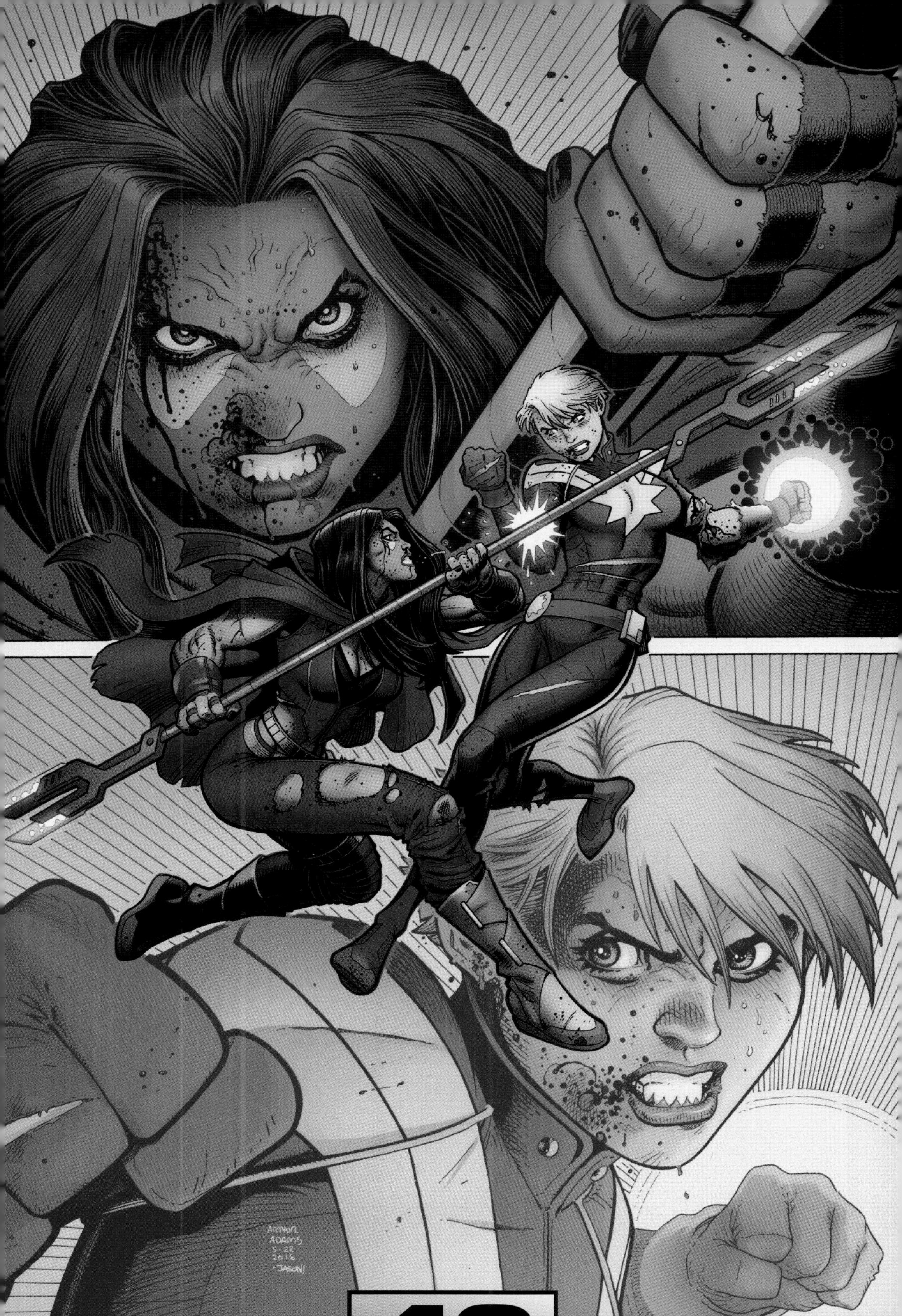
ARTHUR ADAMS 5-22 2016 +JASON!

12

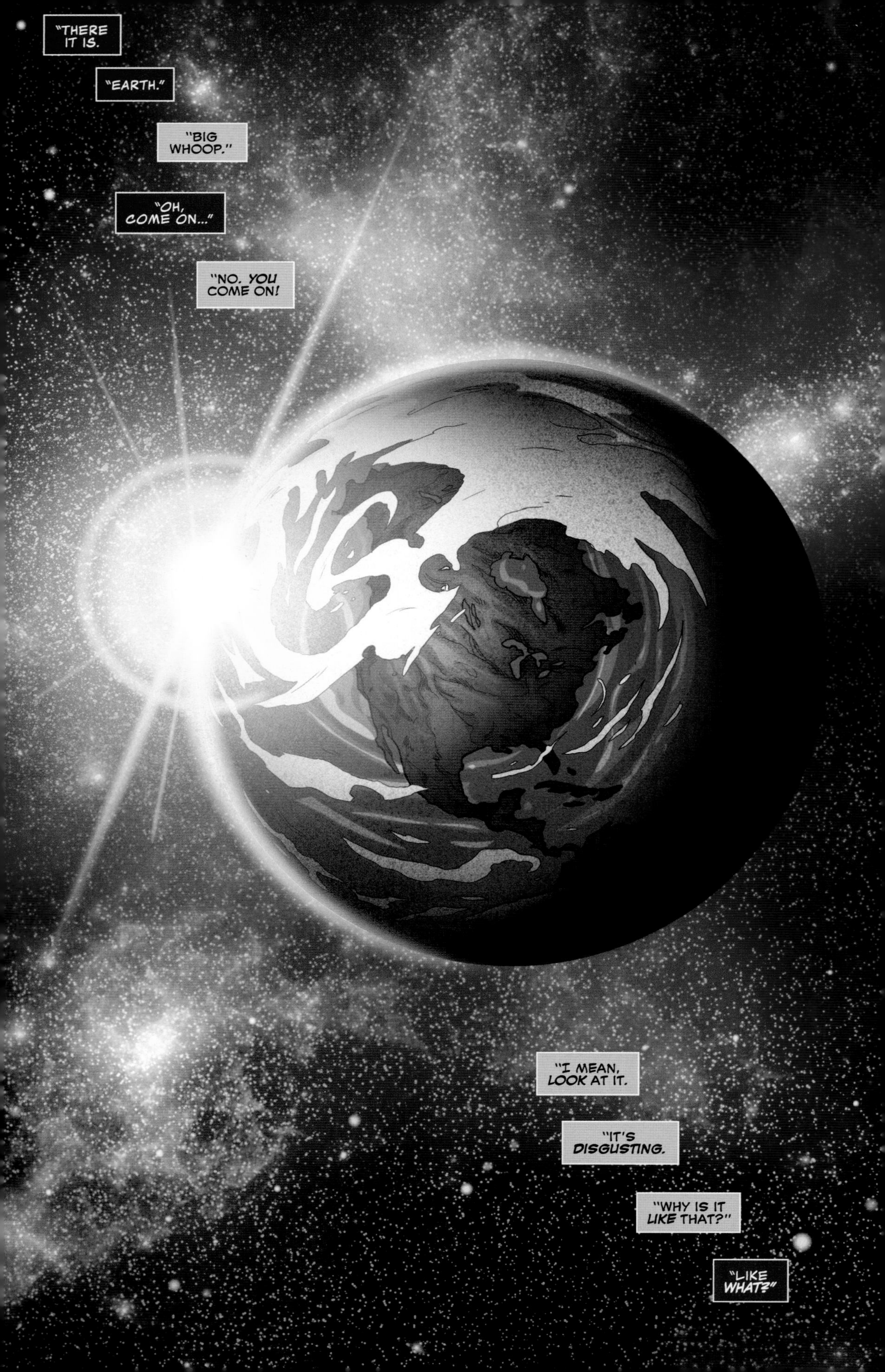
"THERE IT IS.
"EARTH."
"BIG WHOOP."
"OH, COME ON..."
"NO. YOU COME ON!
"I MEAN, LOOK AT IT.
"IT'S DISGUSTING.
"WHY IS IT LIKE THAT?"
"LIKE WHAT?"

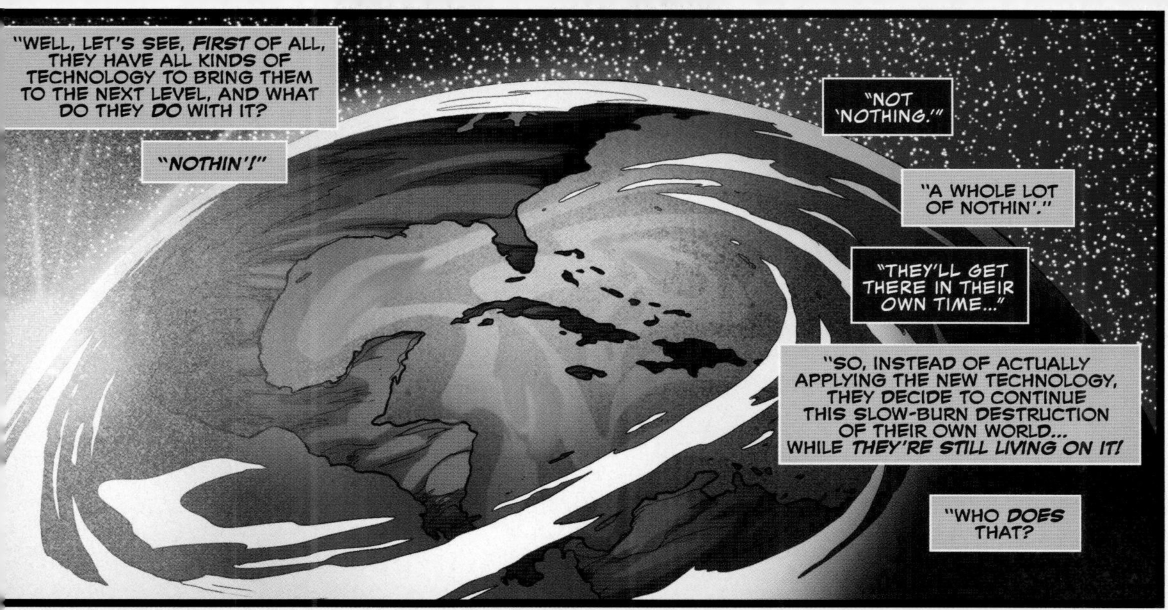
"WELL, LET'S SEE, FIRST OF ALL, THEY HAVE ALL KINDS OF TECHNOLOGY TO BRING THEM TO THE NEXT LEVEL, AND WHAT DO THEY DO WITH IT?
"NOTHIN'!"
"NOT 'NOTHING.'"
"A WHOLE LOT OF NOTHIN'."
"THEY'LL GET THERE IN THEIR OWN TIME..."
"SO, INSTEAD OF ACTUALLY APPLYING THE NEW TECHNOLOGY, THEY DECIDE TO CONTINUE THIS SLOW-BURN DESTRUCTION OF THEIR OWN WORLD... WHILE THEY'RE STILL LIVING ON IT!
"WHO DOES THAT?

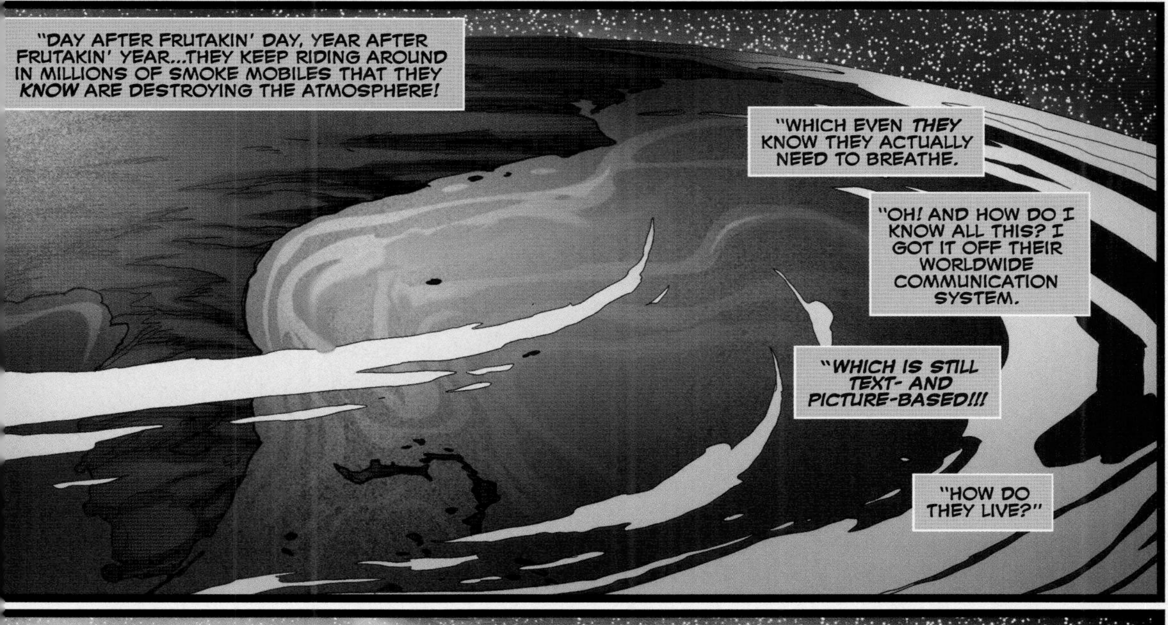
"DAY AFTER FRUTAKIN' DAY, YEAR AFTER FRUTAKIN' YEAR...THEY KEEP RIDING AROUND IN MILLIONS OF SMOKE MOBILES THAT THEY KNOW ARE DESTROYING THE ATMOSPHERE!
"WHICH EVEN THEY KNOW THEY ACTUALLY NEED TO BREATHE.
"OH! AND HOW DO I KNOW ALL THIS? I GOT IT OFF THEIR WORLDWIDE COMMUNICATION SYSTEM.
"WHICH IS STILL TEXT- AND PICTURE-BASED!!!
"HOW DO THEY LIVE?"

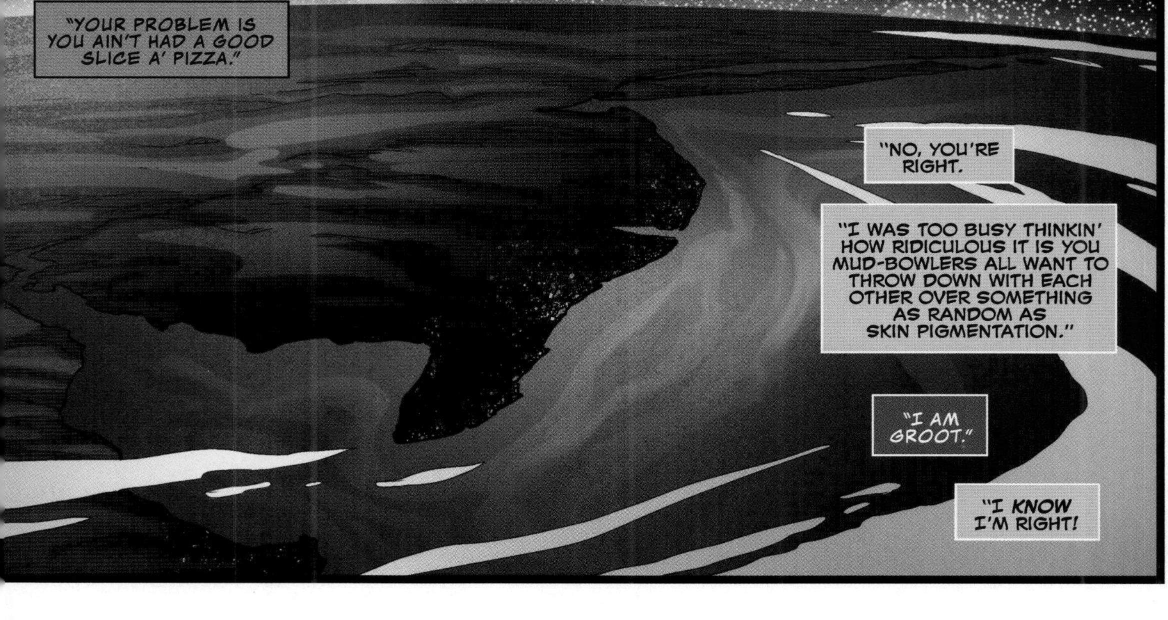
"YOUR PROBLEM IS YOU AIN'T HAD A GOOD SLICE A' PIZZA."
"NO, YOU'RE RIGHT.
"I WAS TOO BUSY THINKIN' HOW RIDICULOUS IT IS YOU MUD-BOWLERS ALL WANT TO THROW DOWN WITH EACH OTHER OVER SOMETHING AS RANDOM AS SKIN PIGMENTATION."
"I AM GROOT."
"I KNOW I'M RIGHT!

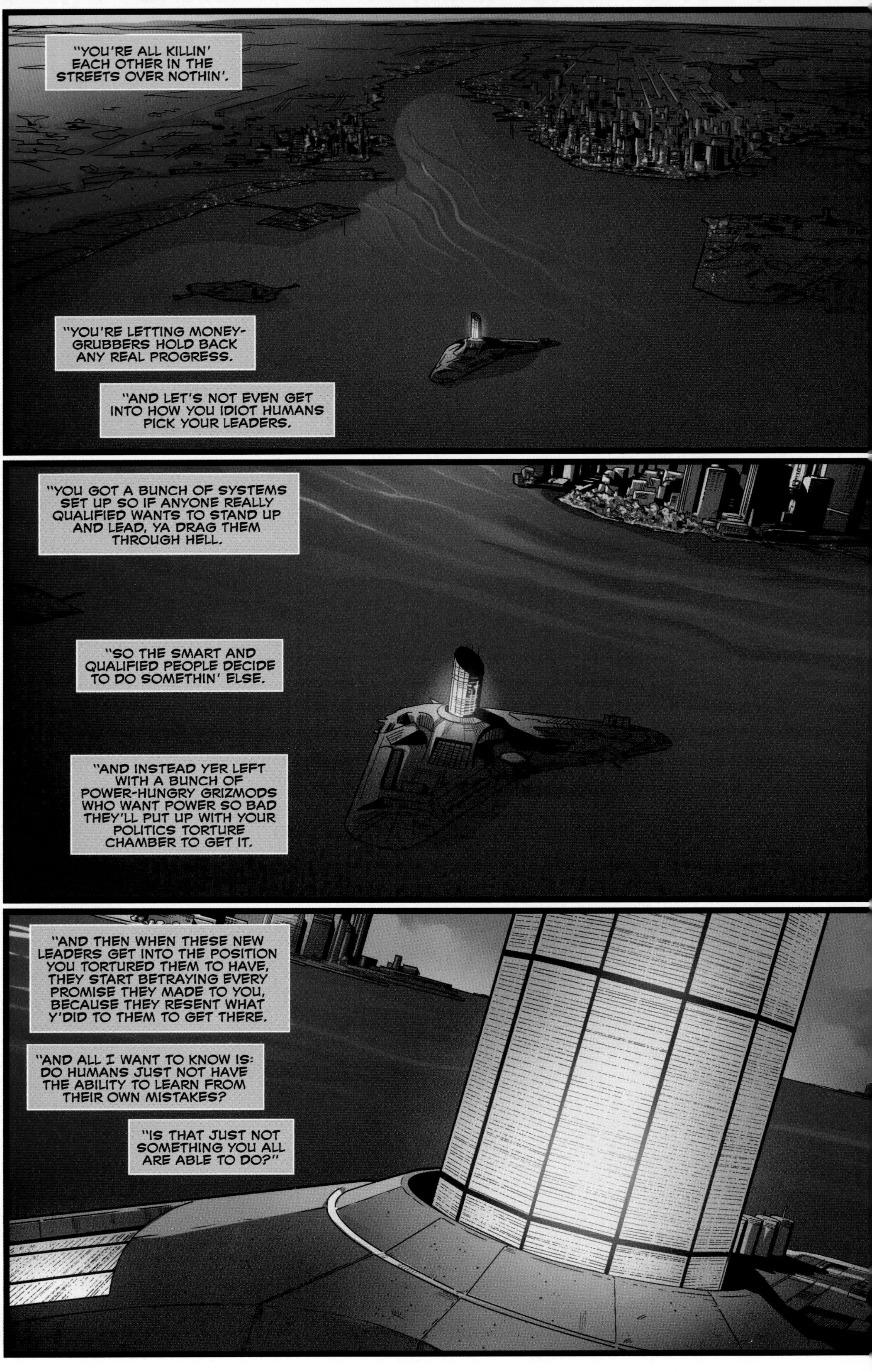
"YOU'RE ALL KILLIN' EACH OTHER IN THE STREETS OVER NOTHIN'.
"YOU'RE LETTING MONEY-GRUBBERS HOLD BACK ANY REAL PROGRESS.
"AND LET'S NOT EVEN GET INTO HOW YOU IDIOT HUMANS PICK YOUR LEADERS.
"YOU GOT A BUNCH OF SYSTEMS SET UP SO IF ANYONE REALLY QUALIFIED WANTS TO STAND UP AND LEAD, YA DRAG THEM THROUGH HELL.
"SO THE SMART AND QUALIFIED PEOPLE DECIDE TO DO SOMETHIN' ELSE.
"AND INSTEAD YER LEFT WITH A BUNCH OF POWER-HUNGRY GRIZMODS WHO WANT POWER SO BAD THEY'LL PUT UP WITH YOUR POLITICS TORTURE CHAMBER TO GET IT.
"AND THEN WHEN THESE NEW LEADERS GET INTO THE POSITION YOU TORTURED THEM TO HAVE, THEY START BETRAYING EVERY PROMISE THEY MADE TO YOU, BECAUSE THEY RESENT WHAT Y'DID TO THEM TO GET THERE.
"AND ALL I WANT TO KNOW IS: DO HUMANS JUST NOT HAVE THE ABILITY TO LEARN FROM THEIR OWN MISTAKES?
"IS THAT JUST NOT SOMETHING YOU ALL ARE ABLE TO DO?"

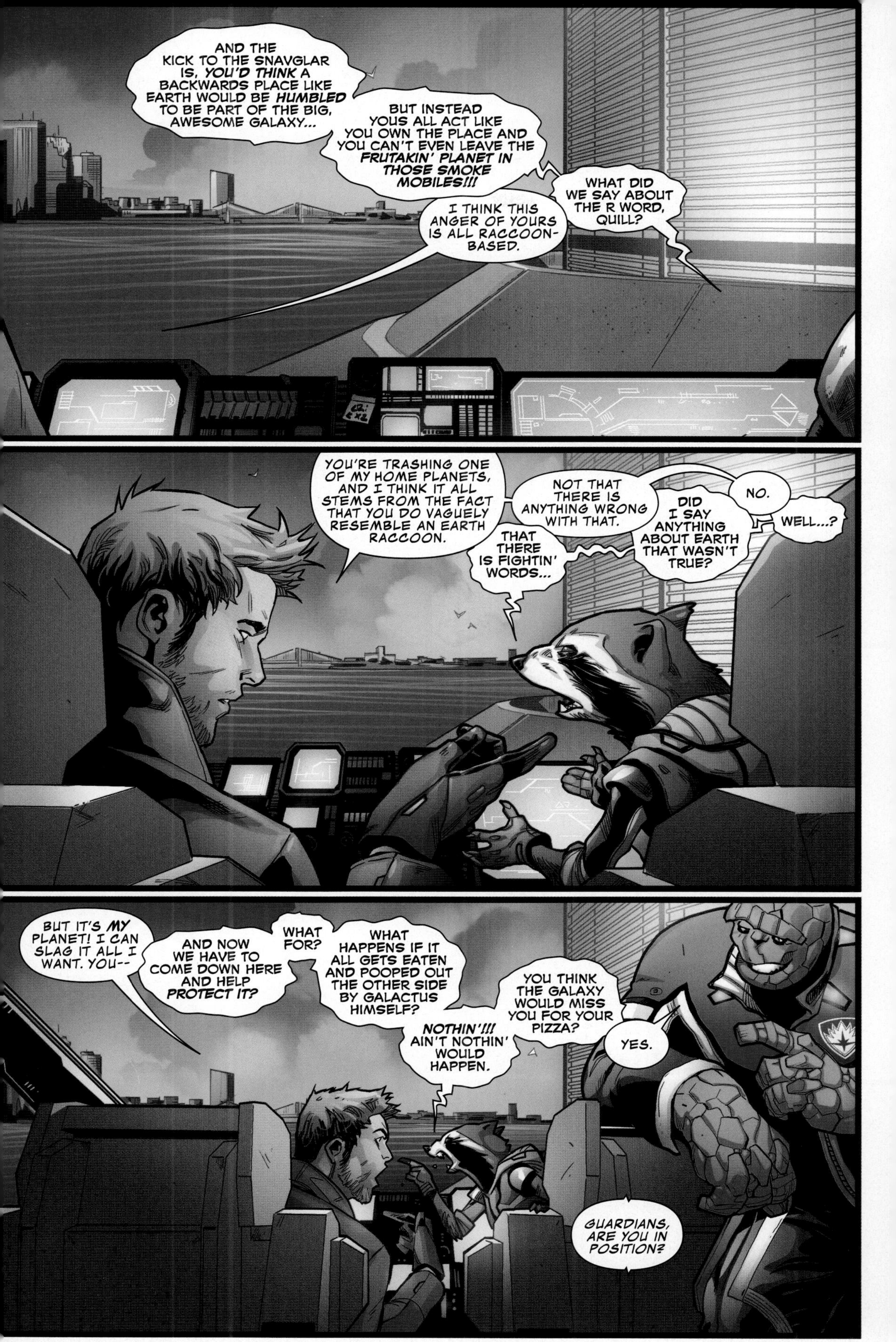
AND THE KICK TO THE SNAVGLAR IS, YOU'D THINK A BACKWARDS PLACE LIKE EARTH WOULD BE HUMBLED TO BE PART OF THE BIG, AWESOME GALAXY...
BUT INSTEAD YOUS ALL ACT LIKE YOU OWN THE PLACE AND YOU CAN'T EVEN LEAVE THE FRUTAKIN' PLANET IN THOSE SMOKE MOBILES!!!
I THINK THIS ANGER OF YOURS IS ALL RACCOON-BASED.
WHAT DID WE SAY ABOUT THE R WORD, QUILL?
YOU'RE TRASHING ONE OF MY HOME PLANETS, AND I THINK IT ALL STEMS FROM THE FACT THAT YOU DO VAGUELY RESEMBLE AN EARTH RACCOON.
NOT THAT THERE IS ANYTHING WRONG WITH THAT.
NO.
THAT THERE IS FIGHTIN' WORDS...
DID I SAY ANYTHING ABOUT EARTH THAT WASN'T TRUE?
WELL...?
BUT IT'S MY PLANET! I CAN SLAG IT ALL I WANT. YOU--
AND NOW WE HAVE TO COME DOWN HERE AND HELP PROTECT IT?
WHAT FOR?
WHAT HAPPENS IF IT ALL GETS EATEN AND POOPED OUT THE OTHER SIDE BY GALACTUS HIMSELF?
NOTHIN'!!! AIN'T NOTHIN' WOULD HAPPEN.
YOU THINK THE GALAXY WOULD MISS YOU FOR YOUR PIZZA?
YES.
GUARDIANS, ARE YOU IN POSITION?

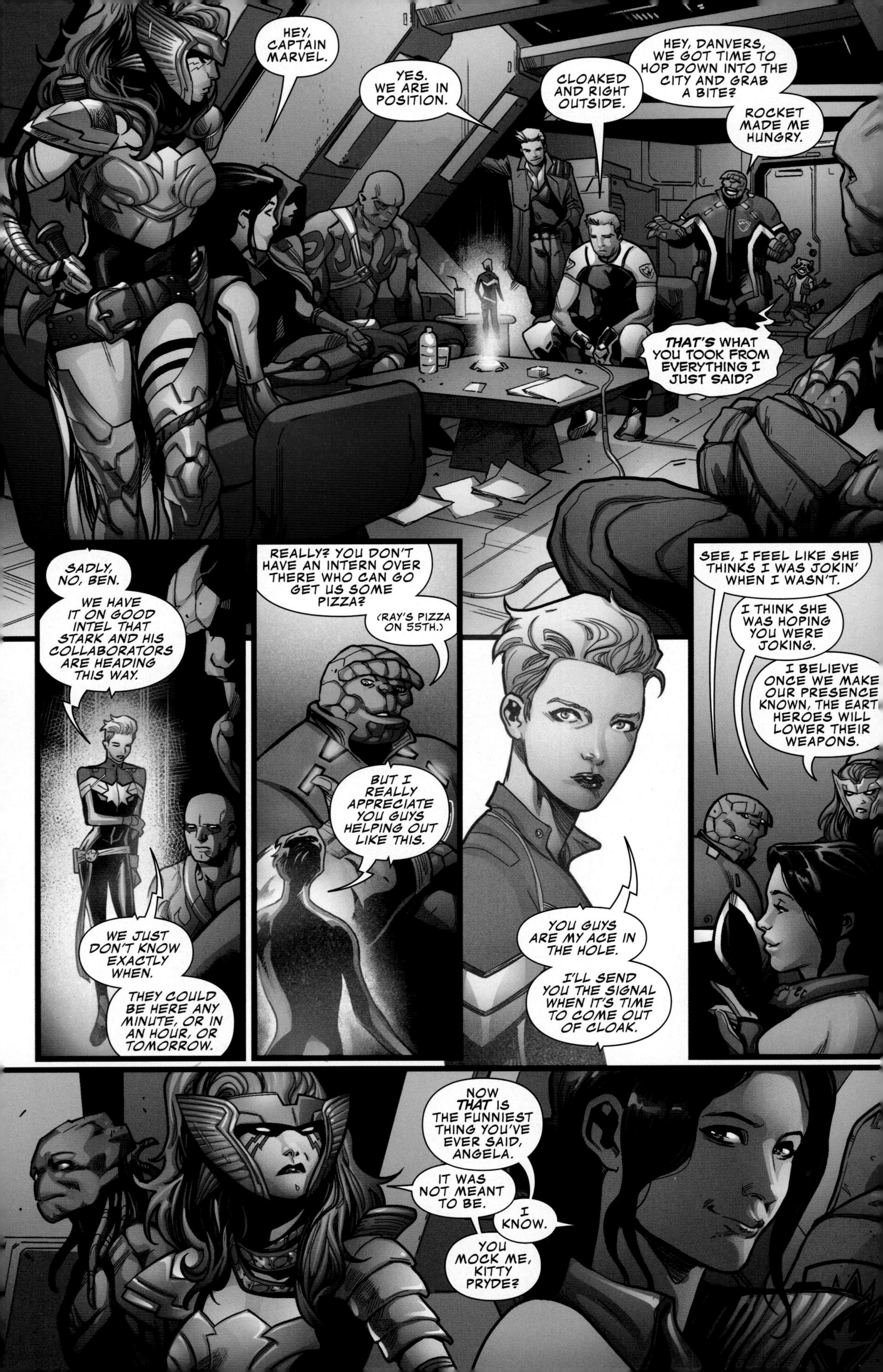

HEY, CAPTAIN MARVEL.
YES. WE ARE IN POSITION.
CLOAKED AND RIGHT OUTSIDE.
HEY, DANVERS, WE GOT TIME TO HOP DOWN INTO THE CITY AND GRAB A BITE?
ROCKET MADE ME HUNGRY.
THAT'S WHAT YOU TOOK FROM EVERYTHING I JUST SAID?
SADLY, NO, BEN.
WE HAVE IT ON GOOD INTEL THAT STARK AND HIS COLLABORATORS ARE HEADING THIS WAY.
WE JUST DON'T KNOW EXACTLY WHEN.
THEY COULD BE HERE ANY MINUTE, OR IN AN HOUR, OR TOMORROW.
REALLY? YOU DON'T HAVE AN INTERN OVER THERE WHO CAN GO GET US SOME PIZZA?
(RAY'S PIZZA ON 55TH.)
BUT I REALLY APPRECIATE YOU GUYS HELPING OUT LIKE THIS.
YOU GUYS ARE MY ACE IN THE HOLE.
I'LL SEND YOU THE SIGNAL WHEN IT'S TIME TO COME OUT OF CLOAK.
SEE, I FEEL LIKE SHE THINKS I WAS JOKIN' WHEN I WASN'T.
I THINK SHE WAS HOPING YOU WERE JOKING.
I BELIEVE ONCE WE MAKE OUR PRESENCE KNOWN, THE EART HEROES WILL LOWER THEIR WEAPONS.
NOW THAT IS THE FUNNIEST THING YOU'VE EVER SAID, ANGELA.
IT WAS NOT MEANT TO BE.
I KNOW.
YOU MOCK ME, KITTY PRYDE?

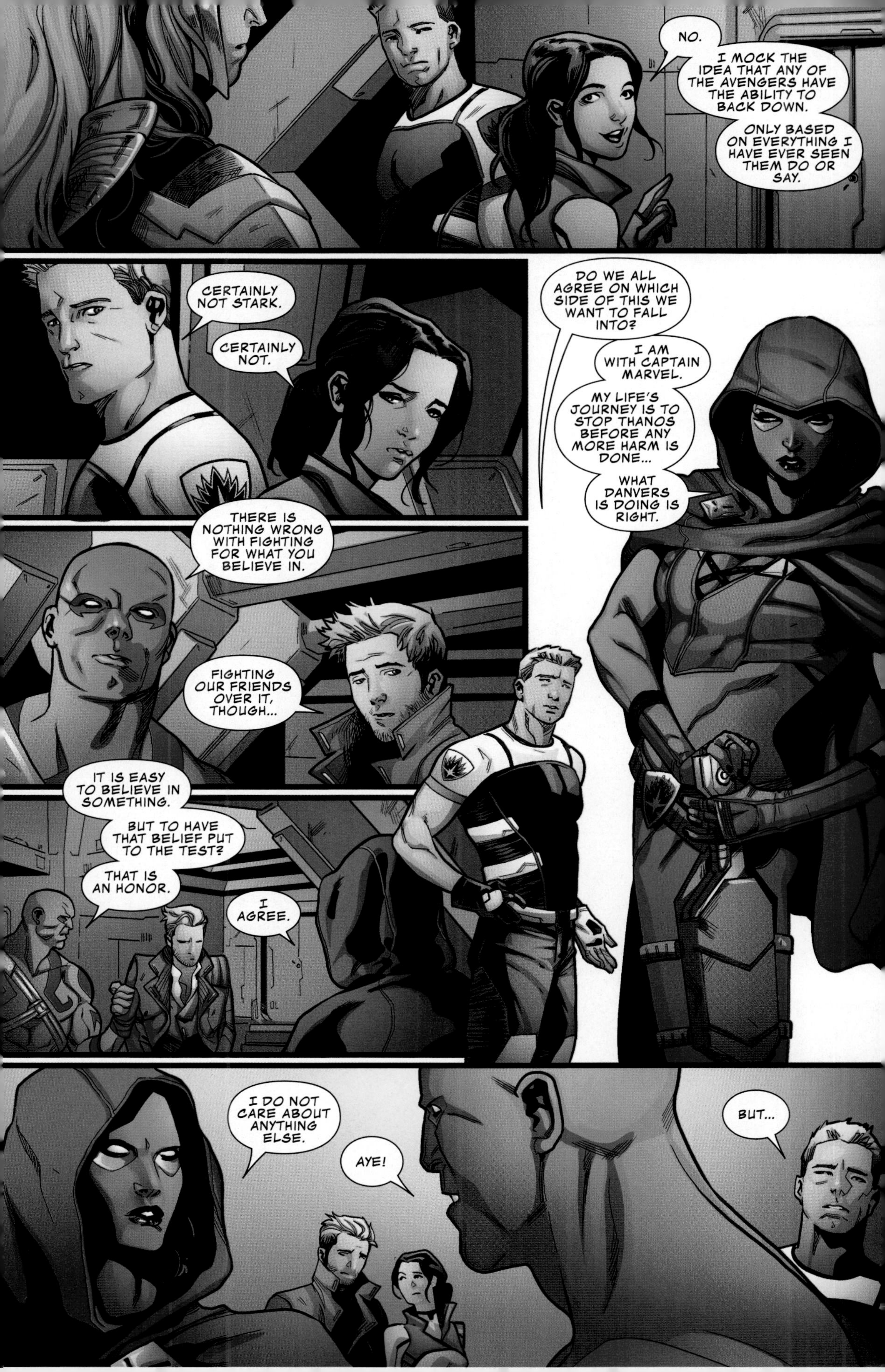
NO.
I MOCK THE IDEA THAT ANY OF THE AVENGERS HAVE THE ABILITY TO BACK DOWN.
ONLY BASED ON EVERYTHING I HAVE EVER SEEN THEM DO OR SAY.
CERTAINLY NOT STARK.
CERTAINLY NOT.
DO WE ALL AGREE ON WHICH SIDE OF THIS WE WANT TO FALL INTO?
I AM WITH CAPTAIN MARVEL.
MY LIFE'S JOURNEY IS TO STOP THANOS BEFORE ANY MORE HARM IS DONE...
WHAT DANVERS IS DOING IS RIGHT.
THERE IS NOTHING WRONG WITH FIGHTING FOR WHAT YOU BELIEVE IN.
FIGHTING OUR FRIENDS OVER IT, THOUGH...
IT IS EASY TO BELIEVE IN SOMETHING.
BUT TO HAVE THAT BELIEF PUT TO THE TEST?
THAT IS AN HONOR.
I AGREE.
I DO NOT CARE ABOUT ANYTHING ELSE.
AYE!
BUT...

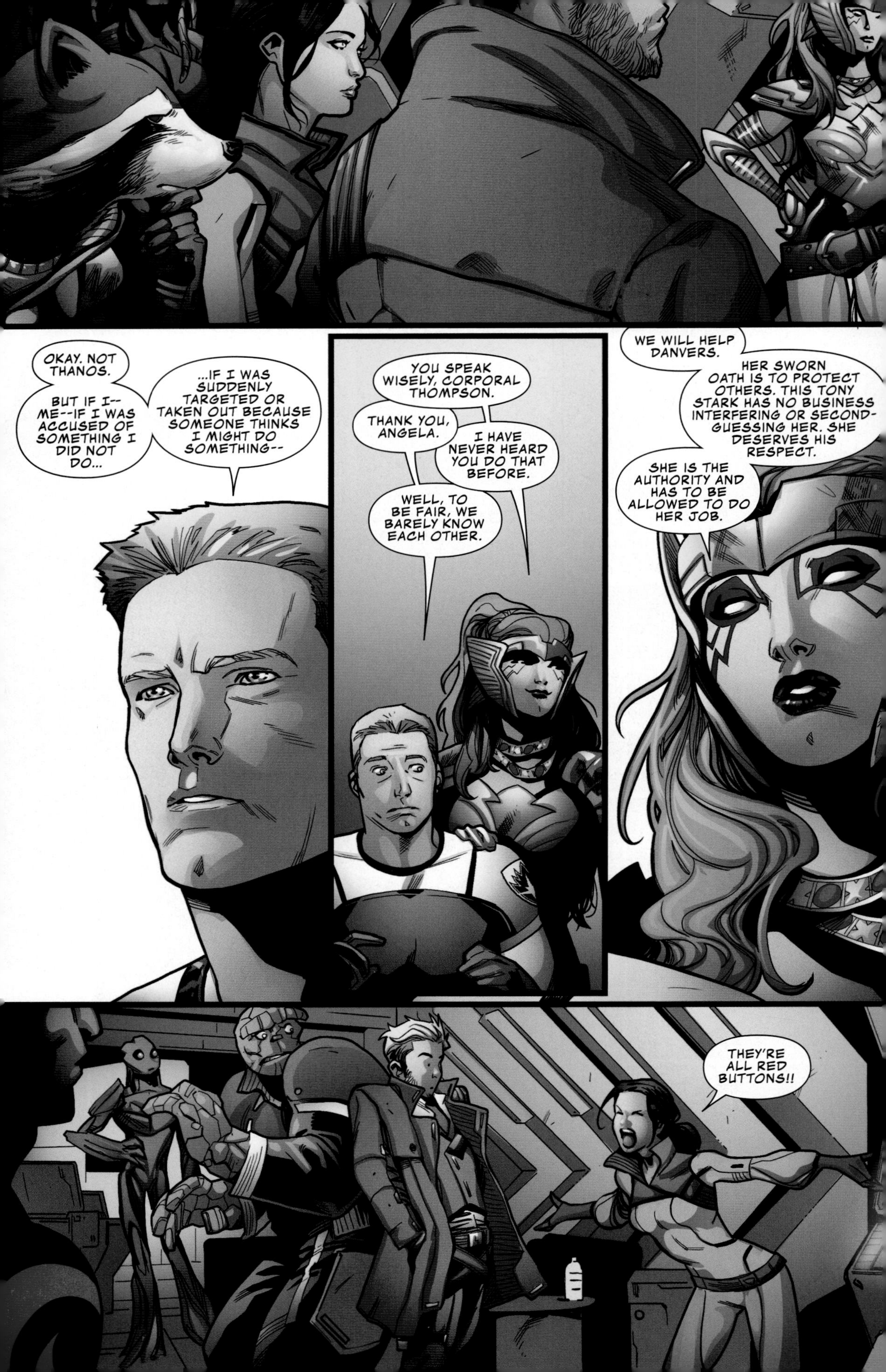
OKAY. NOT THANOS.
BUT IF I--ME--IF I WAS ACCUSED OF SOMETHING I DID NOT DO...
...IF I WAS SUDDENLY TARGETED OR TAKEN OUT BECAUSE SOMEONE THINKS I MIGHT DO SOMETHING--
YOU SPEAK WISELY, CORPORAL THOMPSON.
THANK YOU, ANGELA.
I HAVE NEVER HEARD YOU DO THAT BEFORE.
WELL, TO BE FAIR, WE BARELY KNOW EACH OTHER.
WE WILL HELP DANVERS.
HER SWORN OATH IS TO PROTECT OTHERS. THIS TONY STARK HAS NO BUSINESS INTERFERING OR SECOND-GUESSING HER. SHE DESERVES HIS RESPECT.
SHE IS THE AUTHORITY AND HAS TO BE ALLOWED TO DO HER JOB.
THEY'RE ALL RED BUTTONS!!

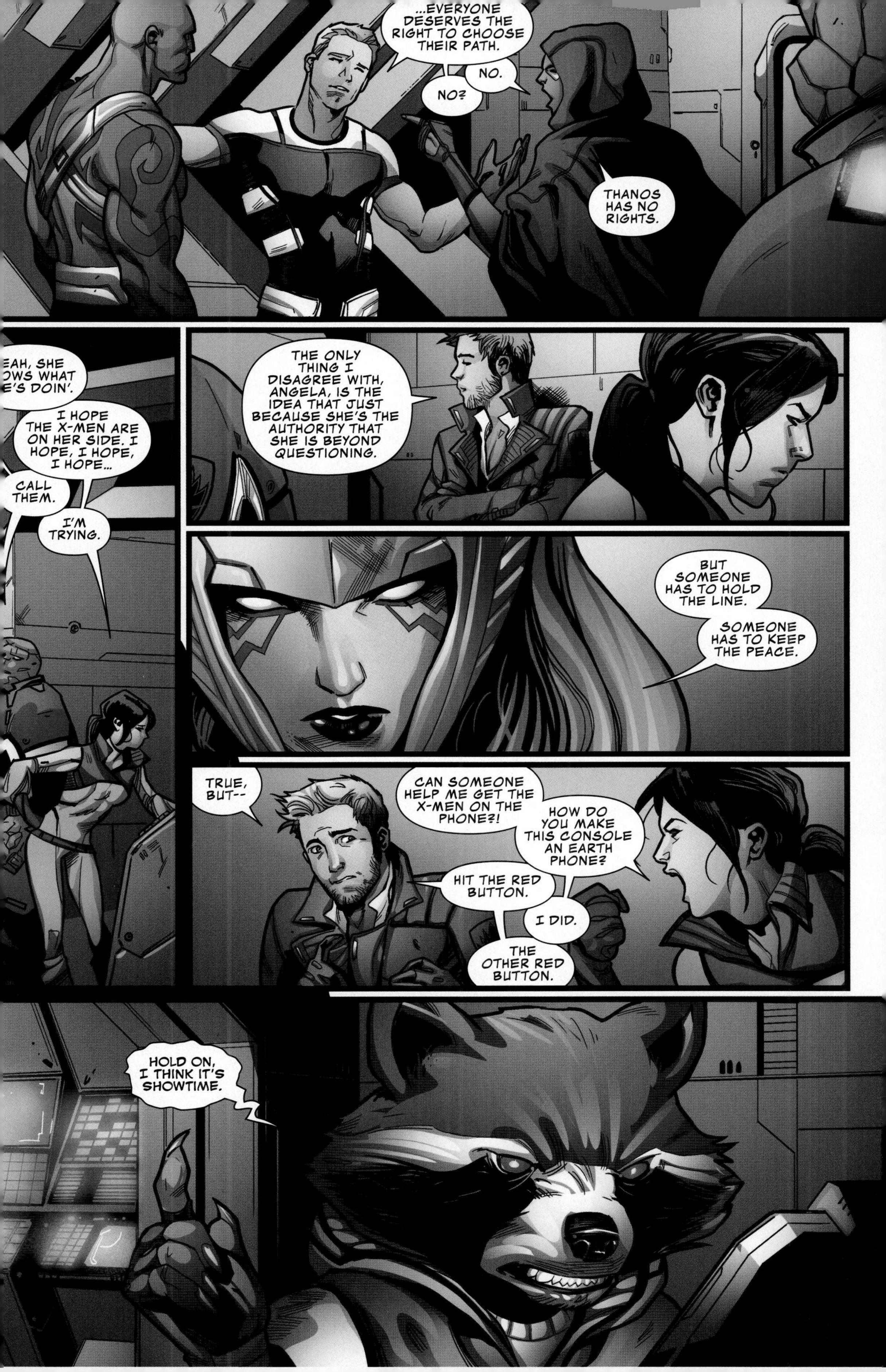
...EVERYONE DESERVES THE RIGHT TO CHOOSE THEIR PATH.
NO.
NO?
THANOS HAS NO RIGHTS.
EAH, SHE OWS WHAT E'S DOIN'.
I HOPE THE X-MEN ARE ON HER SIDE. I HOPE, I HOPE, I HOPE...
CALL THEM.
I'M TRYING.
THE ONLY THING I DISAGREE WITH, ANGELA, IS THE IDEA THAT JUST BECAUSE SHE'S THE AUTHORITY THAT SHE IS BEYOND QUESTIONING.
BUT SOMEONE HAS TO HOLD THE LINE.
SOMEONE HAS TO KEEP THE PEACE.
TRUE, BUT--
CAN SOMEONE HELP ME GET THE X-MEN ON THE PHONE?!
HOW DO YOU MAKE THIS CONSOLE AN EARTH PHONE?
HIT THE RED BUTTON.
I DID.
THE OTHER RED BUTTON.
HOLD ON, I THINK IT'S SHOWTIME.

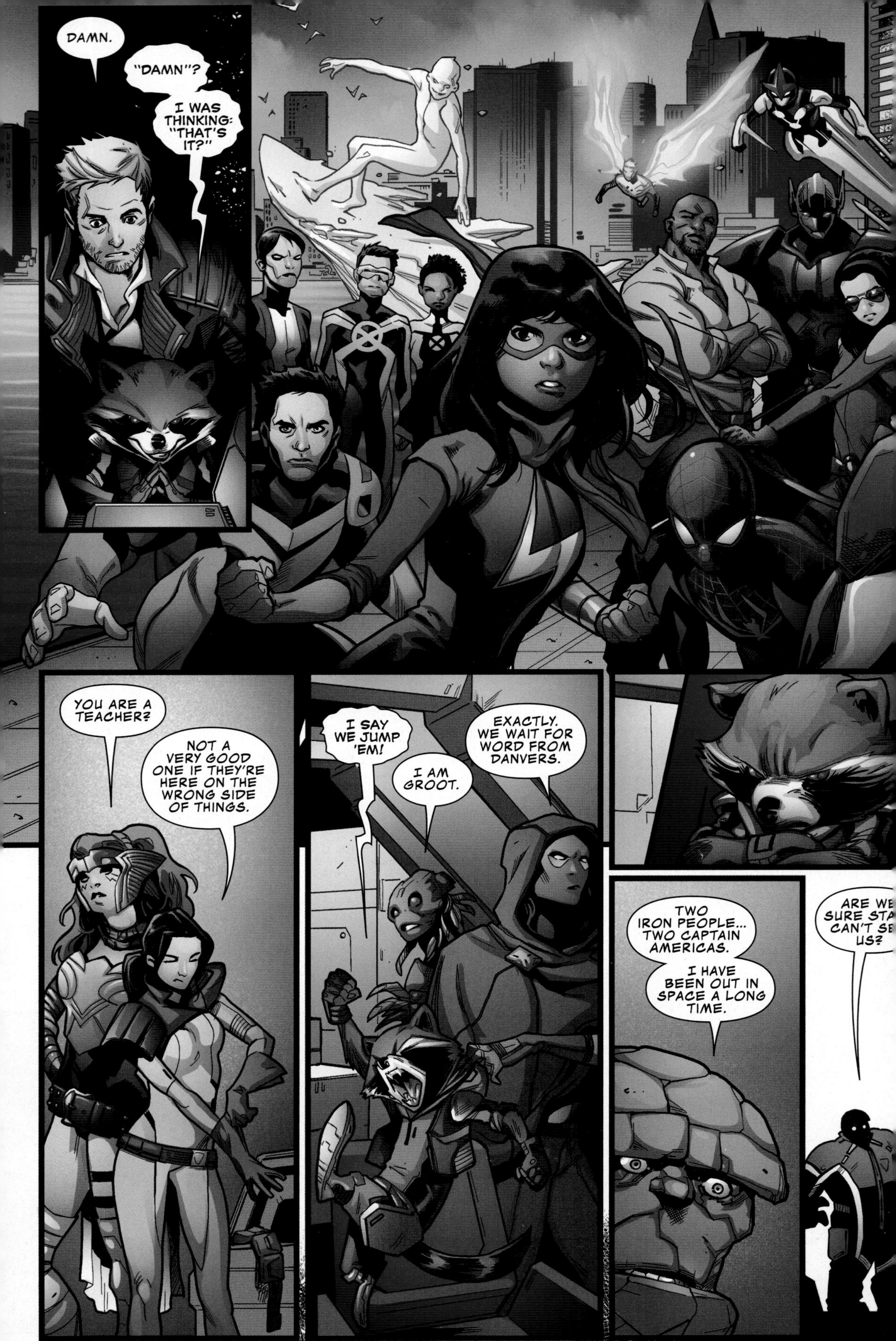
DAMN.
"DAMN"?
I WAS THINKING: "THAT'S IT?"
YOU ARE A TEACHER?
NOT A VERY GOOD ONE IF THEY'RE HERE ON THE WRONG SIDE OF THINGS.
I SAY WE JUMP 'EM!
I AM GROOT.
EXACTLY. WE WAIT FOR WORD FROM DANVERS.
TWO IRON PEOPLE... TWO CAPTAIN AMERICAS.
I HAVE BEEN OUT IN SPACE A LONG TIME.

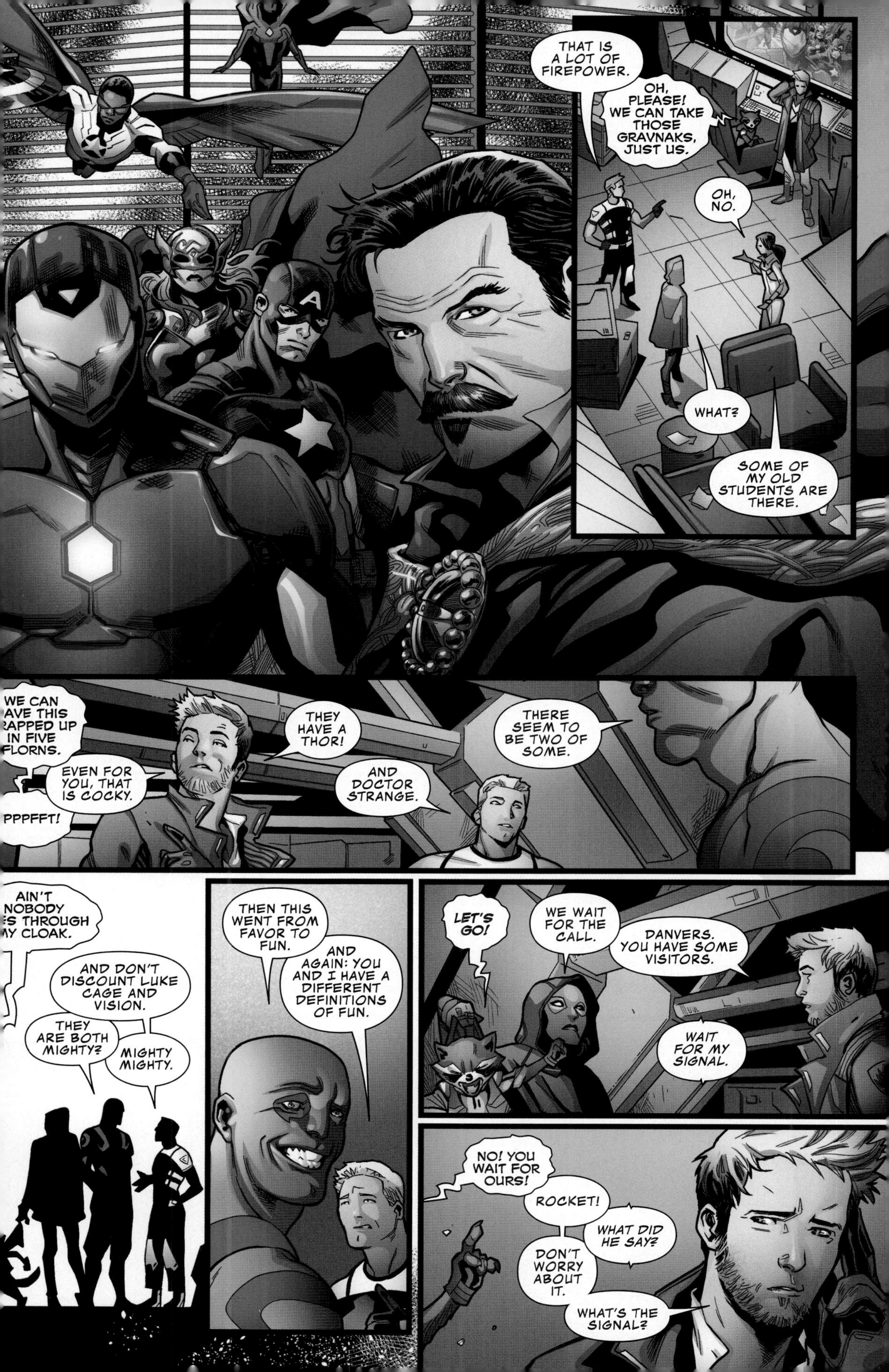
THAT IS A LOT OF FIREPOWER.
OH, PLEASE! WE CAN TAKE THOSE GRAVNAKS, JUST US.
OH, NO.
WHAT?
SOME OF MY OLD STUDENTS ARE THERE.
WE CAN AVE THIS RAPPED UP IN FIVE FLORNS.
EVEN FOR YOU, THAT IS COCKY.
PPPFFT!
THEY HAVE A THOR!
AND DOCTOR STRANGE.
THERE SEEM TO BE TWO OF SOME.
AIN'T NOBODY ES THROUGH MY CLOAK.
AND DON'T DISCOUNT LUKE CAGE AND VISION.
THEY ARE BOTH MIGHTY?
MIGHTY MIGHTY.
THEN THIS WENT FROM FAVOR TO FUN.
AND AGAIN: YOU AND I HAVE A DIFFERENT DEFINITIONS OF FUN.
LET'S GO!
WE WAIT FOR THE CALL.
DANVERS. YOU HAVE SOME VISITORS.
WAIT FOR MY SIGNAL.
NO! YOU WAIT FOR OURS!
ROCKET!
WHAT DID HE SAY?
DON'T WORRY ABOUT IT.
WHAT'S THE SIGNAL?

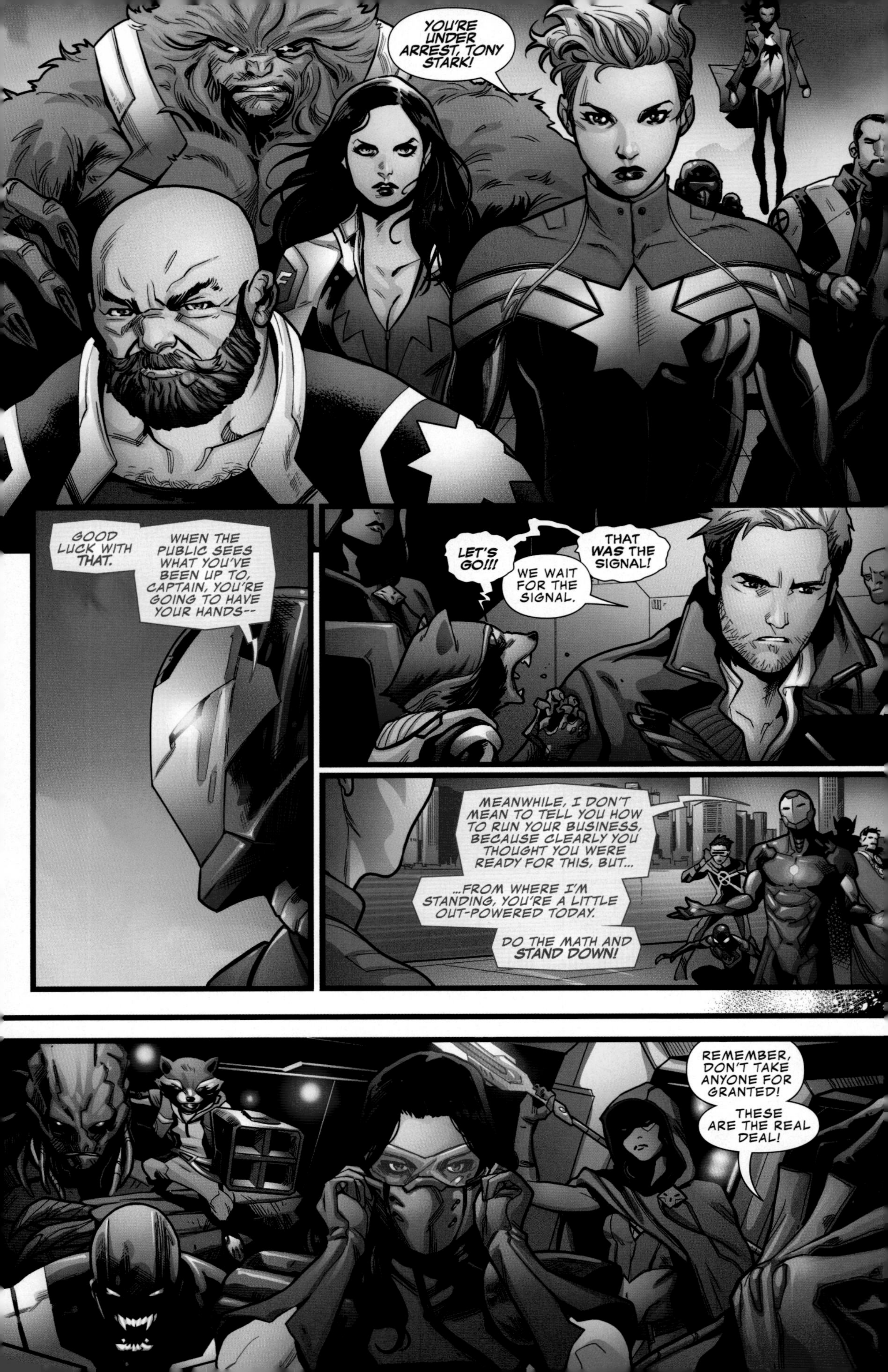
YOU'RE UNDER ARREST, TONY STARK!
GOOD LUCK WITH THAT.
WHEN THE PUBLIC SEES WHAT YOU'VE BEEN UP TO, CAPTAIN, YOU'RE GOING TO HAVE YOUR HANDS--
LET'S GO!!!
WE WAIT FOR THE SIGNAL.
THAT WAS THE SIGNAL!
MEANWHILE, I DON'T MEAN TO TELL YOU HOW TO RUN YOUR BUSINESS, BECAUSE CLEARLY YOU THOUGHT YOU WERE READY FOR THIS, BUT...
...FROM WHERE I'M STANDING, YOU'RE A LITTLE OUT-POWERED TODAY.
DO THE MATH AND STAND DOWN!
REMEMBER, DON'T TAKE ANYONE FOR GRANTED!
THESE ARE THE REAL DEAL!

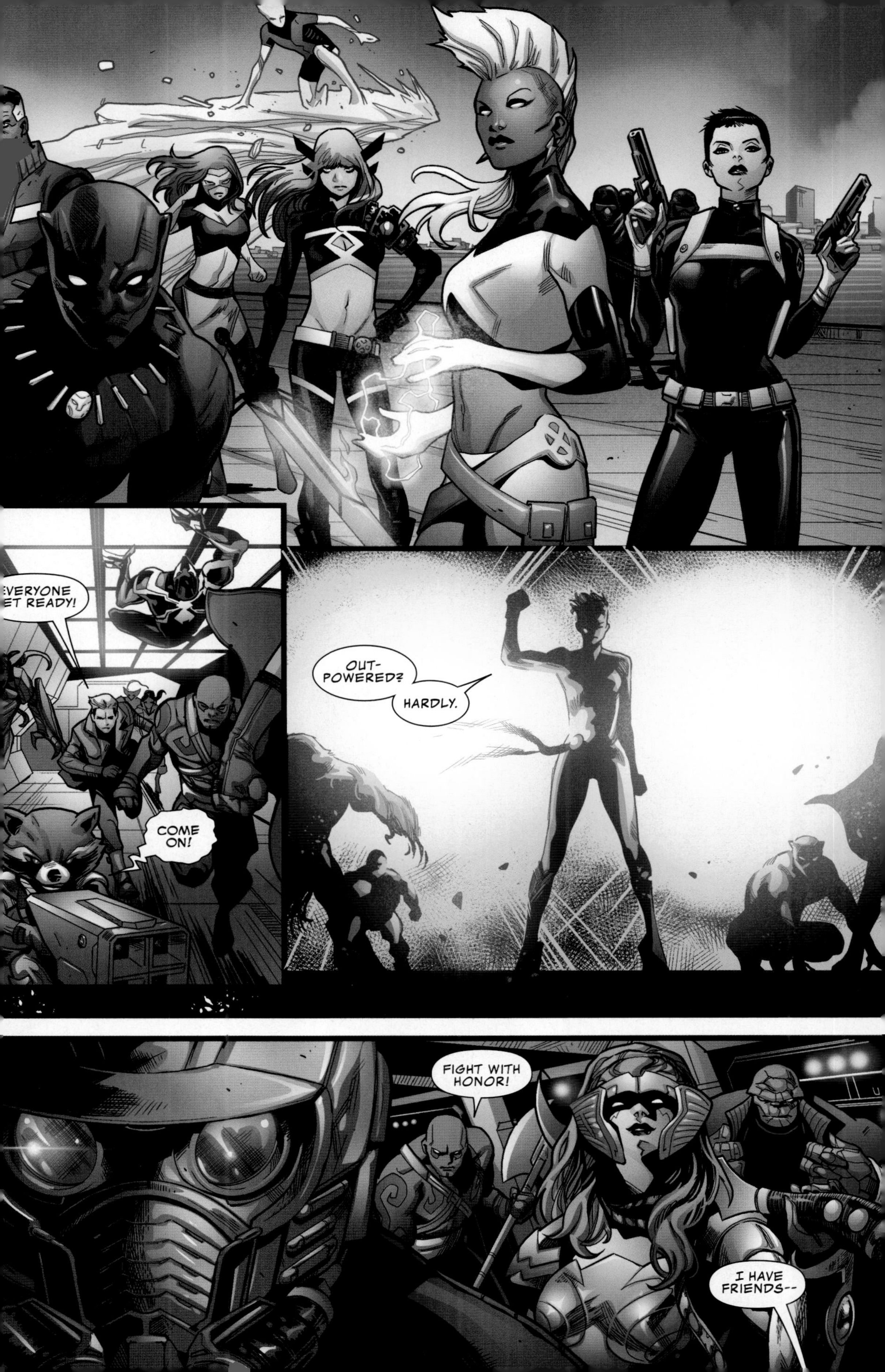

EVERYONE
ET READY!
COME ON!
OUT-POWERED?
HARDLY.
FIGHT WITH HONOR!
I HAVE FRIENDS--

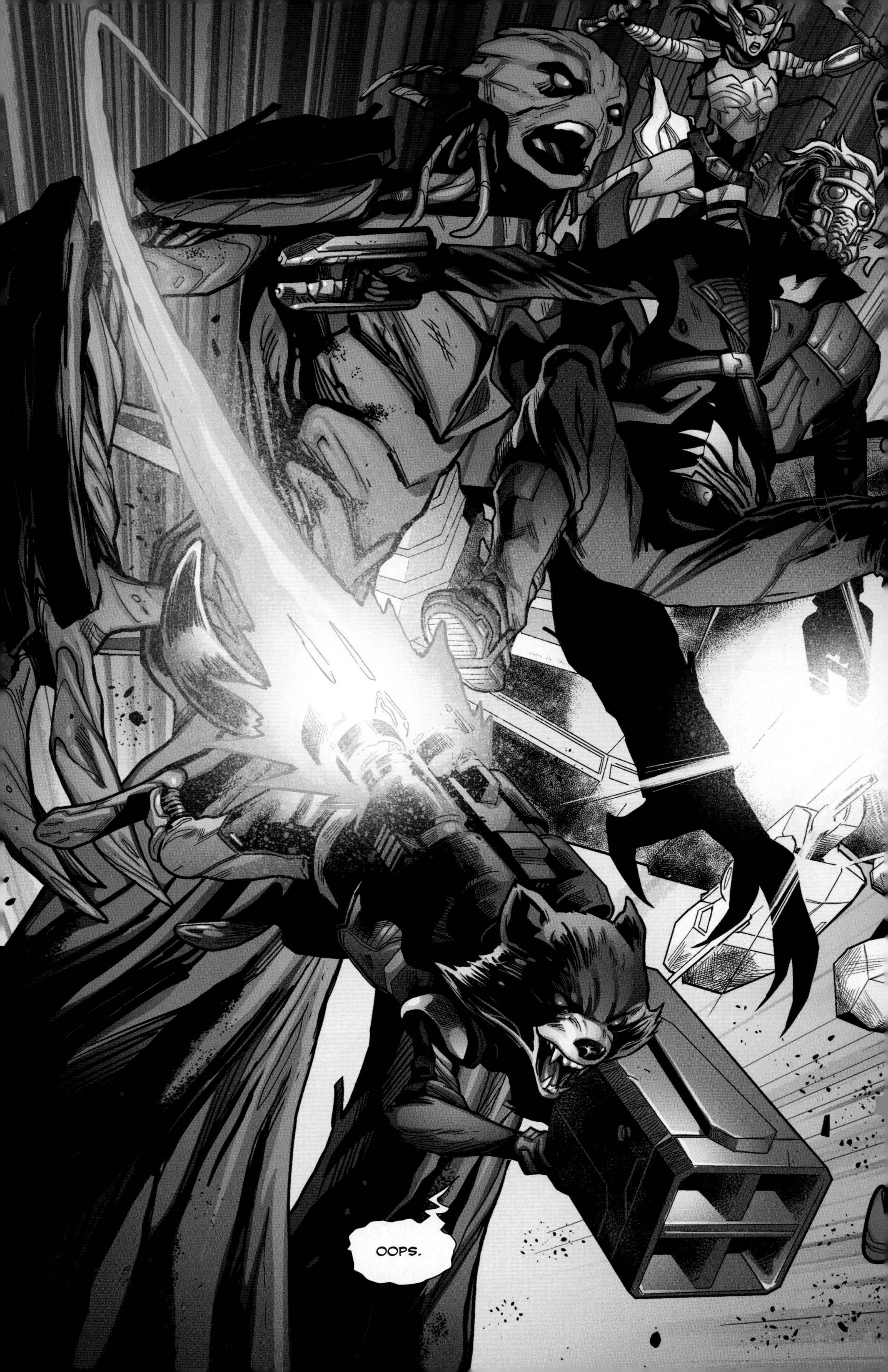
OOPS.

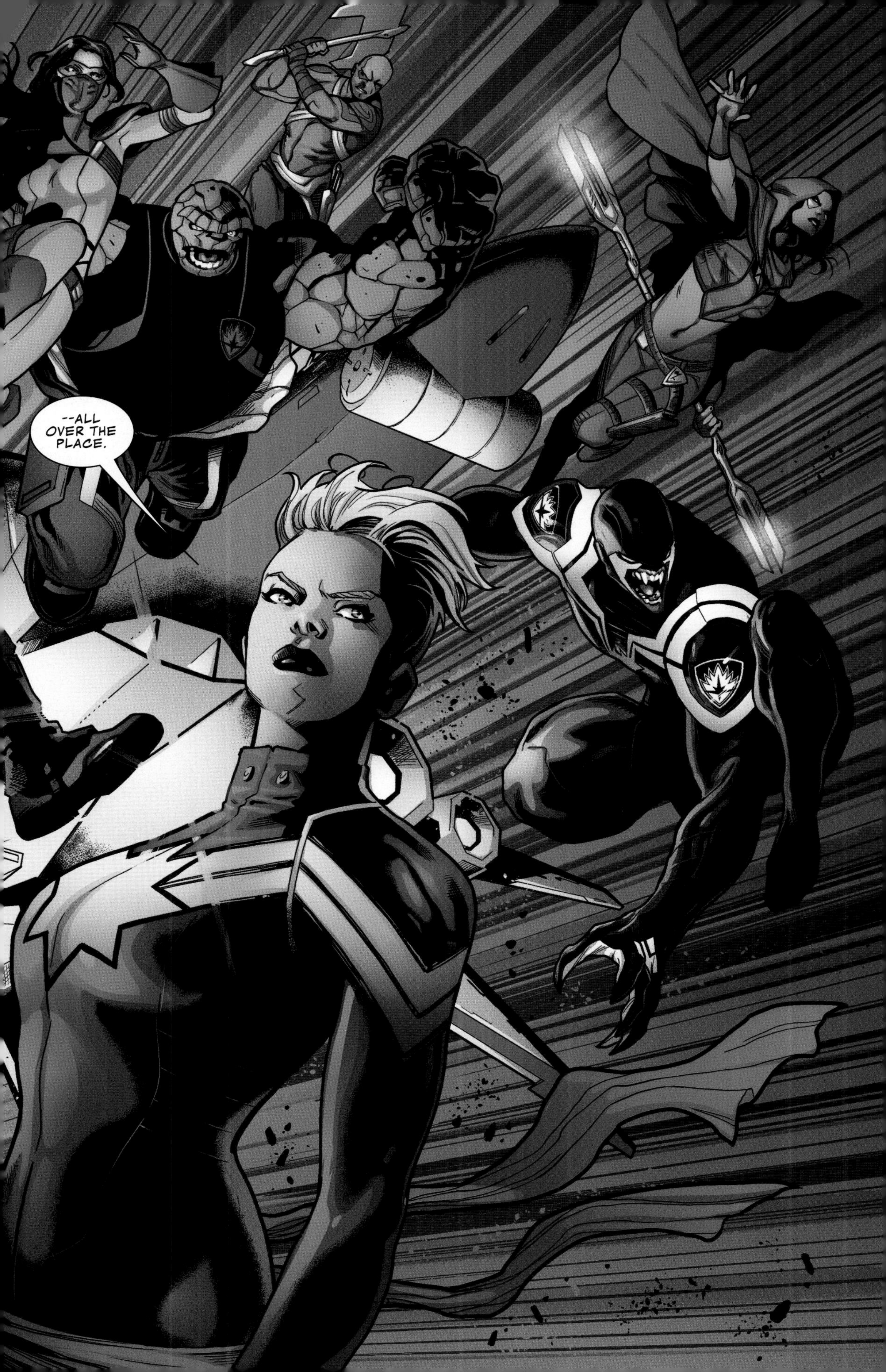
--ALL OVER THE PLACE.

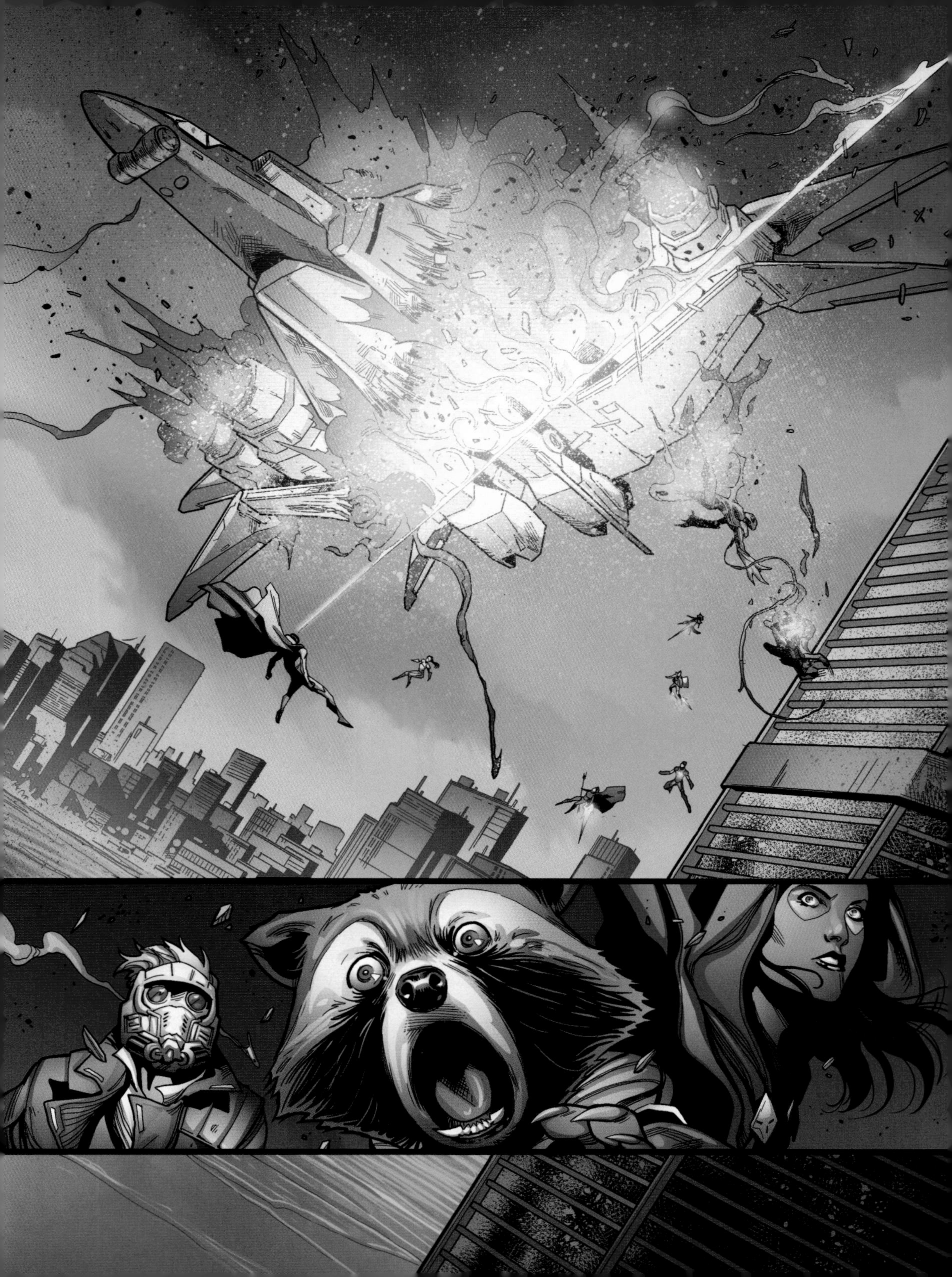

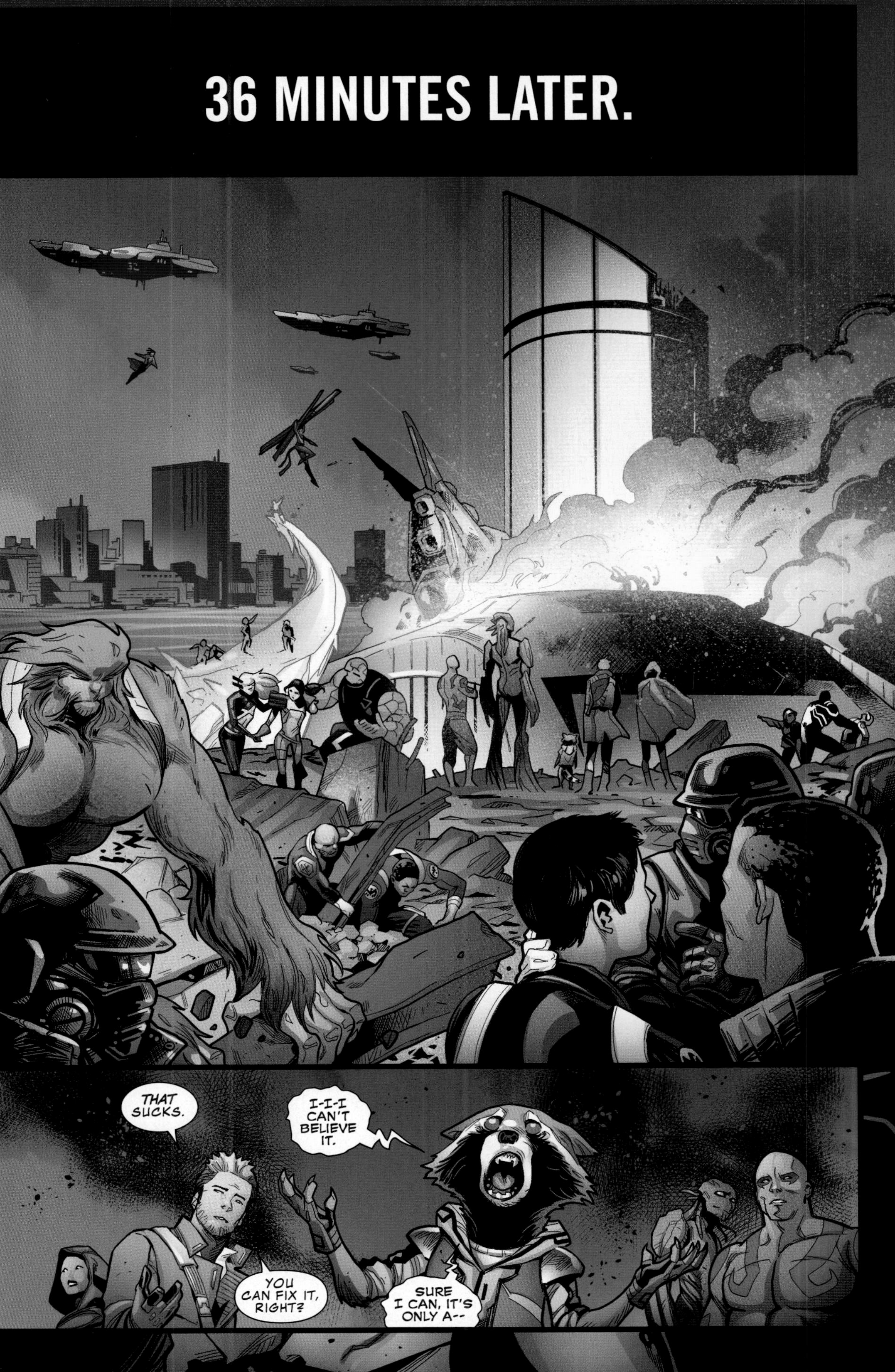
36 MINUTES LATER.
THAT SUCKS.
I-I-I CAN'T BELIEVE IT.
YOU CAN FIX IT, RIGHT?
SURE I CAN, IT'S ONLY A--

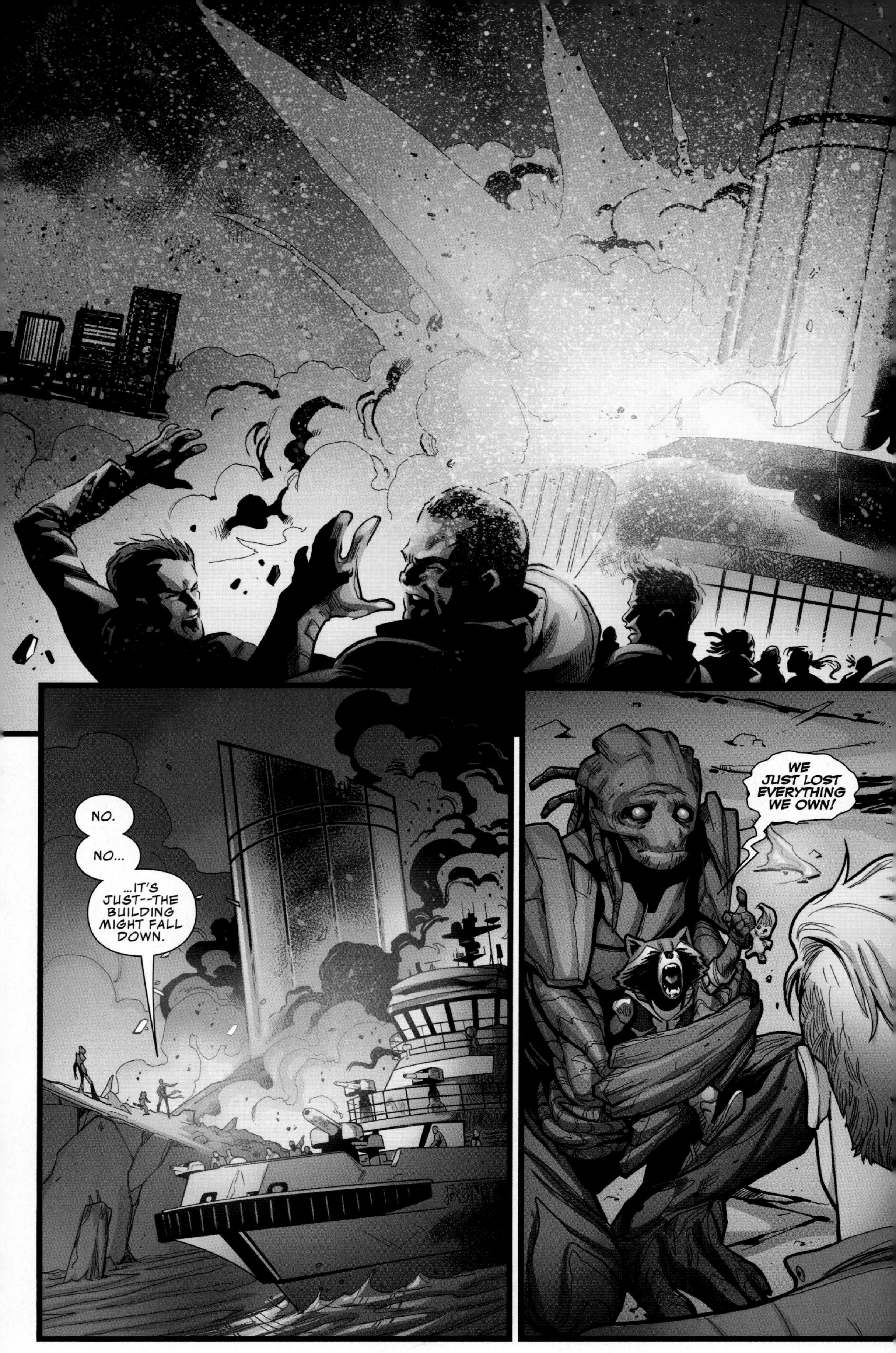
NO.
NO...
...IT'S JUST--THE BUILDING MIGHT FALL DOWN.
WE JUST LOST EVERYTHING WE OWN!

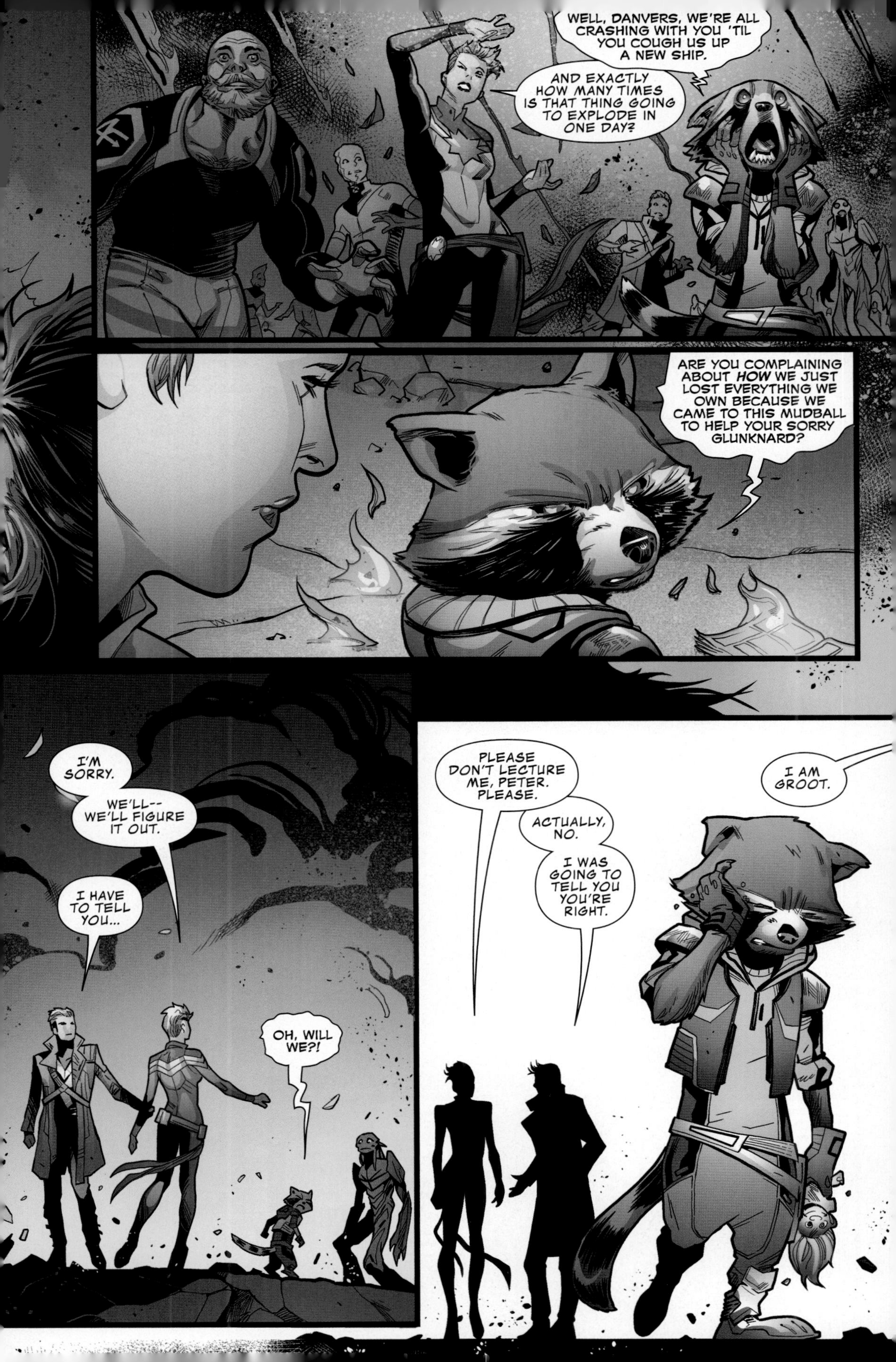
WELL, DANVERS, WE'RE ALL CRASHING WITH YOU 'TIL YOU COUGH US UP A NEW SHIP.
AND EXACTLY HOW MANY TIMES IS THAT THING GOING TO EXPLODE IN ONE DAY?
ARE YOU COMPLAINING ABOUT *HOW* WE JUST LOST EVERYTHING WE OWN BECAUSE WE CAME TO THIS MUDBALL TO HELP YOUR SORRY GLUNKNARD?
I'M SORRY.
WE'LL-- WE'LL FIGURE IT OUT.
I HAVE TO TELL YOU...
OH, WILL WE?!
PLEASE DON'T LECTURE ME, PETER. PLEASE.
ACTUALLY, NO.
I WAS GOING TO TELL YOU YOU'RE RIGHT.
I AM GROOT.

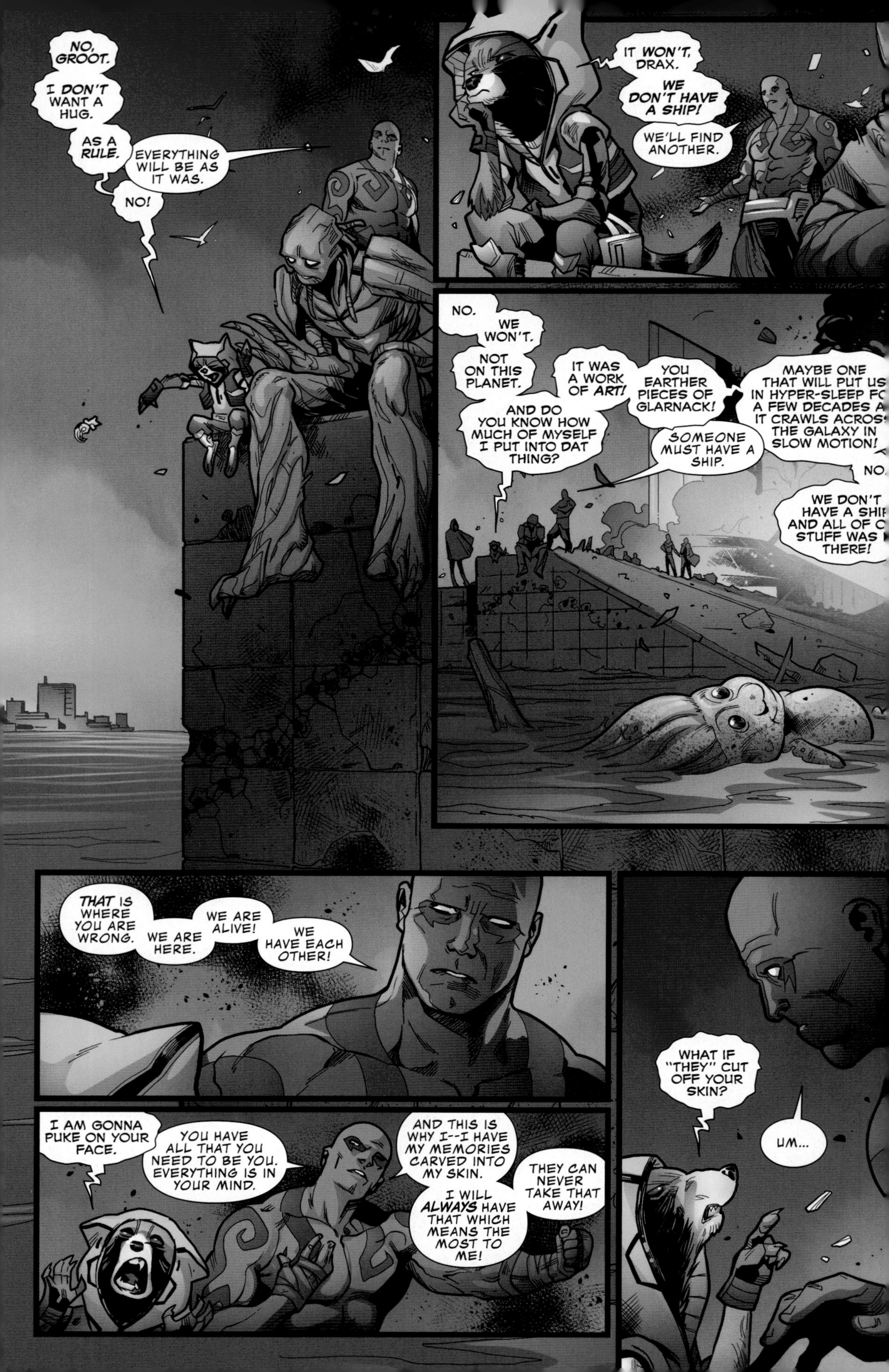
NO, GROOT.
I DON'T WANT A HUG.
AS A RULE.
EVERYTHING WILL BE AS IT WAS.
NO!
IT WON'T, DRAX.
WE DON'T HAVE A SHIP!
WE'LL FIND ANOTHER.
NO.
WE WON'T.
NOT ON THIS PLANET.
IT WAS A WORK OF ART!
AND DO YOU KNOW HOW MUCH OF MYSELF I PUT INTO DAT THING?
YOU EARTHER PIECES OF GLARNACK!
SOMEONE MUST HAVE A SHIP.
MAYBE ONE THAT WILL PUT US IN HYPER-SLEEP FO A FEW DECADES A IT CRAWLS ACROS THE GALAXY IN SLOW MOTION!
NO.
WE DON'T HAVE A SHI AND ALL OF O STUFF WAS THERE!
THAT IS WHERE YOU ARE WRONG.
WE ARE HERE.
WE ARE ALIVE!
WE HAVE EACH OTHER!
I AM GONNA PUKE ON YOUR FACE.
YOU HAVE ALL THAT YOU NEED TO BE YOU. EVERYTHING IS IN YOUR MIND.
AND THIS IS WHY I--I HAVE MY MEMORIES CARVED INTO MY SKIN.
I WILL ALWAYS HAVE THAT WHICH MEANS THE MOST TO ME!
THEY CAN NEVER TAKE THAT AWAY!
WHAT IF "THEY" CUT OFF YOUR SKIN?
UM...

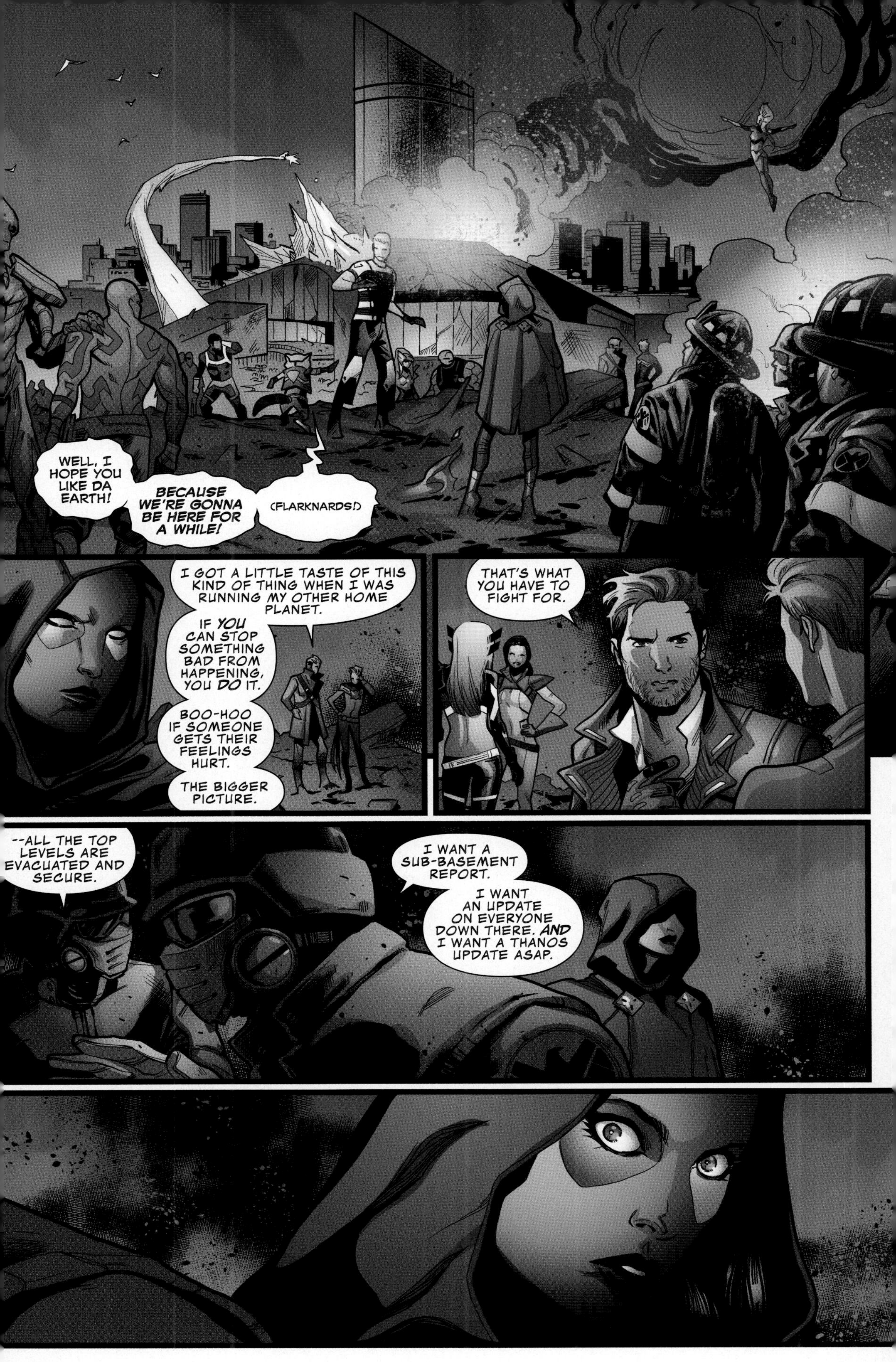
WELL, I HOPE YOU LIKE DA EARTH!
BECAUSE WE'RE GONNA BE HERE FOR A WHILE!
(FLARKNARDS!)
I GOT A LITTLE TASTE OF THIS KIND OF THING WHEN I WAS RUNNING MY OTHER HOME PLANET.
IF YOU CAN STOP SOMETHING BAD FROM HAPPENING, YOU DO IT.
BOO-HOO IF SOMEONE GETS THEIR FEELINGS HURT.
THE BIGGER PICTURE.
THAT'S WHAT YOU HAVE TO FIGHT FOR.
--ALL THE TOP LEVELS ARE EVACUATED AND SECURE.
I WANT A SUB-BASEMENT REPORT.
I WANT AN UPDATE ON EVERYONE DOWN THERE. AND I WANT A THANOS UPDATE ASAP.

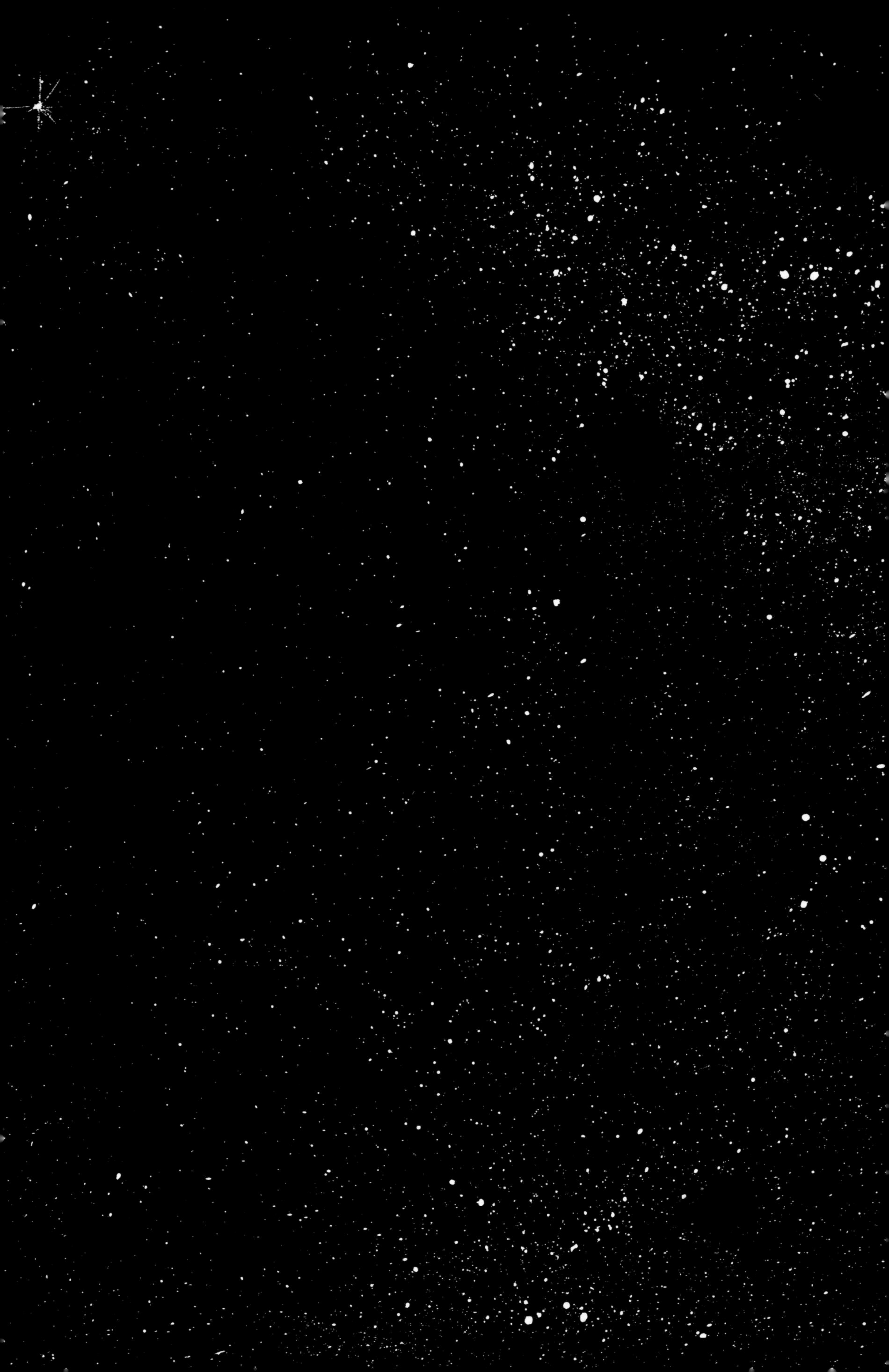

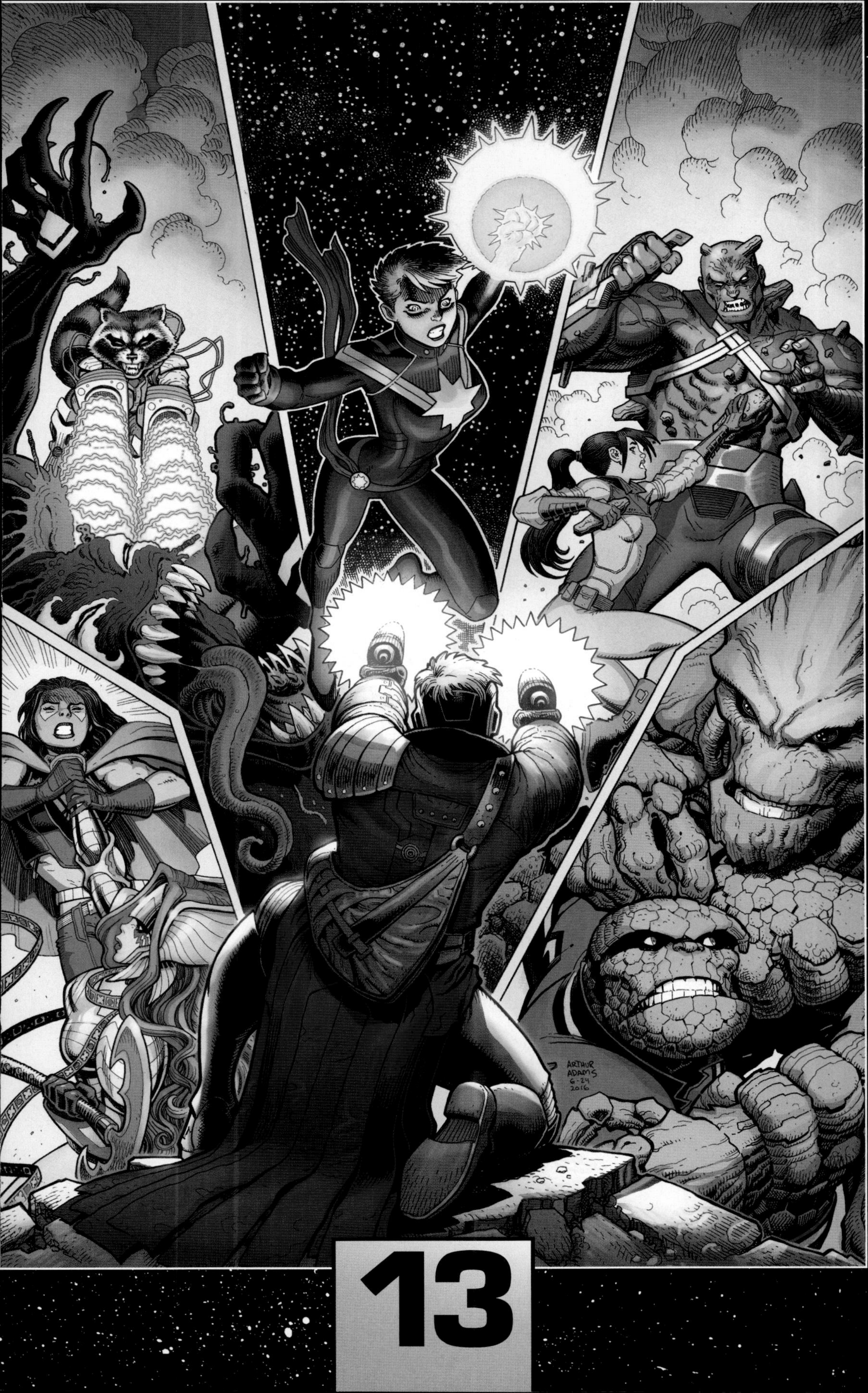
ARTHUR
ADAMS
6-24
2016

13

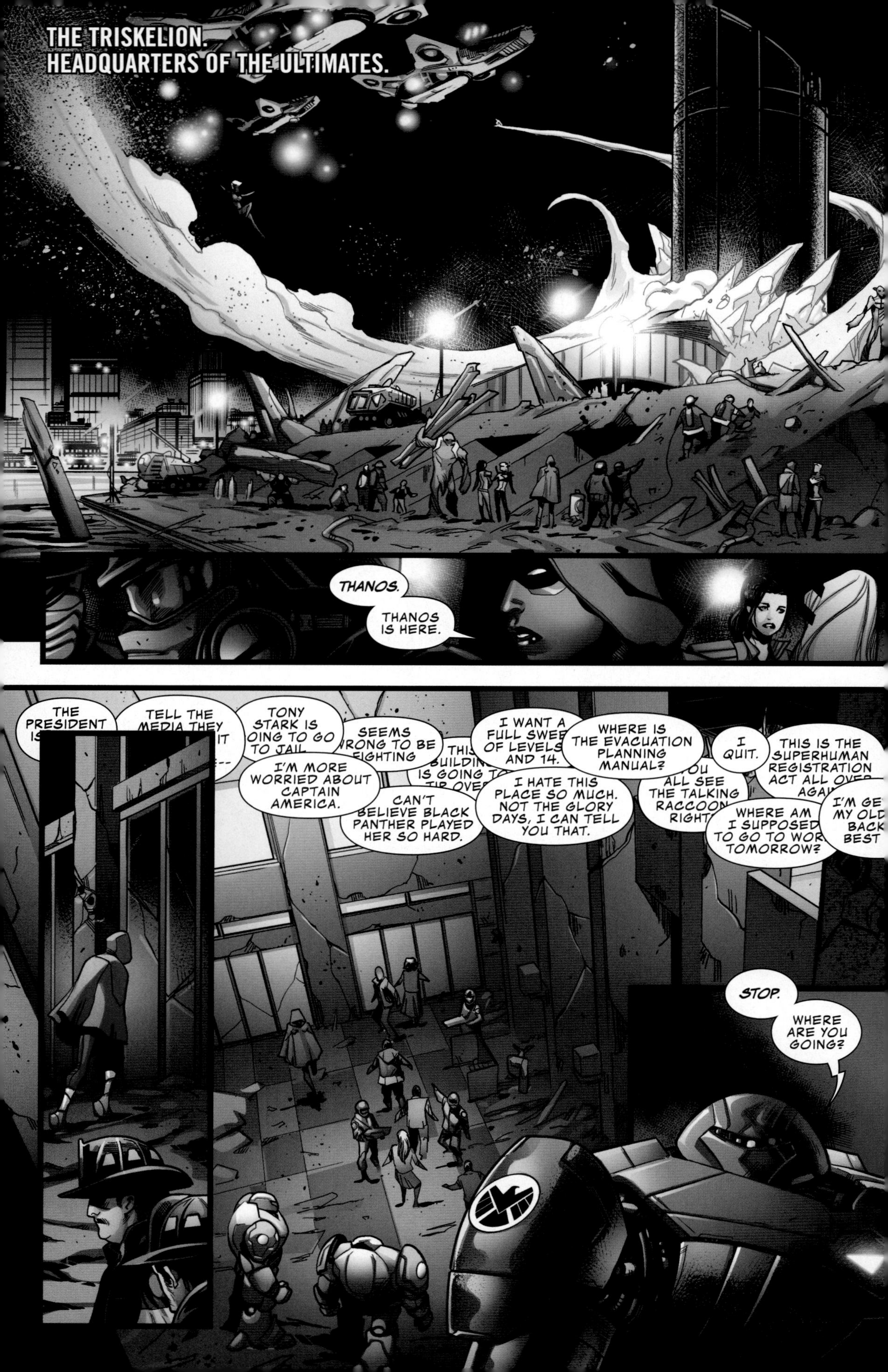
THE TRISKELION.
HEADQUARTERS OF THE ULTIMATES.
THANOS.
THANOS IS HERE.
THE PRESIDENT
TELL THE MEDIA THEY
TONY STARK IS
I'M MORE WORRIED ABOUT CAPTAIN AMERICA.
CAN'T BELIEVE BLACK PANTHER PLAYED HER SO HARD.
I WANT A FULL
AND 14.
WHERE IS THE EVACUATION PLANNING MANUAL?
I HATE THIS PLACE SO MUCH. NOT THE GLORY DAYS, I CAN TELL YOU THAT.
ALL SEE THE TALKING
I QUIT.
THIS IS THE SUPERHUMAN REGISTRATION ACT ALL
WHERE AM TO GO TO TOMORROW?
MY OLD
BEST
STOP.
WHERE ARE YOU GOING?

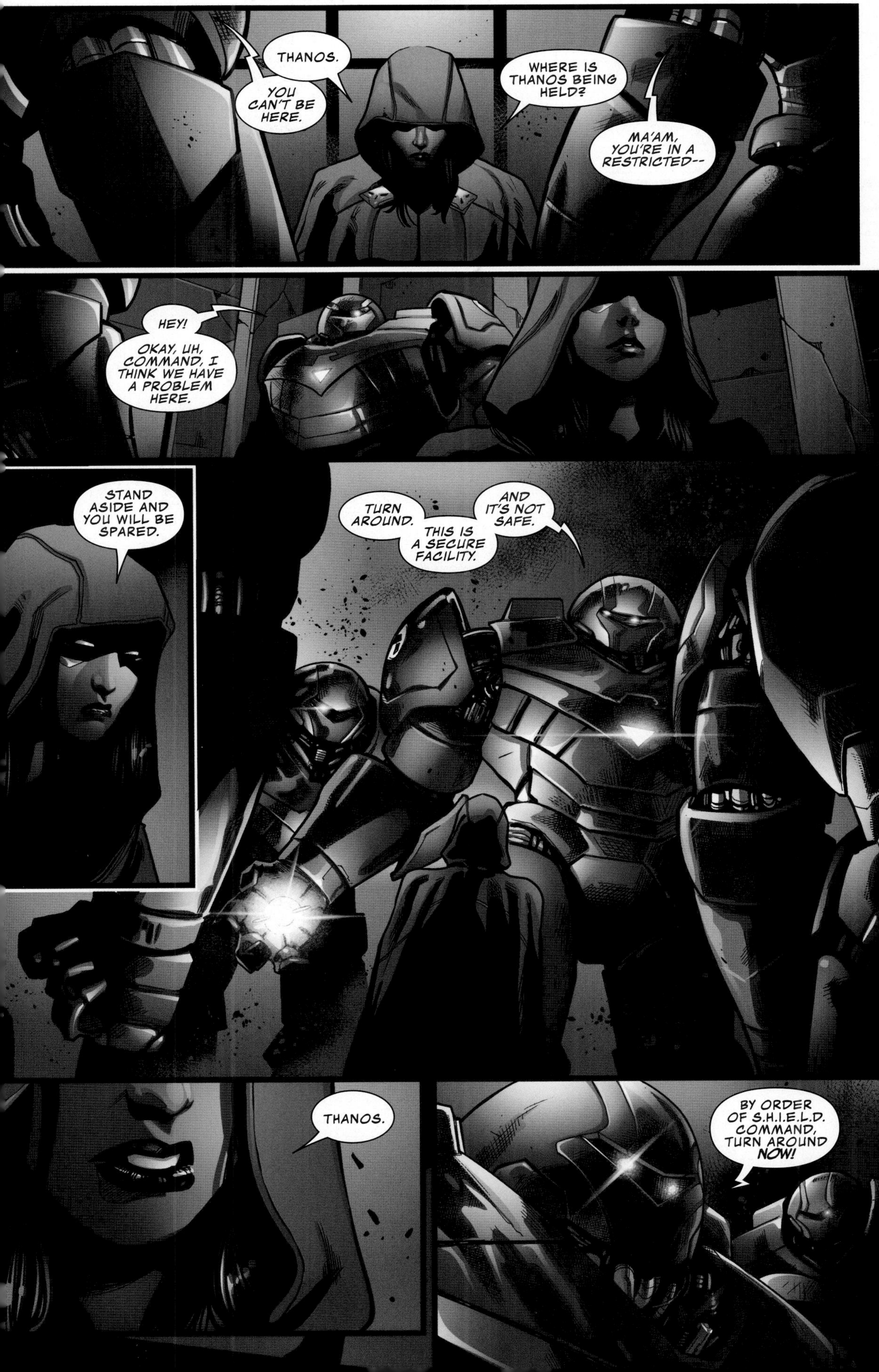
THANOS.
YOU CAN'T BE HERE.
WHERE IS THANOS BEING HELD?
MA'AM, YOU'RE IN A RESTRICTED--
HEY!
OKAY, UH, COMMAND, I THINK WE HAVE A PROBLEM HERE.
STAND ASIDE AND YOU WILL BE SPARED.
TURN AROUND.
THIS IS A SECURE FACILITY.
AND IT'S NOT SAFE.
THANOS.
BY ORDER OF S.H.I.E.L.D. COMMAND, TURN AROUND NOW!

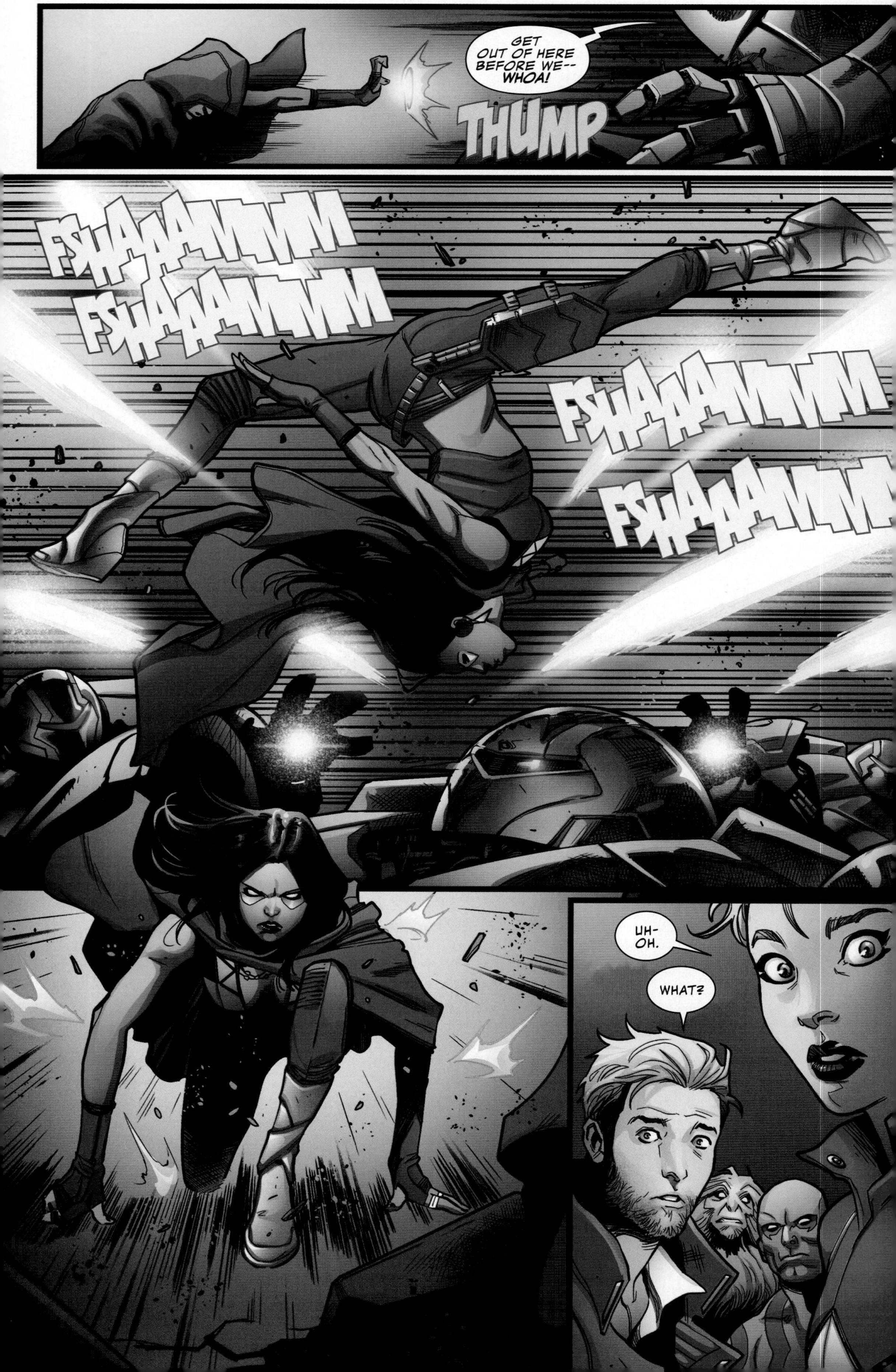
GET OUT OF HERE BEFORE WE-- WHOA!
THUMP
FSHAAAMMM
FSHAAAMMM
FSHAAAMMM
FSHAAAMMM
UH-OH.
WHAT?

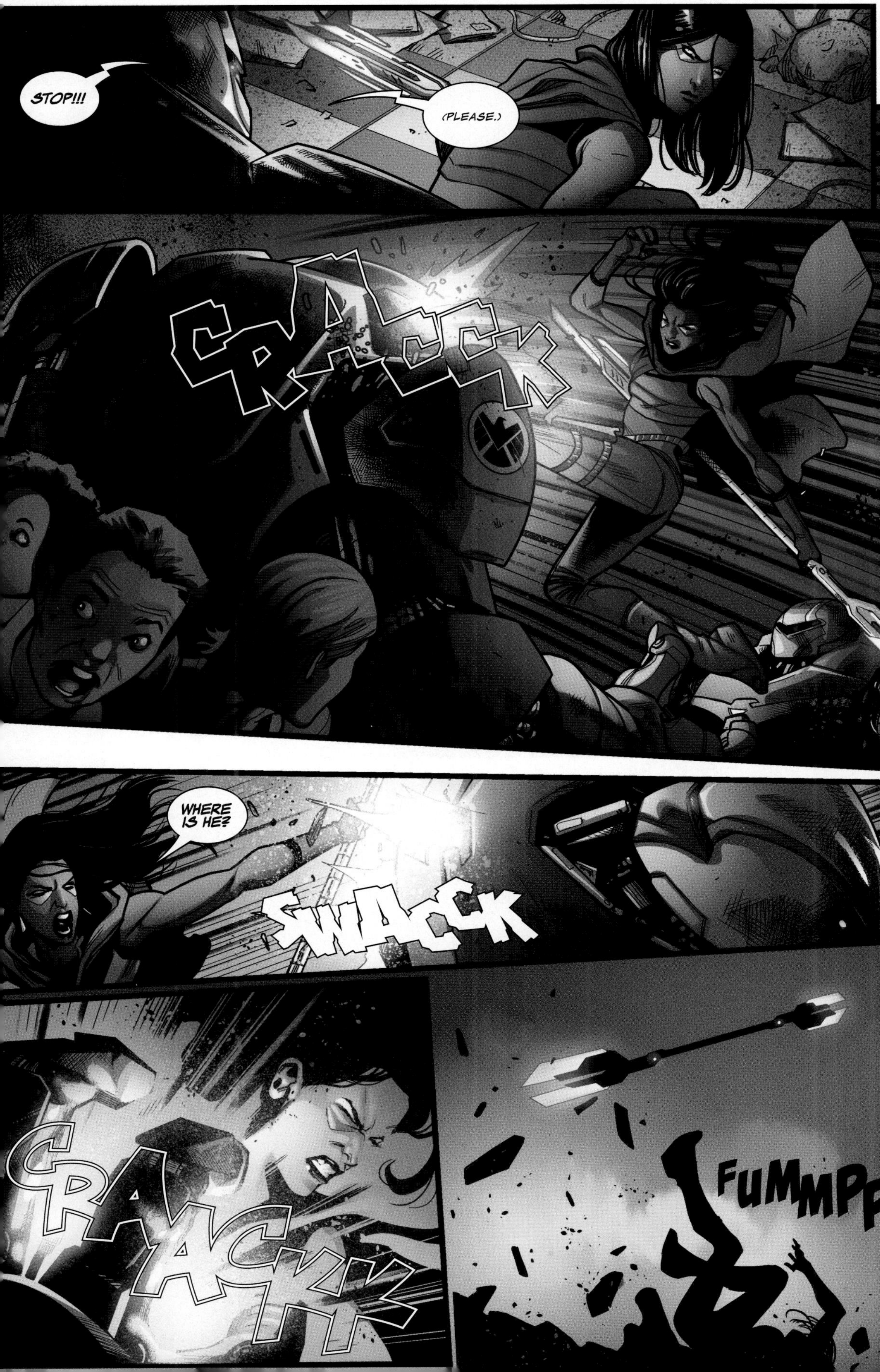
STOP!!!
(PLEASE.)
CRACCK
WHERE IS HE?
SWACCK
CRACKK
FUMMPP

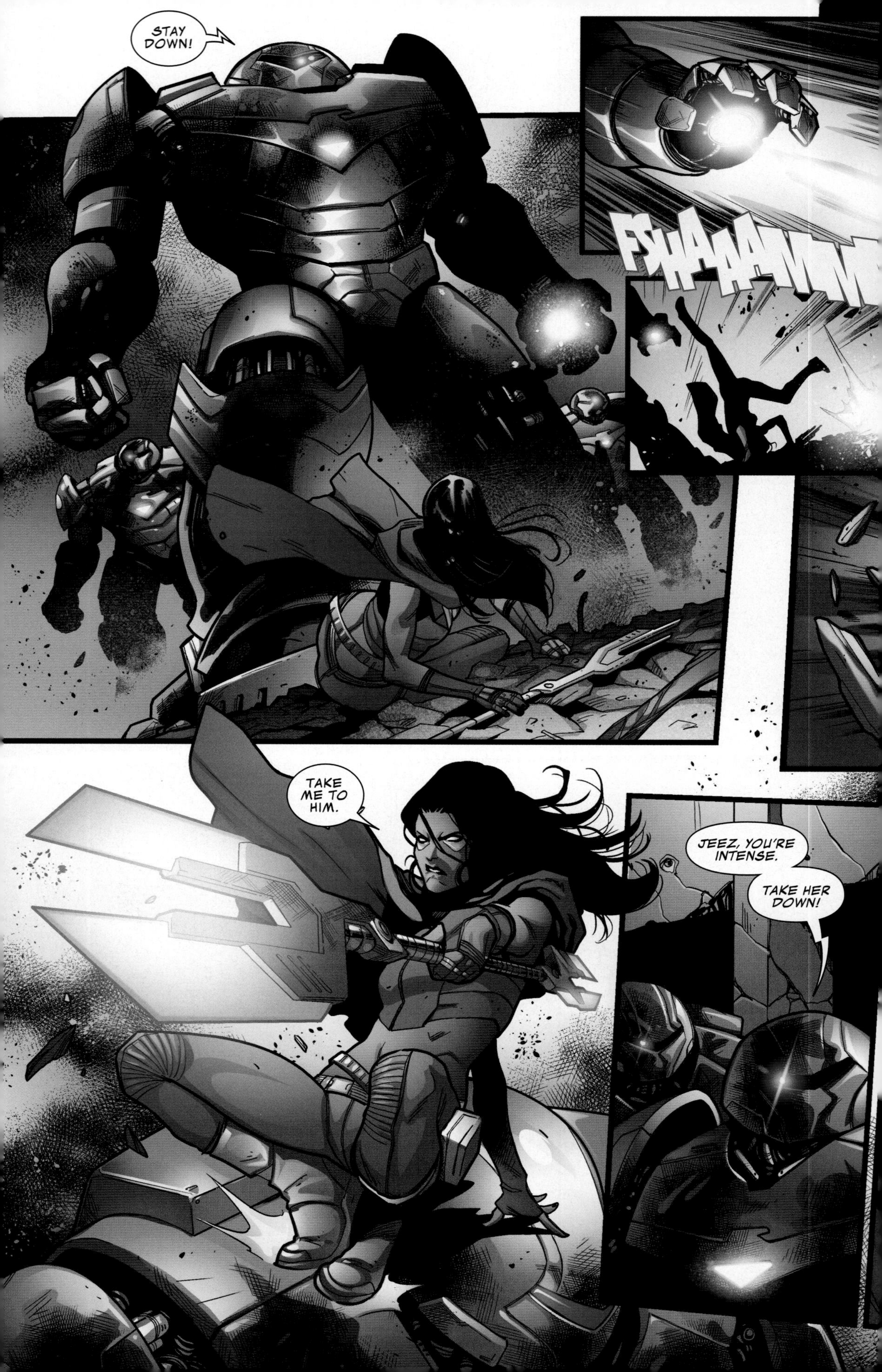
STAY DOWN!
FSHAAAAMM
TAKE ME TO HIM.
JEEZ, YOU'RE INTENSE.
TAKE HER DOWN!

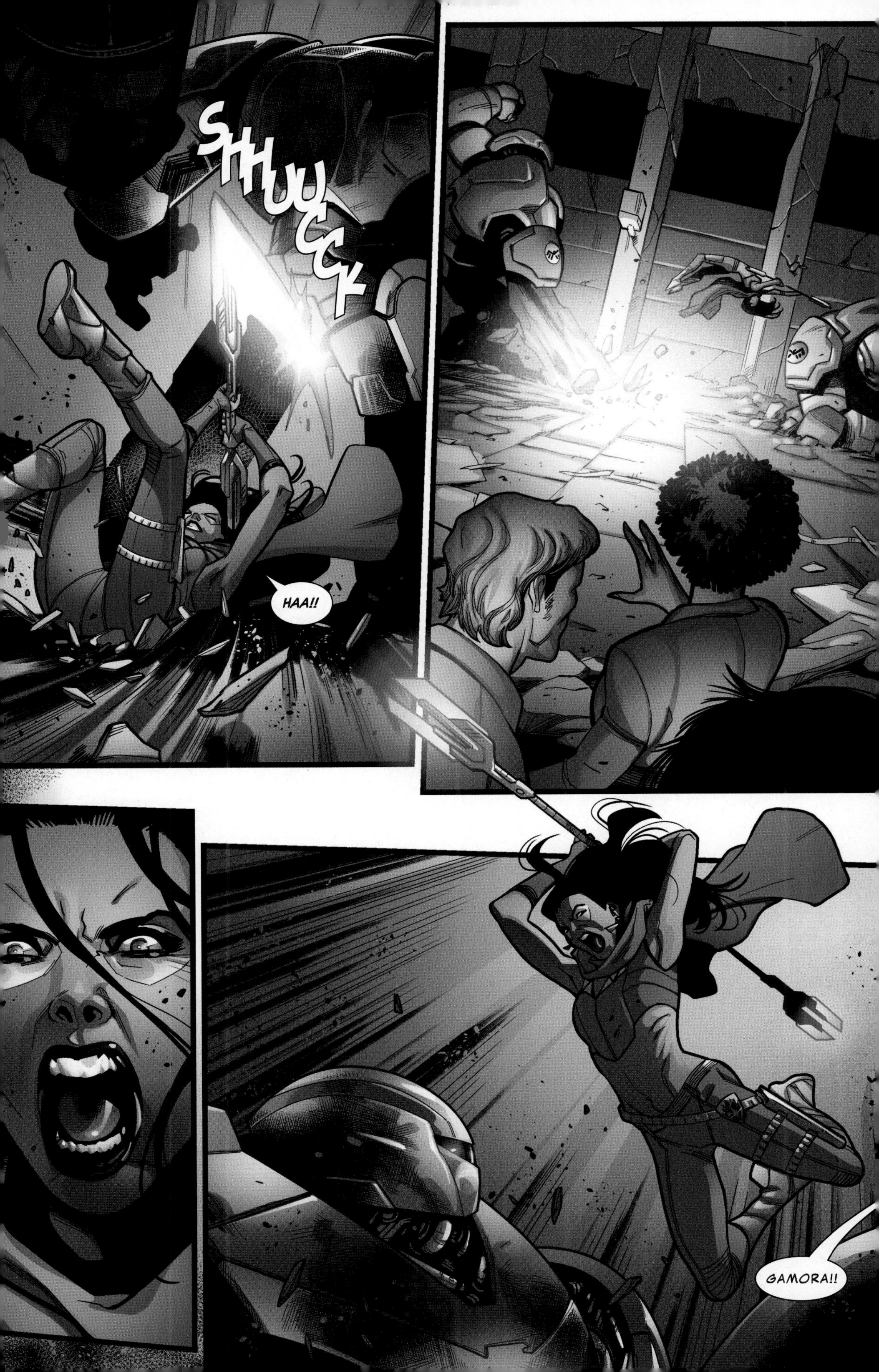
SHHUCCK
HAA!!
GAMORA!!

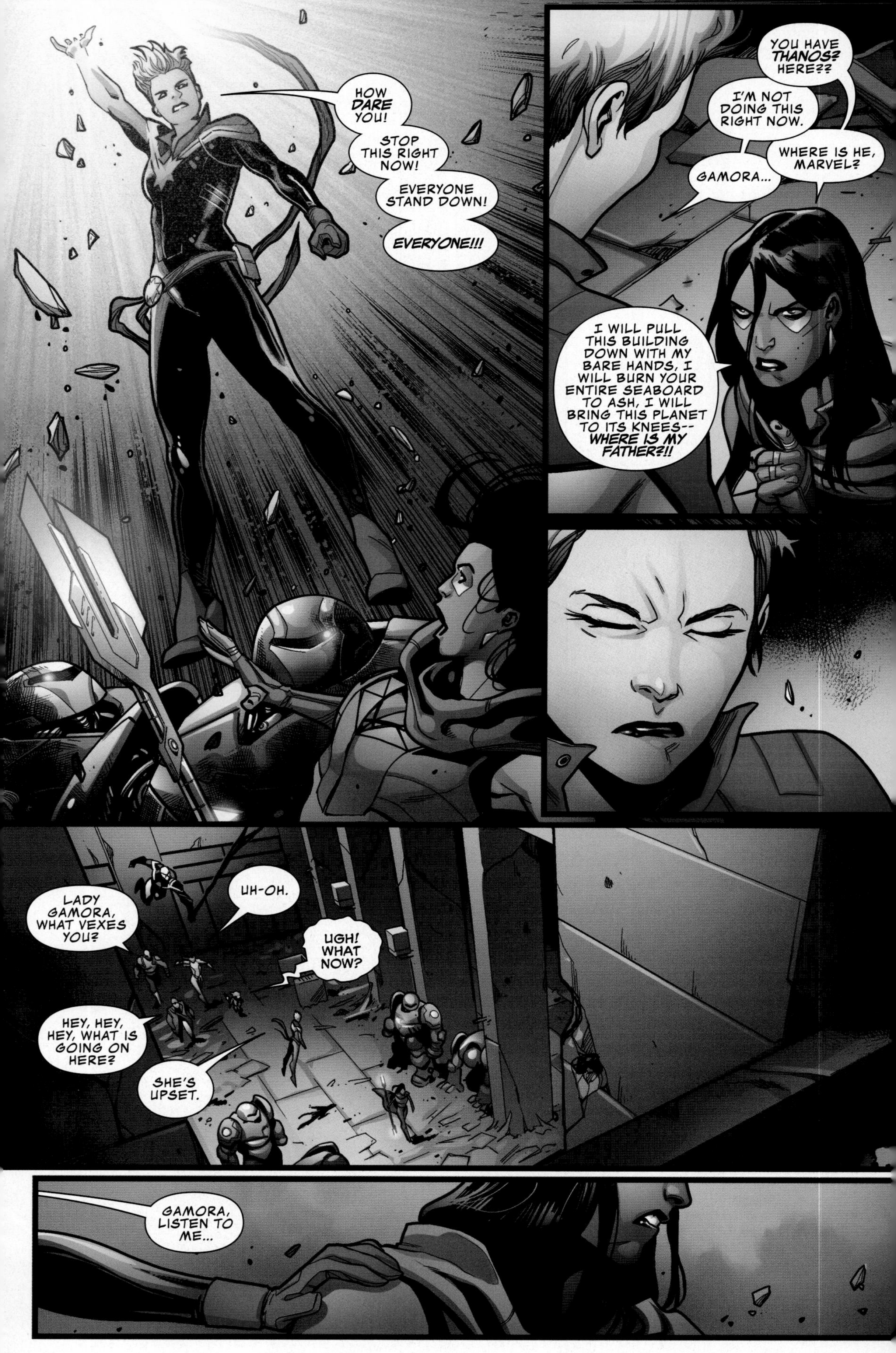
HOW DARE YOU!
STOP THIS RIGHT NOW!
EVERYONE STAND DOWN!
EVERYONE!!!
YOU HAVE THANOS? HERE??
I'M NOT DOING THIS RIGHT NOW.
WHERE IS HE, MARVEL?
GAMORA...
I WILL PULL THIS BUILDING DOWN WITH MY BARE HANDS, I WILL BURN YOUR ENTIRE SEABOARD TO ASH, I WILL BRING THIS PLANET TO ITS KNEES-- WHERE IS MY FATHER?!!
LADY GAMORA, WHAT VEXES YOU?
UH-OH.
UGH! WHAT NOW?
HEY, HEY, HEY, WHAT IS GOING ON HERE?
SHE'S UPSET.
GAMORA, LISTEN TO ME...

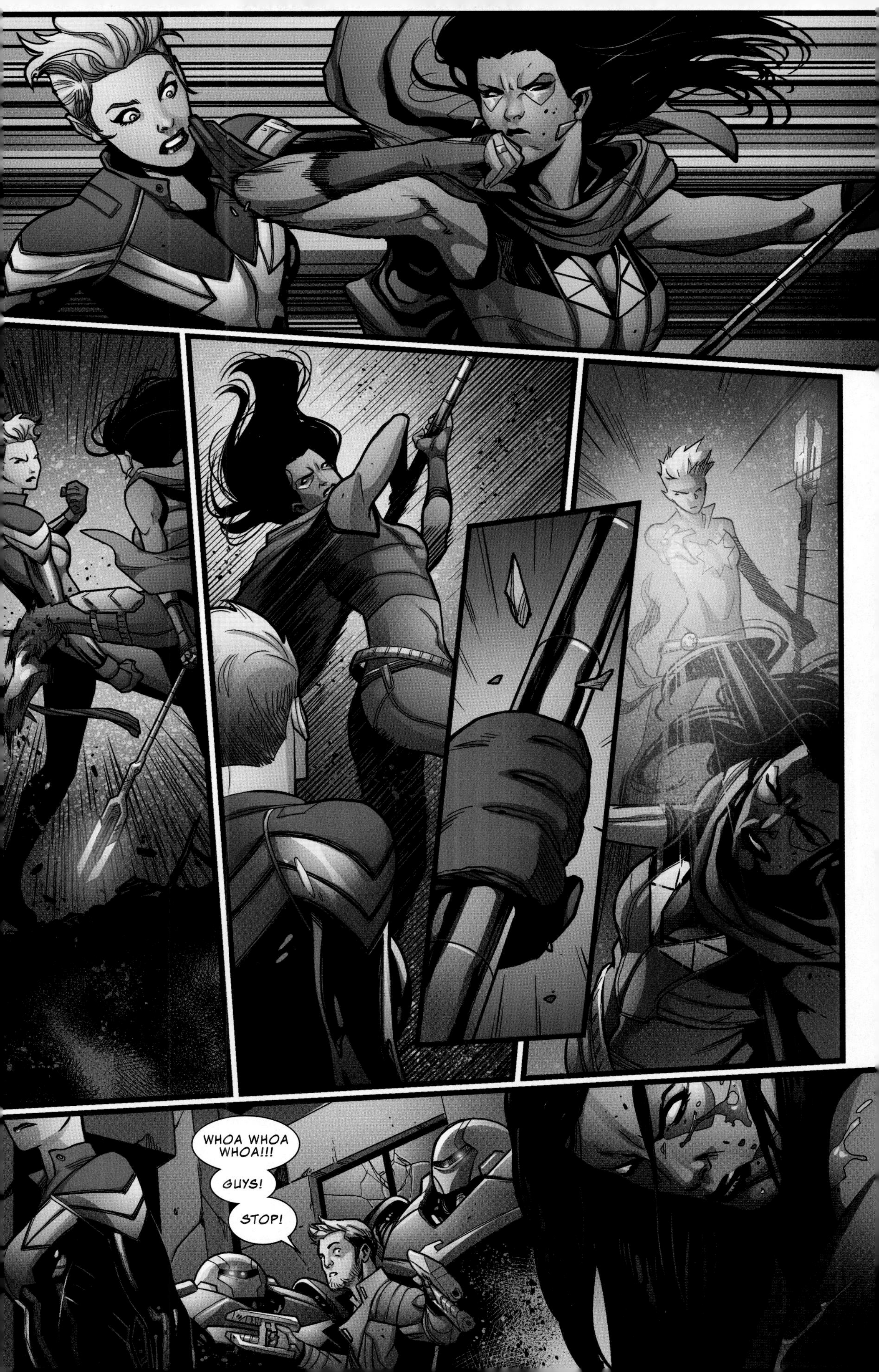
WHOA WHOA WHOA!!!
GUYS!
STOP!

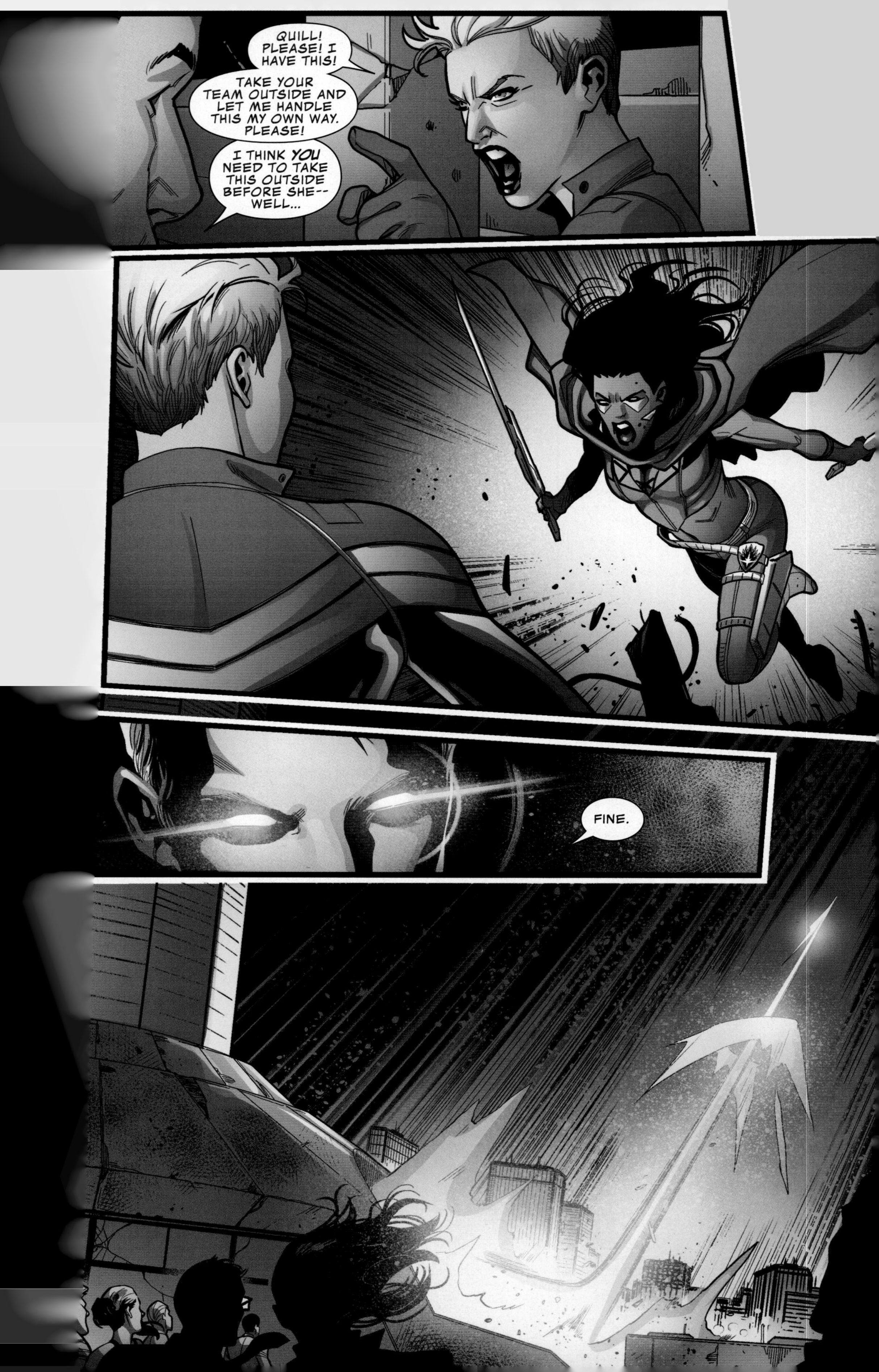
QUILL! PLEASE! I HAVE THIS!
TAKE YOUR TEAM OUTSIDE AND LET ME HANDLE THIS MY OWN WAY. PLEASE!
I THINK YOU NEED TO TAKE THIS OUTSIDE BEFORE SHE-- WELL...
FINE.

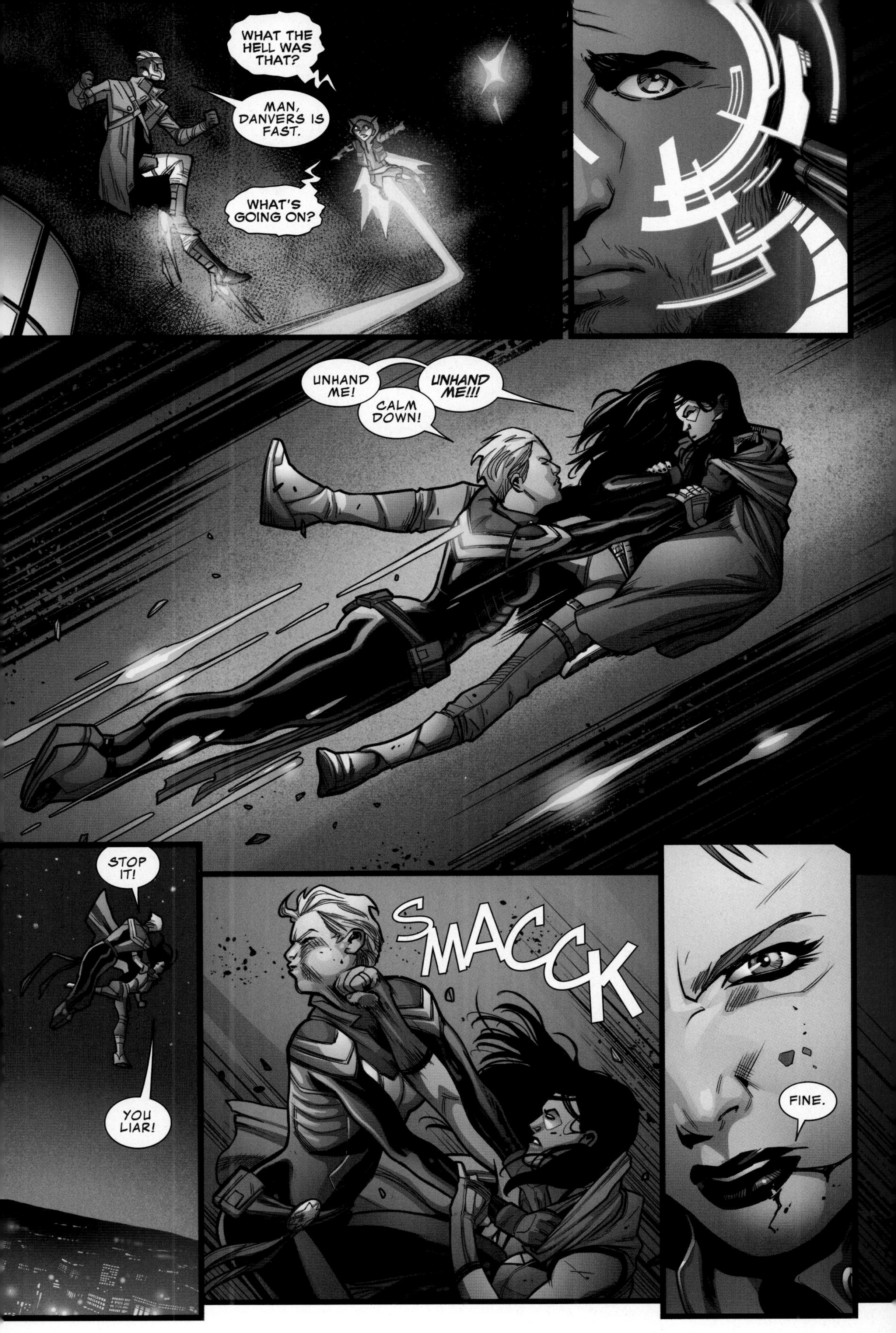
WHAT THE HELL WAS THAT?
MAN, DANVERS IS FAST.
WHAT'S GOING ON?
UNHAND ME!
CALM DOWN!
UNHAND ME!!!
STOP IT!
YOU LIAR!
SMACCK
FINE.

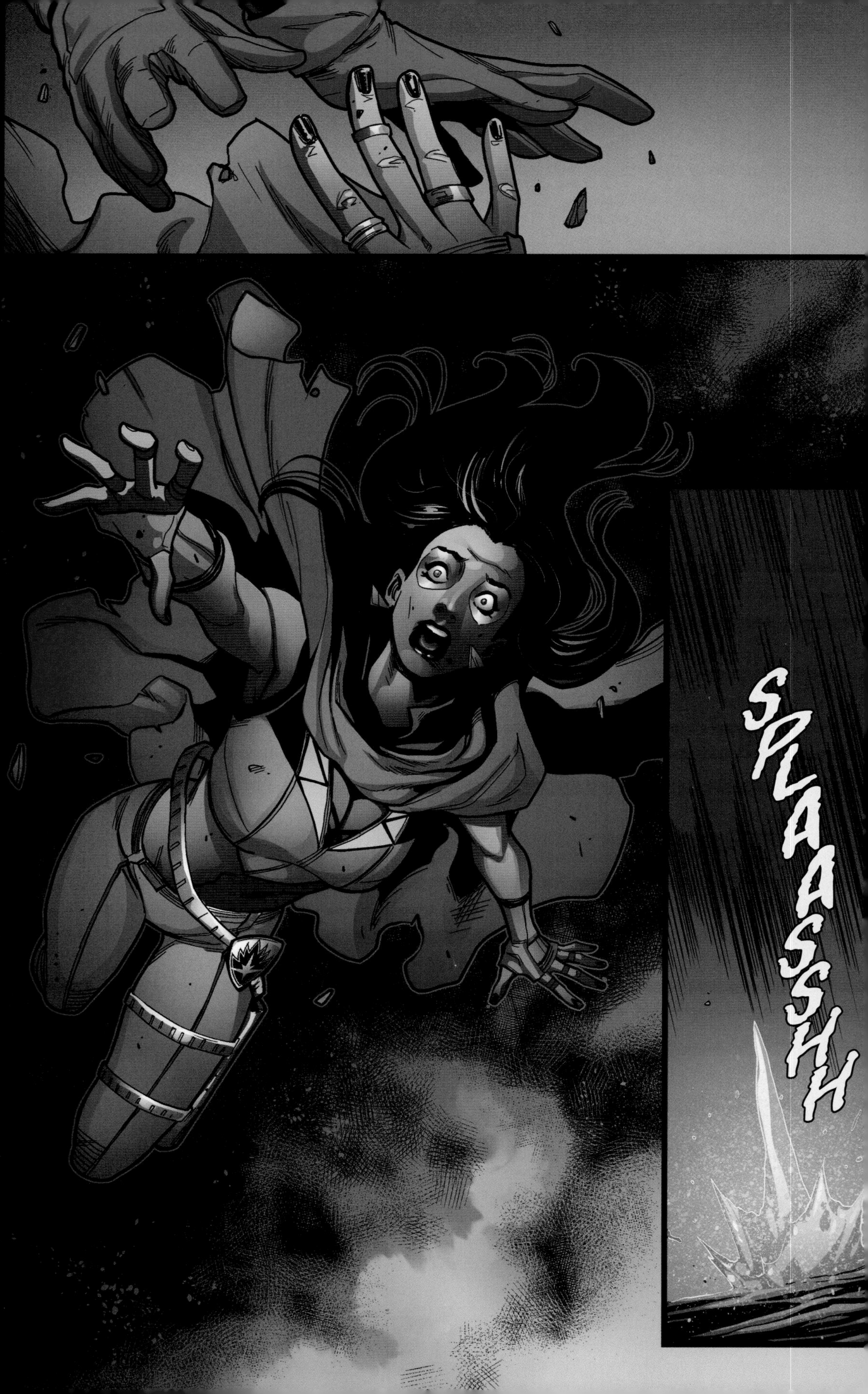
SPLAASSHH

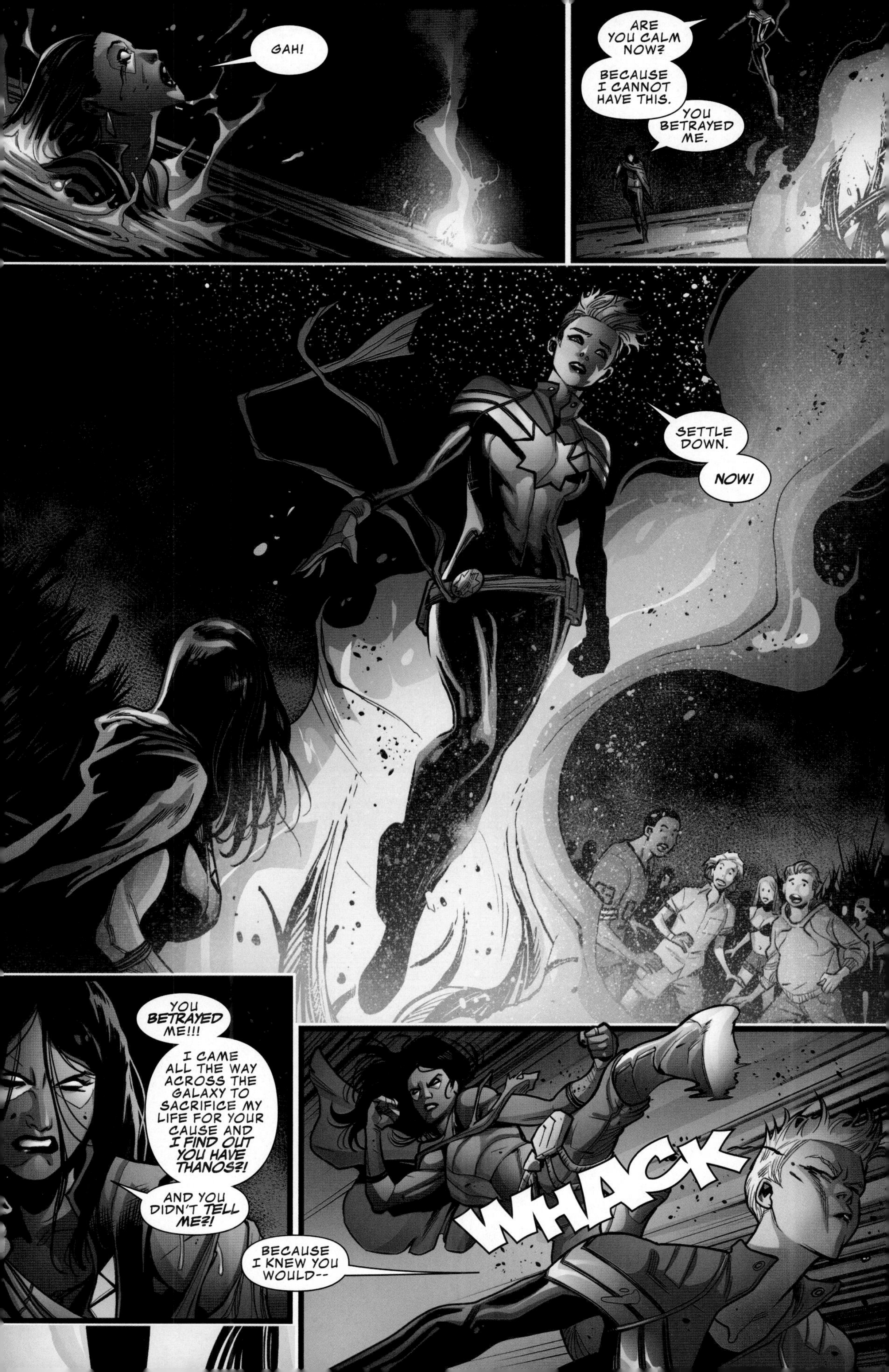
GAH!
ARE YOU CALM NOW?
BECAUSE I CANNOT HAVE THIS.
YOU BETRAYED ME.
SETTLE DOWN.
NOW!
YOU BETRAYED ME!!!
I CAME ALL THE WAY ACROSS THE GALAXY TO SACRIFICE MY LIFE FOR YOUR CAUSE AND I FIND OUT YOU HAVE THANOS?!
AND YOU DIDN'T TELL ME?!
WHACK
BECAUSE I KNEW YOU WOULD--

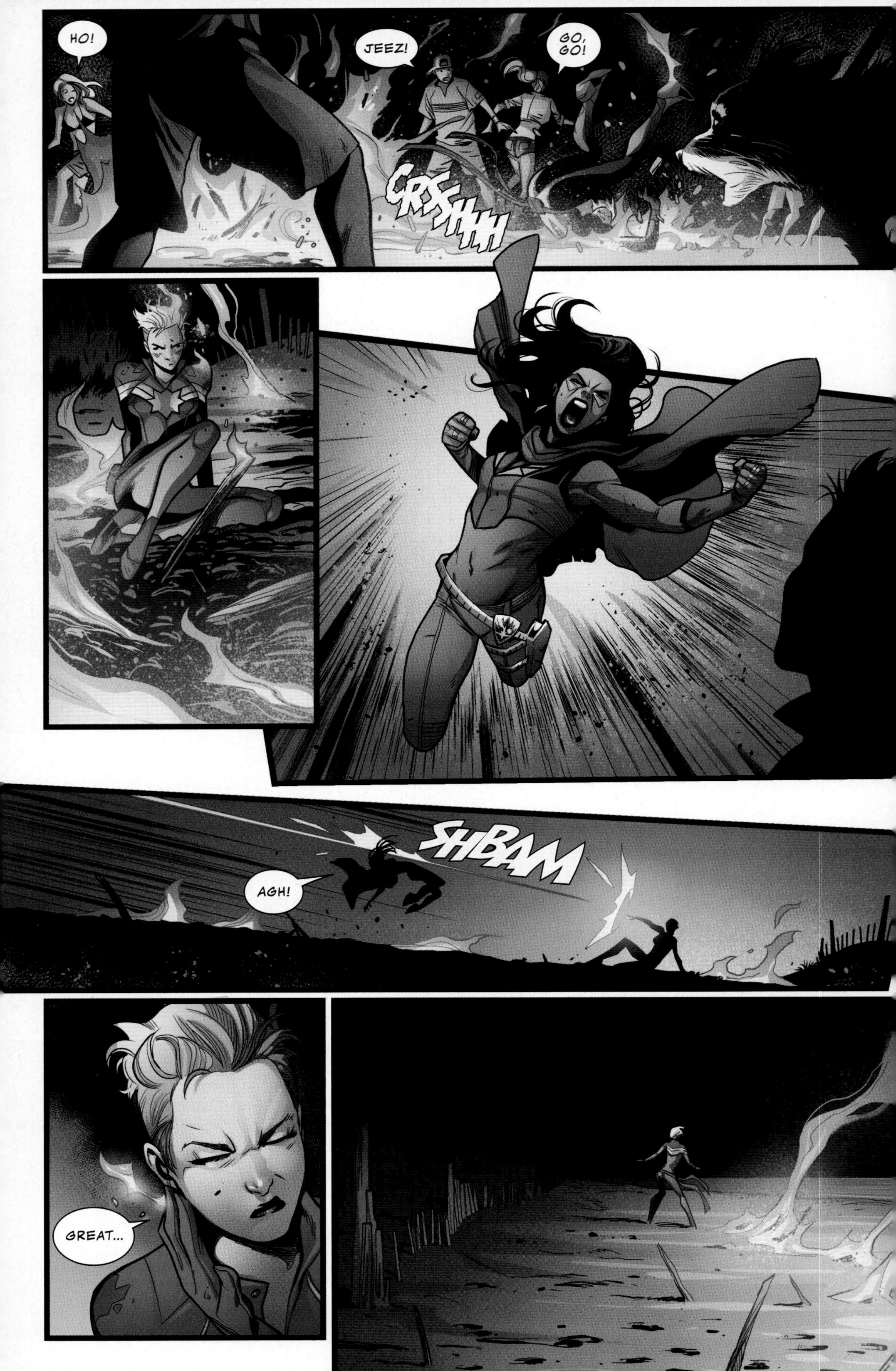
HO!
JEEZ!
GO, GO!
CRSSHHH
SHBAM
AGH!
GREAT...

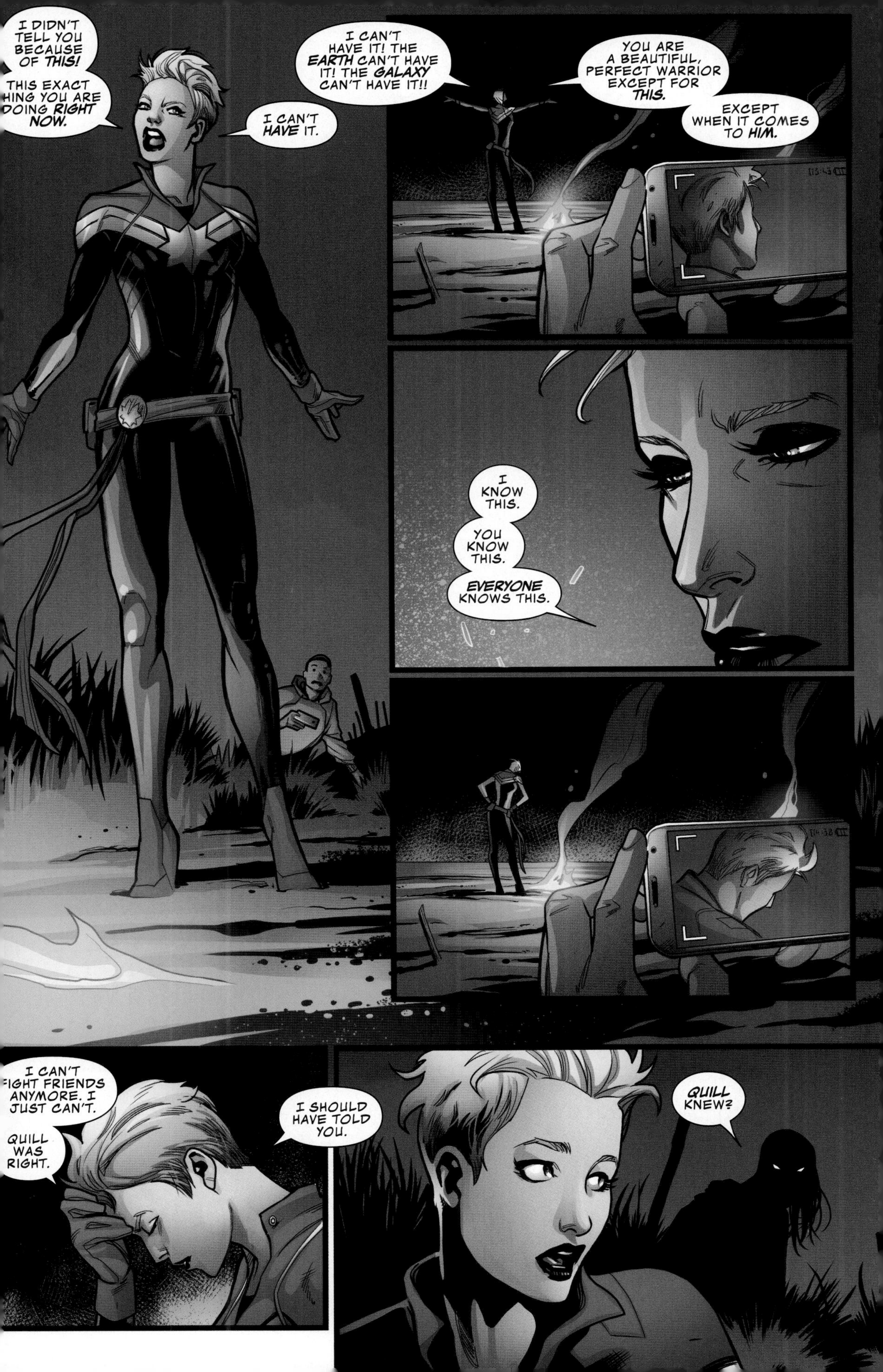
I DIDN'T TELL YOU BECAUSE OF THIS!
THIS EXACT THING YOU ARE DOING RIGHT NOW.
I CAN'T HAVE IT.
I CAN'T HAVE IT! THE EARTH CAN'T HAVE IT! THE GALAXY CAN'T HAVE IT!!
YOU ARE A BEAUTIFUL, PERFECT WARRIOR EXCEPT FOR THIS.
EXCEPT WHEN IT COMES TO HIM.
I KNOW THIS.
YOU KNOW THIS.
EVERYONE KNOWS THIS.
I CAN'T FIGHT FRIENDS ANYMORE. I JUST CAN'T.
QUILL WAS RIGHT.
I SHOULD HAVE TOLD YOU.
QUILL KNEW?

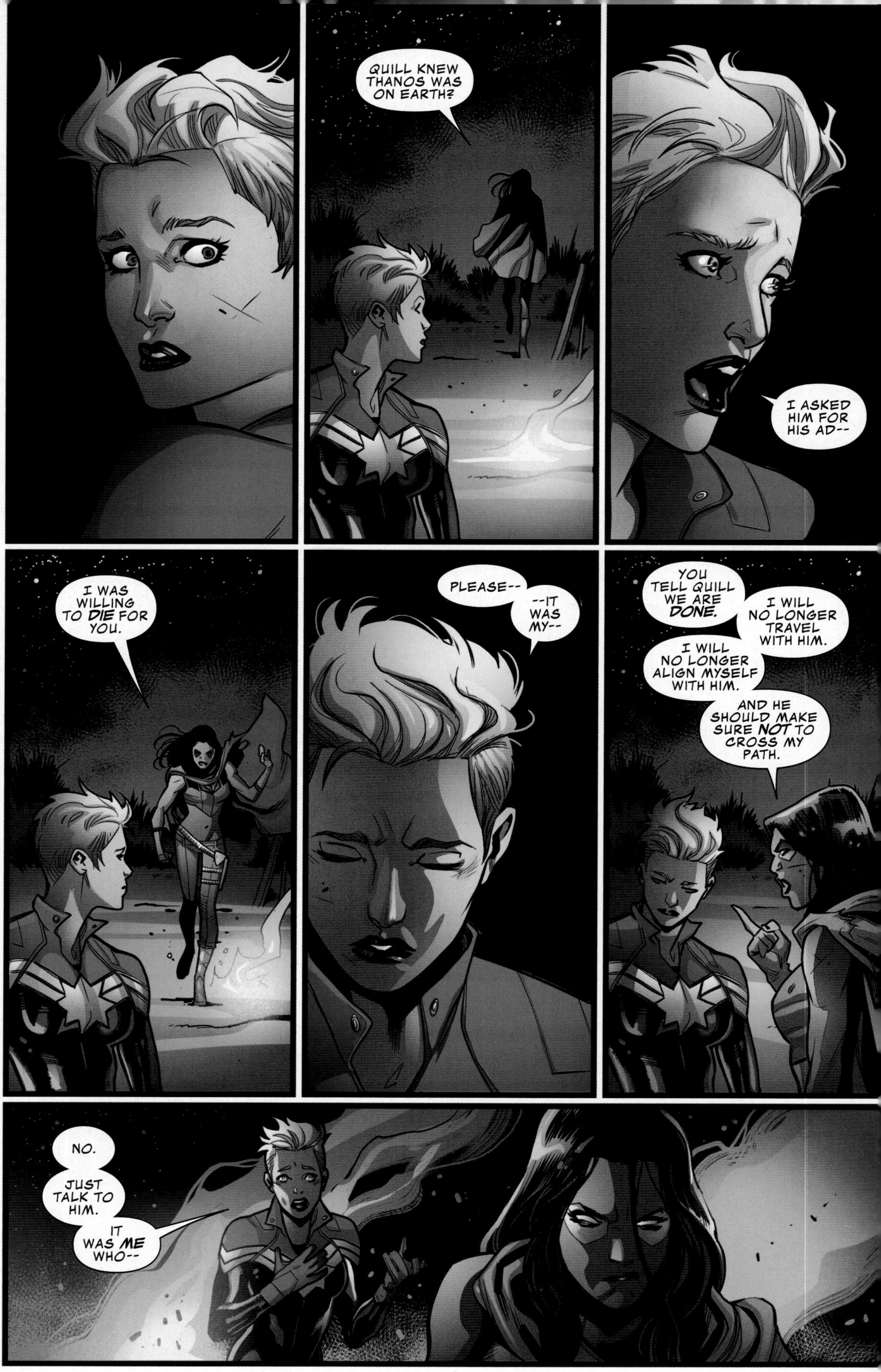
QUILL KNEW THANOS WAS ON EARTH?
I ASKED HIM FOR HIS AD--
I WAS WILLING TO DIE FOR YOU.
PLEASE--
--IT WAS MY--
YOU TELL QUILL WE ARE DONE.
I WILL NO LONGER TRAVEL WITH HIM.
I WILL NO LONGER ALIGN MYSELF WITH HIM.
AND HE SHOULD MAKE SURE NOT TO CROSS MY PATH.
NO.
JUST TALK TO HIM.
IT WAS ME WHO--

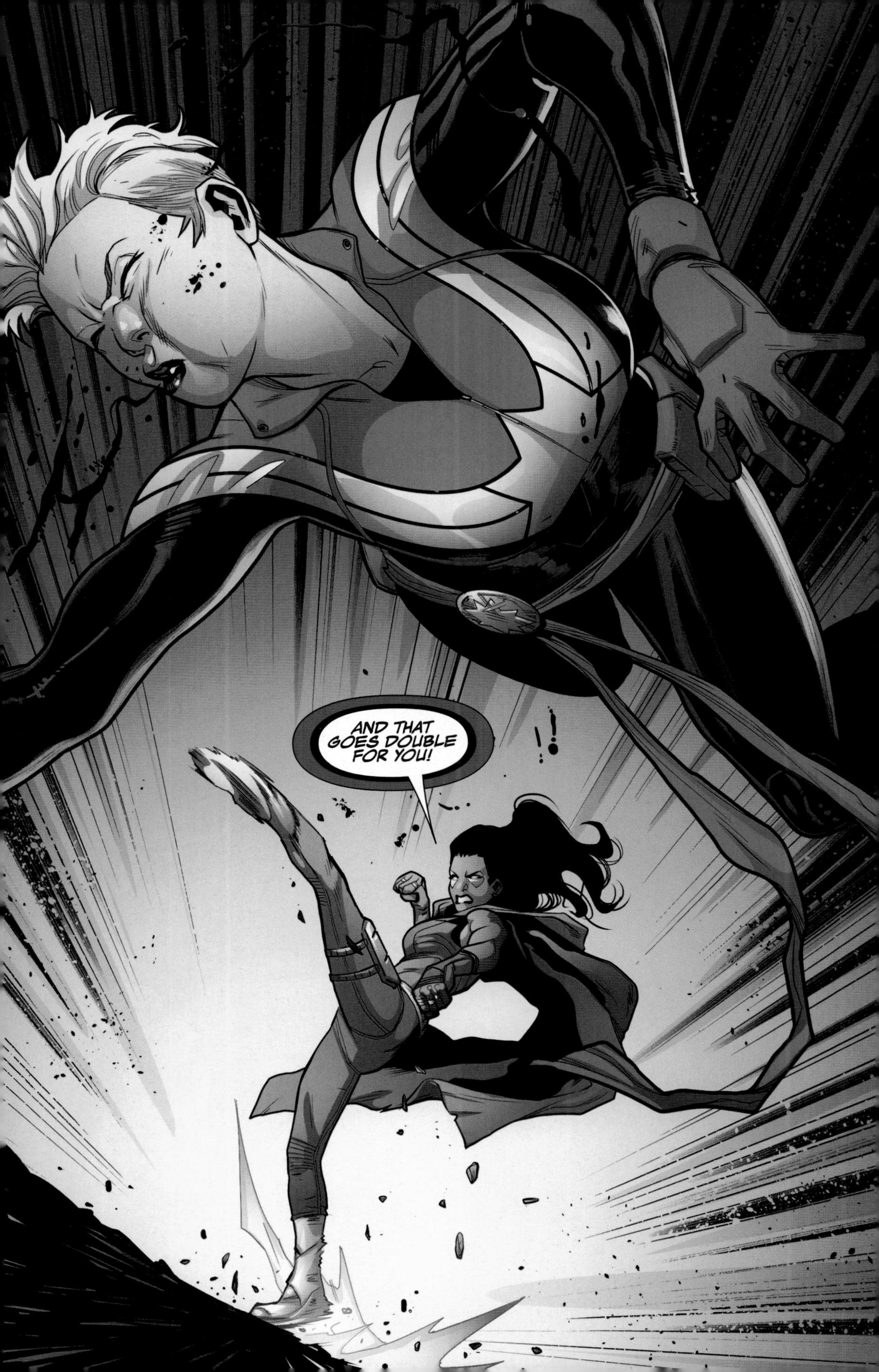
AND THAT GOES DOUBLE FOR YOU!
!!

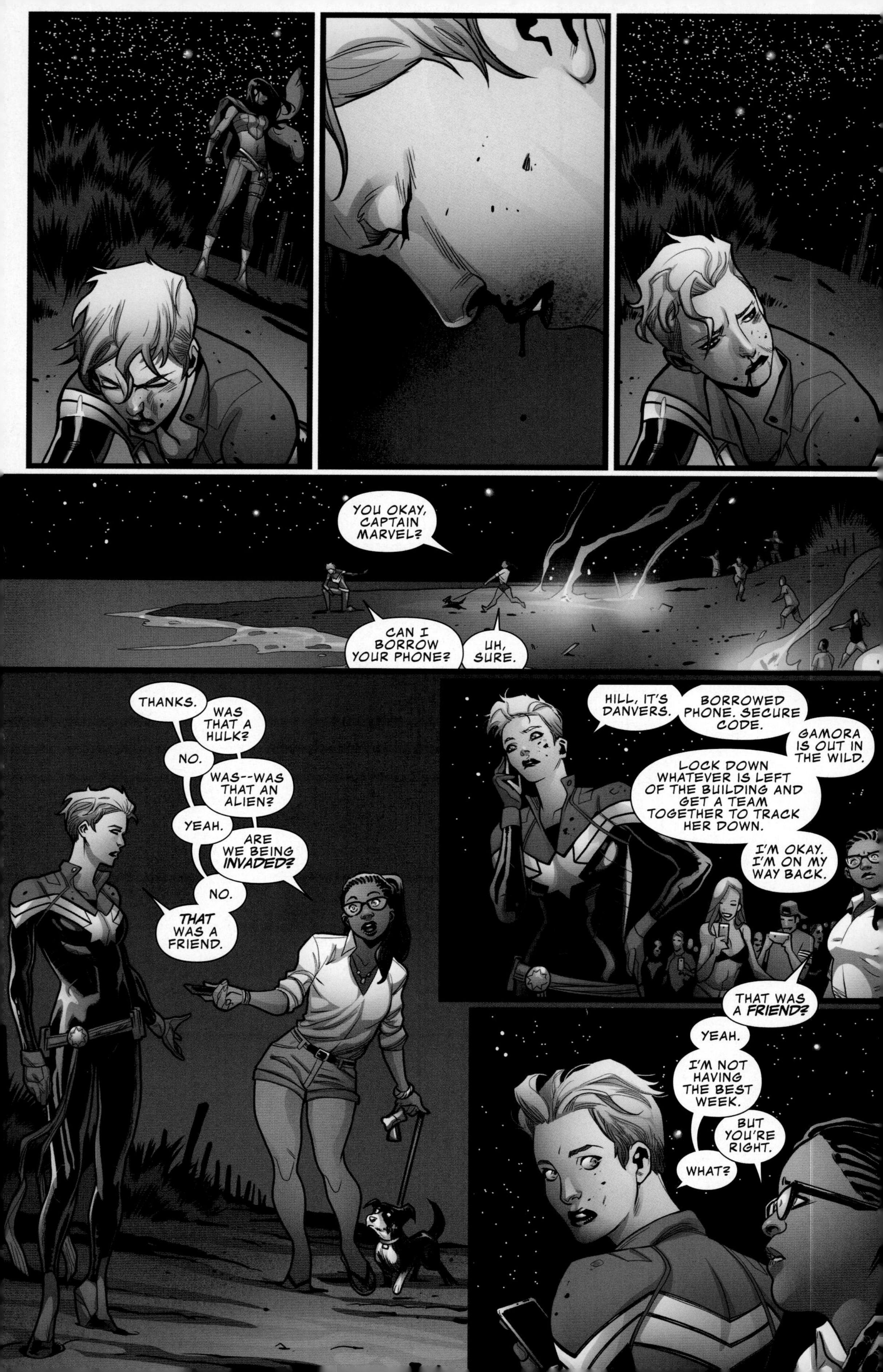
YOU OKAY, CAPTAIN MARVEL?
CAN I BORROW YOUR PHONE?
UH, SURE.
THANKS.
WAS THAT A HULK?
NO.
WAS--WAS THAT AN ALIEN?
YEAH.
ARE WE BEING *INVADED?*
NO.
THAT WAS A FRIEND.
HILL, IT'S DANVERS.
BORROWED PHONE. SECURE CODE.
GAMORA IS OUT IN THE WILD.
LOCK DOWN WHATEVER IS LEFT OF THE BUILDING AND GET A TEAM TOGETHER TO TRACK HER DOWN.
I'M OKAY. I'M ON MY WAY BACK.
THAT WAS A *FRIEND?*
YEAH.
I'M NOT HAVING THE BEST WEEK.
BUT YOU'RE RIGHT.
WHAT?

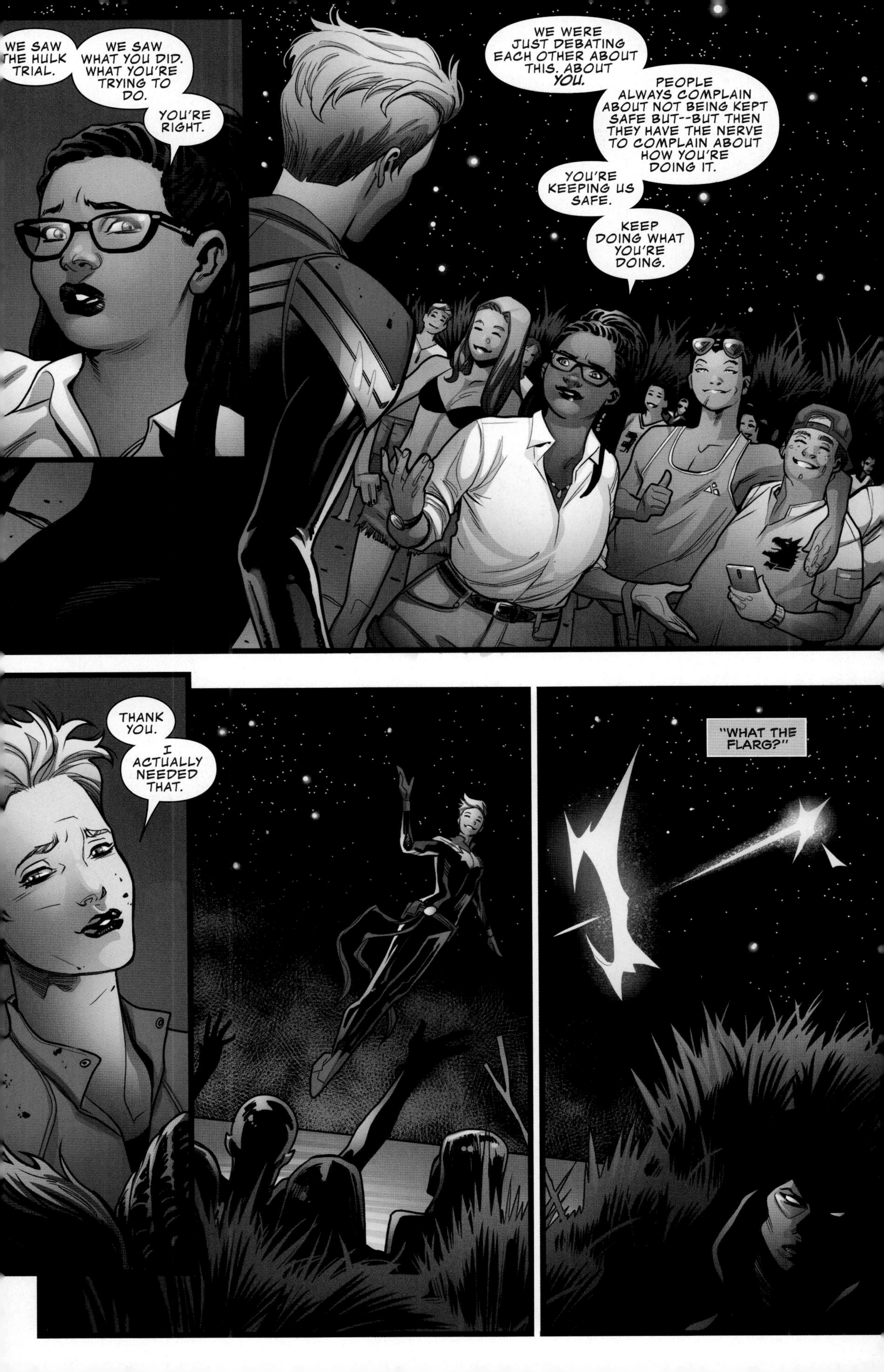
WE SAW THE HULK TRIAL.
WE SAW WHAT YOU DID. WHAT YOU'RE TRYING TO DO.
YOU'RE RIGHT.
WE WERE JUST DEBATING EACH OTHER ABOUT THIS. ABOUT YOU.
PEOPLE ALWAYS COMPLAIN ABOUT NOT BEING KEPT SAFE BUT--BUT THEN THEY HAVE THE NERVE TO COMPLAIN ABOUT HOW YOU'RE DOING IT.
YOU'RE KEEPING US SAFE.
KEEP DOING WHAT YOU'RE DOING.
THANK YOU.
I ACTUALLY NEEDED THAT.
"WHAT THE FLARG?"

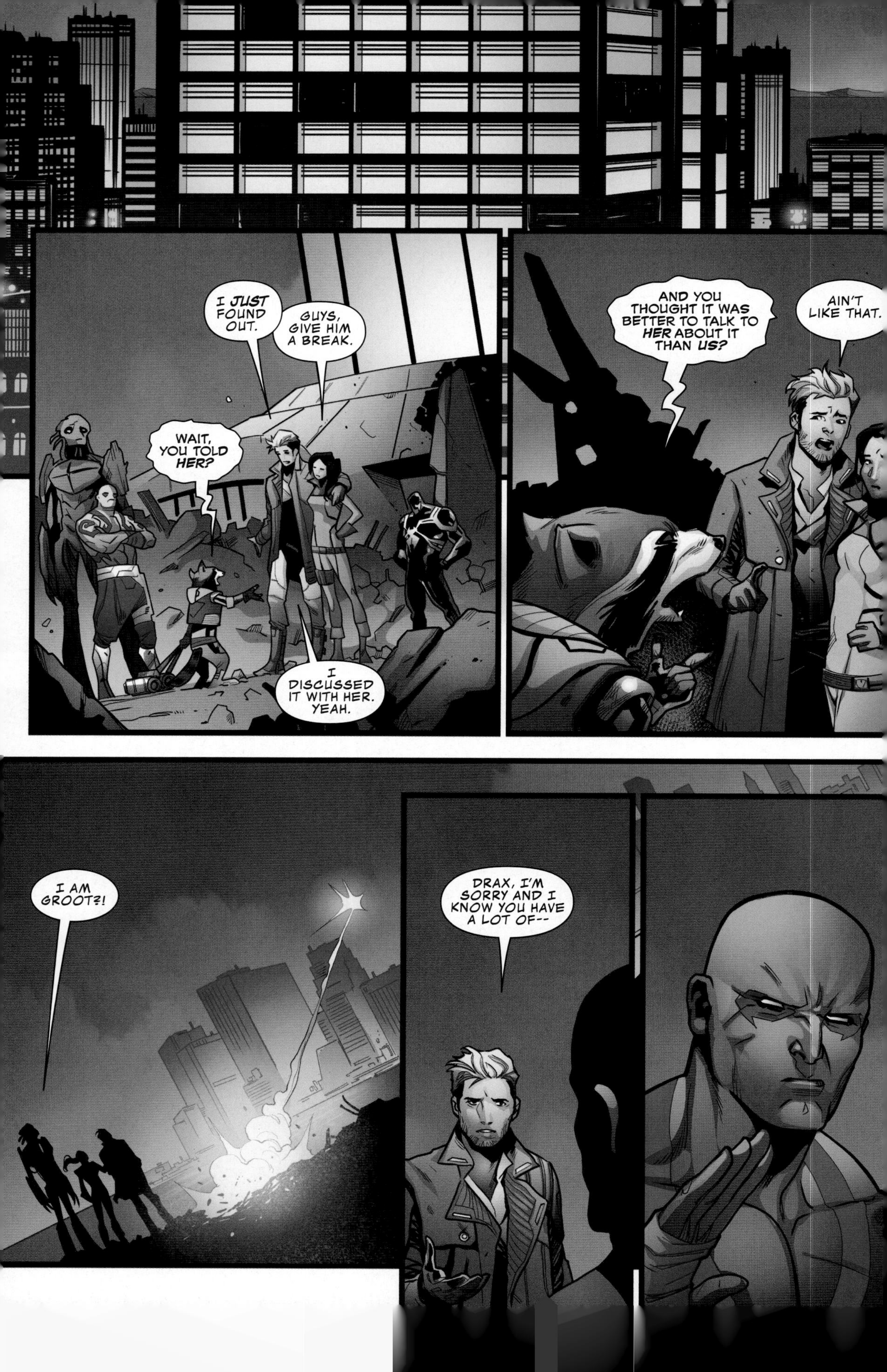
I JUST FOUND OUT.
GUYS, GIVE HIM A BREAK.
WAIT, YOU TOLD HER?
I DISCUSSED IT WITH HER. YEAH.
AND YOU THOUGHT IT WAS BETTER TO TALK TO HER ABOUT IT THAN US?
AIN'T LIKE THAT.
I AM GROOT?!
DRAX, I'M SORRY AND I KNOW YOU HAVE A LOT OF--

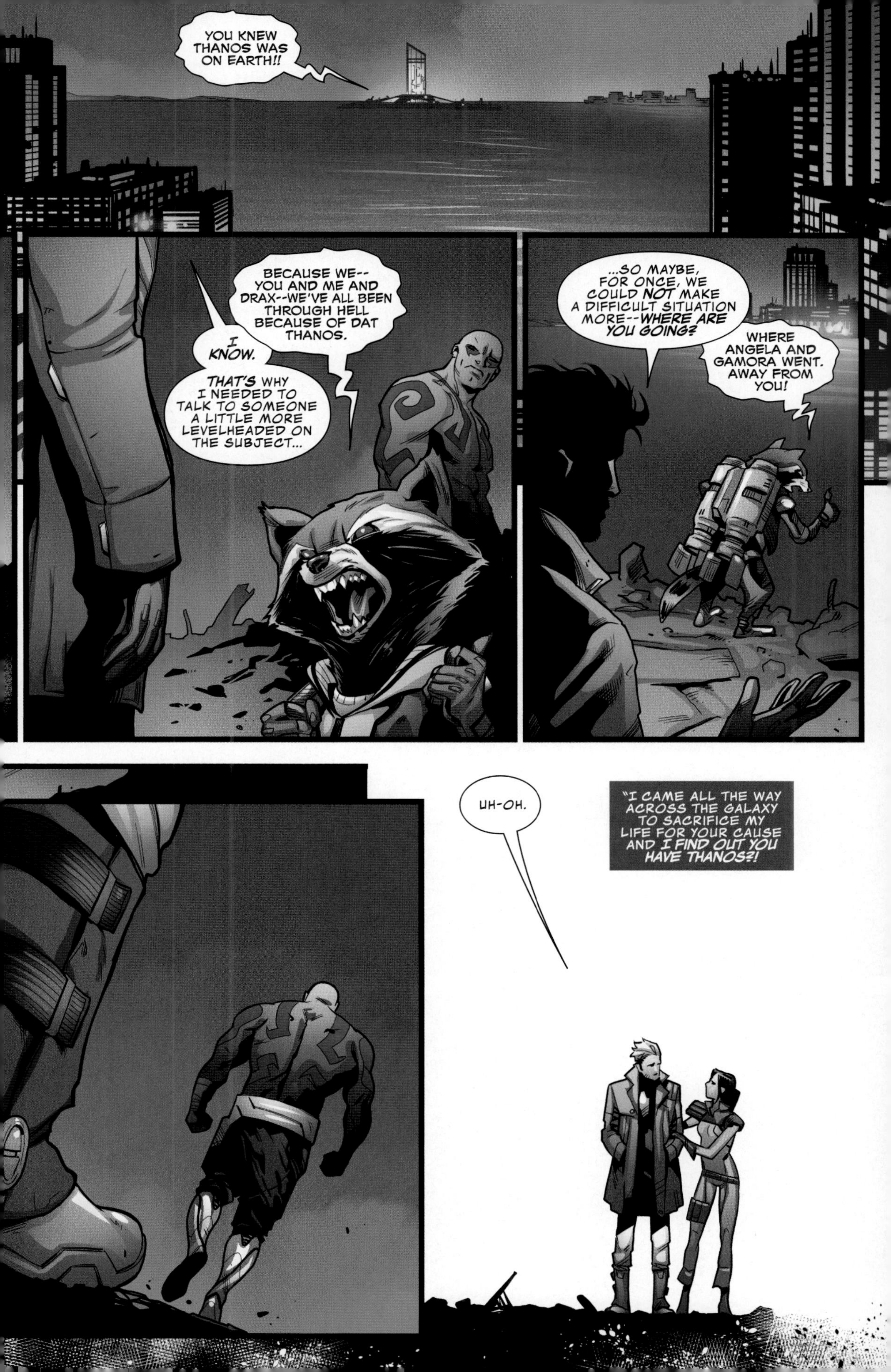
YOU KNEW THANOS WAS ON EARTH!!
BECAUSE WE-- YOU AND ME AND DRAX--WE'VE ALL BEEN THROUGH HELL BECAUSE OF DAT THANOS.
I KNOW.
THAT'S WHY I NEEDED TO TALK TO SOMEONE A LITTLE MORE LEVELHEADED ON THE SUBJECT...
...SO MAYBE, FOR ONCE, WE COULD NOT MAKE A DIFFICULT SITUATION MORE--WHERE ARE YOU GOING?
WHERE ANGELA AND GAMORA WENT. AWAY FROM YOU!
UH-OH.
"I CAME ALL THE WAY ACROSS THE GALAXY TO SACRIFICE MY LIFE FOR YOUR CAUSE AND I FIND OUT YOU HAVE THANOS?!

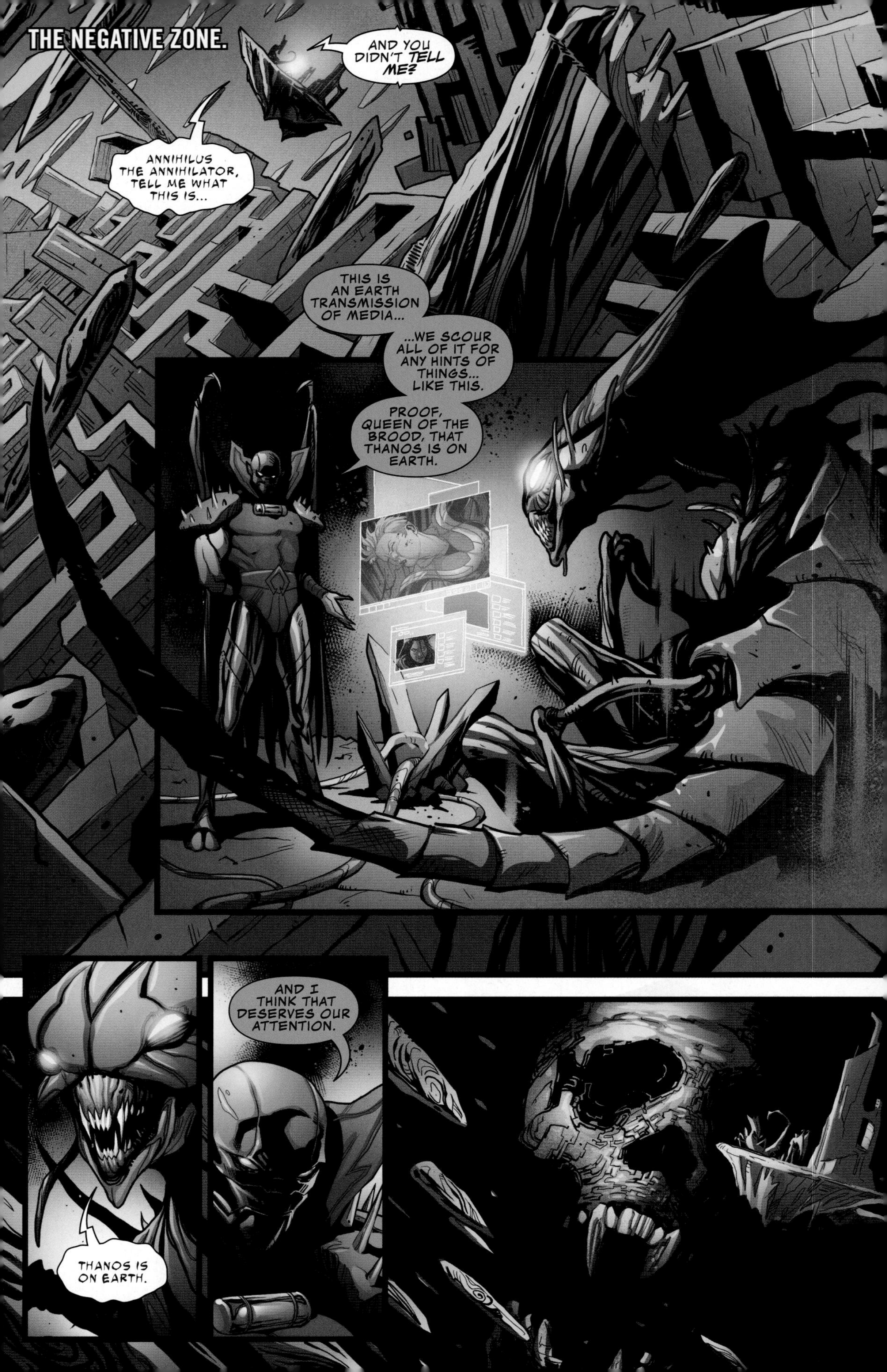
THE NEGATIVE ZONE.
AND YOU DIDN'T TELL ME?
ANNIHILUS THE ANNIHILATOR, TELL ME WHAT THIS IS...
THIS IS AN EARTH TRANSMISSION OF MEDIA...
...WE SCOUR ALL OF IT FOR ANY HINTS OF THINGS... LIKE THIS.
PROOF, QUEEN OF THE BROOD, THAT THANOS IS ON EARTH.
THANOS IS ON EARTH.
AND I THINK THAT DESERVES OUR ATTENTION.

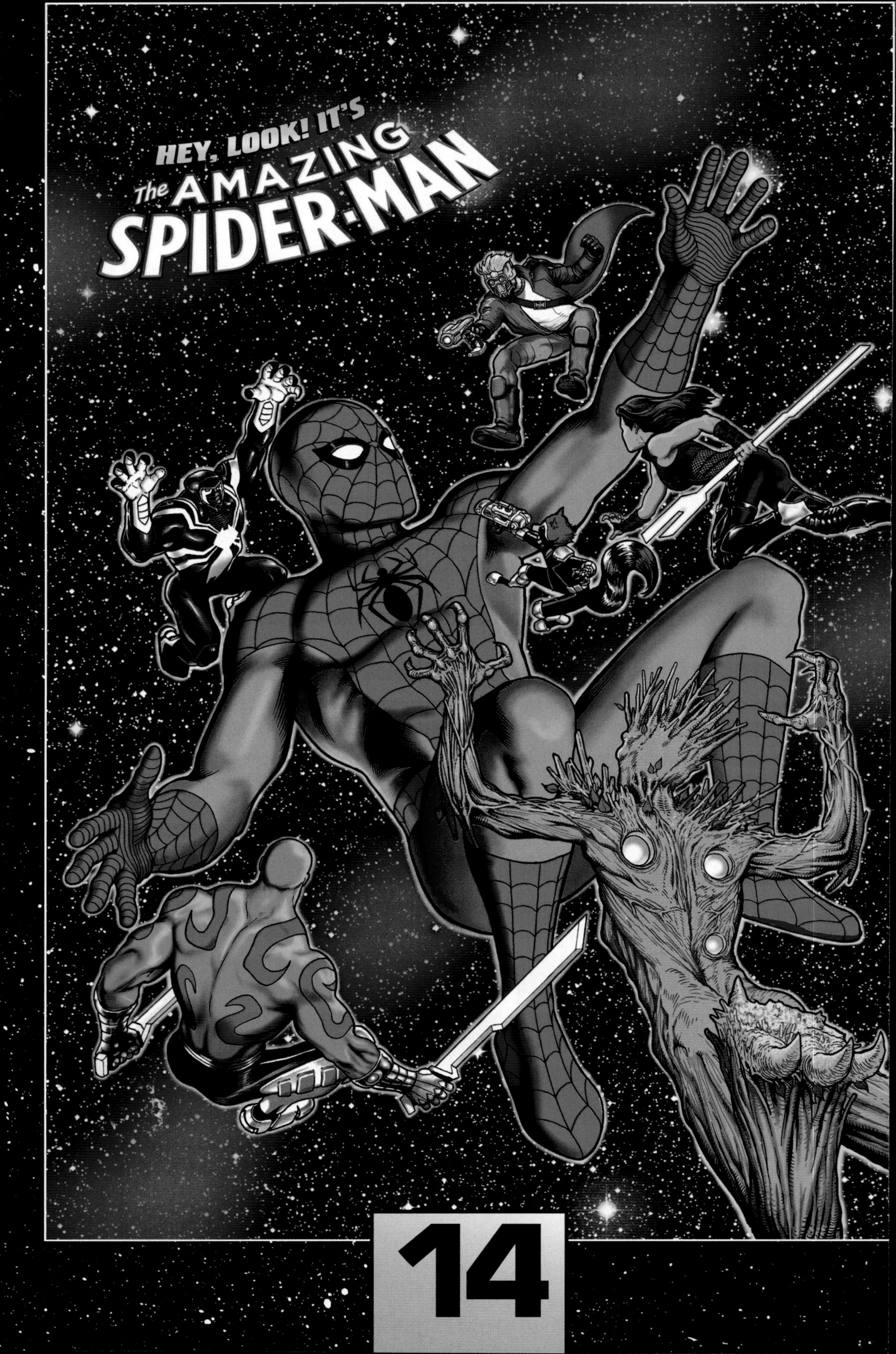
HEY, LOOK! IT'S
The AMAZING
SPIDER-MAN
14

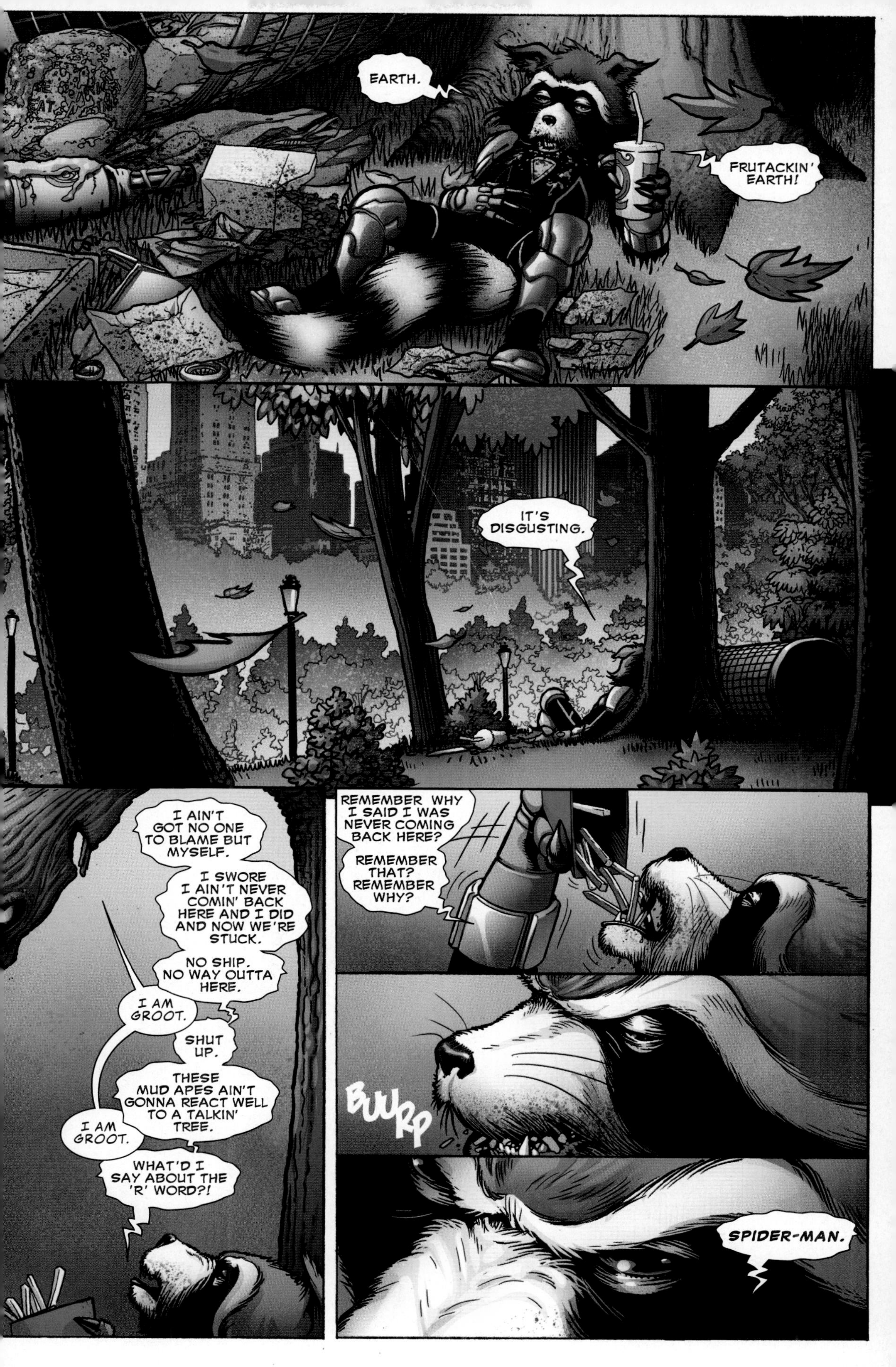
EARTH.
FRUTACKIN' EARTH!
IT'S DISGUSTING.
I AIN'T GOT NO ONE TO BLAME BUT MYSELF.
I SWORE I AIN'T NEVER COMIN' BACK HERE AND I DID AND NOW WE'RE STUCK.
NO SHIP. NO WAY OUTTA HERE.
I AM GROOT.
SHUT UP.
THESE MUD APES AIN'T GONNA REACT WELL TO A TALKIN' TREE.
I AM GROOT.
WHAT'D I SAY ABOUT THE 'R' WORD?!
REMEMBER WHY I SAID I WAS NEVER COMING BACK HERE?
REMEMBER THAT? REMEMBER WHY?
BUURP
SPIDER-MAN.

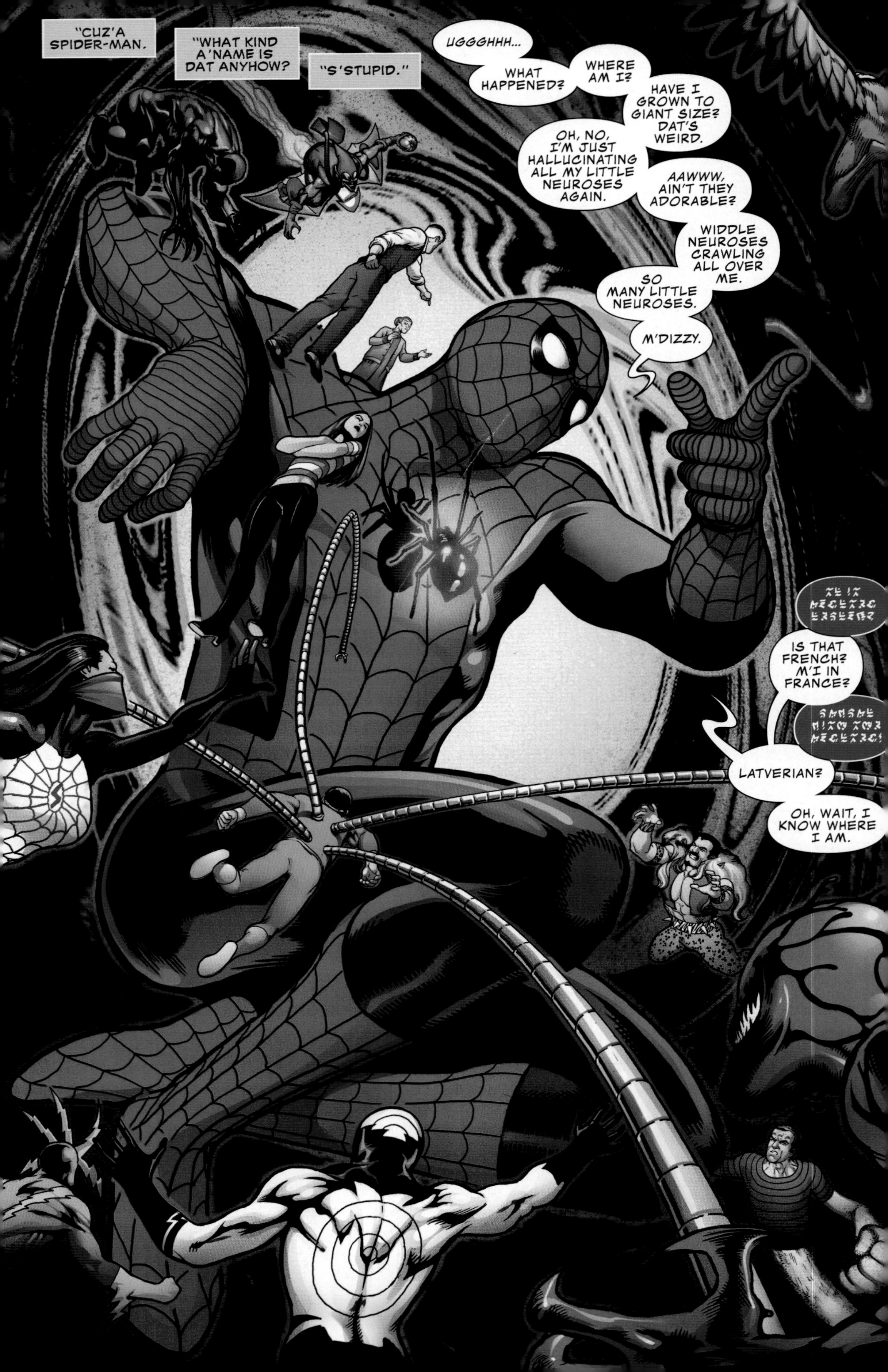
"CUZ'A SPIDER-MAN.
"WHAT KIND A'NAME IS DAT ANYHOW?
"S'STUPID."
UGGGHHH...
WHAT HAPPENED?
WHERE AM I?
HAVE I GROWN TO GIANT SIZE? DAT'S WEIRD.
OH, NO, I'M JUST HALLUCINATING ALL MY LITTLE NEUROSES AGAIN.
AAWWW, AIN'T THEY ADORABLE?
WIDDLE NEUROSES CRAWLING ALL OVER ME.
SO MANY LITTLE NEUROSES.
M'DIZZY.
IS THAT FRENCH? M'I IN FRANCE?
LATVERIAN?
OH, WAIT, I KNOW WHERE I AM.

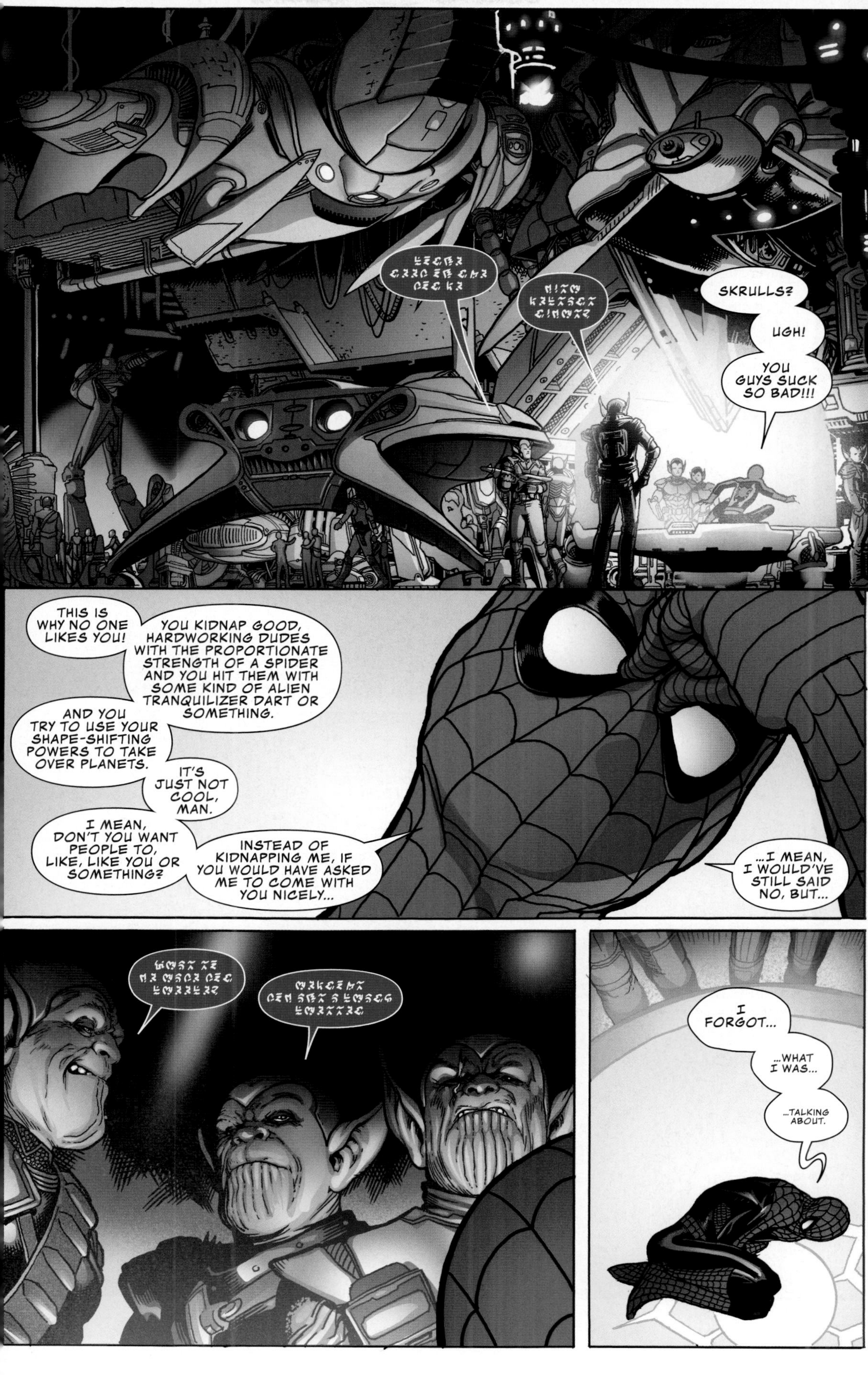
SKRULLS?
UGH!
YOU GUYS SUCK SO BAD!!!
THIS IS WHY NO ONE LIKES YOU!
YOU KIDNAP GOOD, HARDWORKING DUDES WITH THE PROPORTIONATE STRENGTH OF A SPIDER AND YOU HIT THEM WITH SOME KIND OF ALIEN TRANQUILIZER DART OR SOMETHING.
AND YOU TRY TO USE YOUR SHAPE-SHIFTING POWERS TO TAKE OVER PLANETS.
IT'S JUST NOT COOL, MAN.
I MEAN, DON'T YOU WANT PEOPLE TO, LIKE, LIKE YOU OR SOMETHING?
INSTEAD OF KIDNAPPING ME, IF YOU WOULD HAVE ASKED ME TO COME WITH YOU NICELY...
...I MEAN, I WOULD'VE STILL SAID NO, BUT...
I FORGOT...
...WHAT I WAS...
...TALKING ABOUT.

THE GLONTHORP BISTRO AND BREWPUB. ON THE OTHER SIDE OF THE GALAXY.

IT RECEIVED A ONE-STAR RATING IN THE MULLKINI GUIDE.

BUT ONLY BECAUSE THE REVIEWER WAS MURDERED FOR ASKING WHERE THE BATHROOM WAS.

YOU DO NOT TALK ABOUT THE PLANET EARTH THAT WAY!!

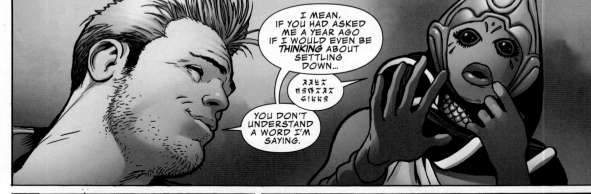

I MEAN, IF YOU HAD ASKED ME A YEAR AGO IF I WOULD EVEN BE *THINKING* ABOUT SETTLING DOWN...

YOU DON'T UNDERSTAND A WORD I'M SAYING.

SHE SEEMED NICE.

WHAT ARE THOSE BOZOS FIGHTING ABOUT NOW, GAMORA?

DOES IT MATTER?

HOW YA DOING OVER THERE, FLASH?

SHOULD WE HELP DRAX?

IF YOU WANT TO.

THEY DO THIS ENTIRELY TOO MUCH.

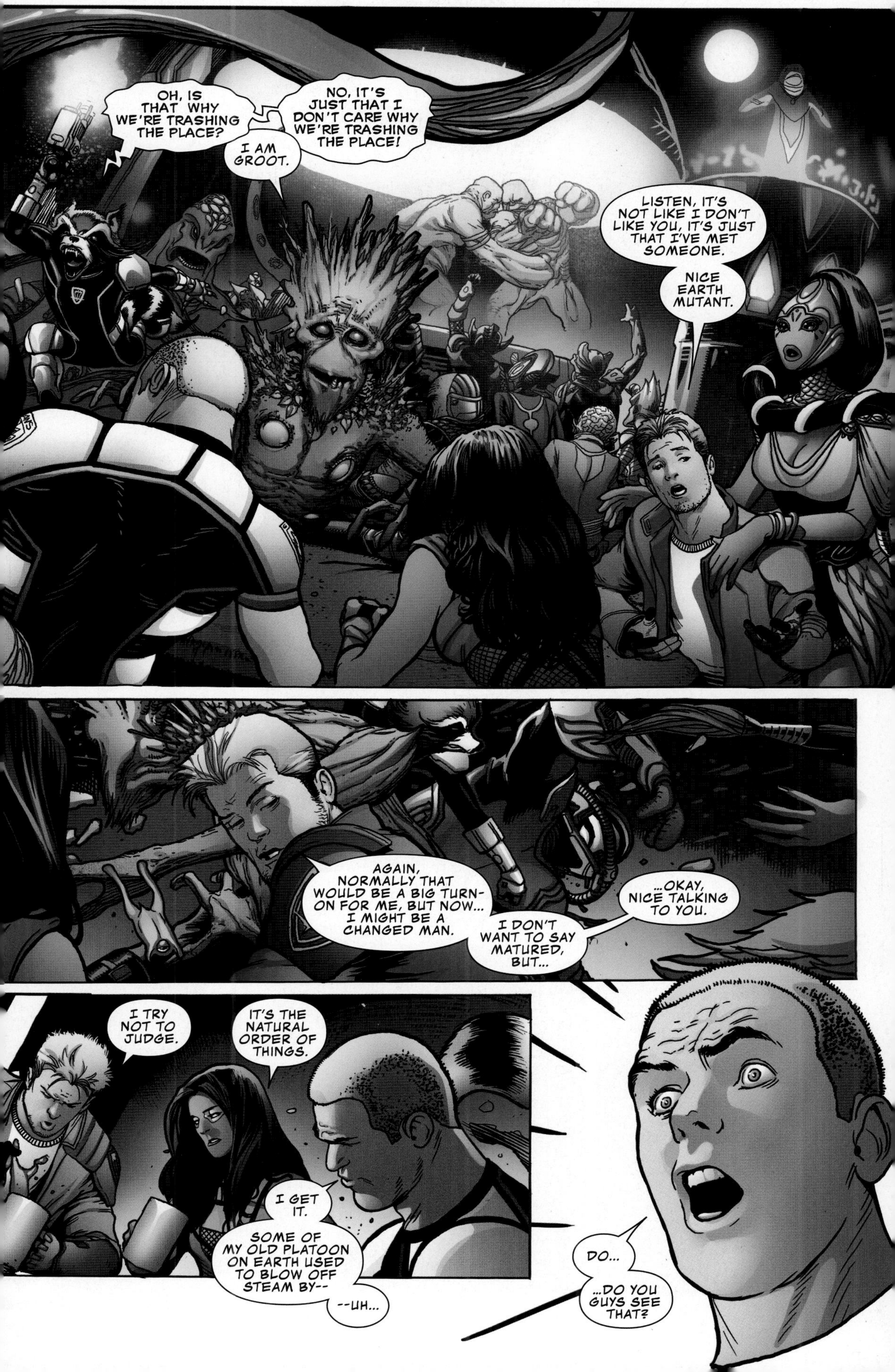
OH, IS THAT WHY WE'RE TRASHING THE PLACE?
NO, IT'S JUST THAT I DON'T CARE WHY WE'RE TRASHING THE PLACE!
I AM GROOT.
LISTEN, IT'S NOT LIKE I DON'T LIKE YOU, IT'S JUST THAT I'VE MET SOMEONE.
NICE EARTH MUTANT.
AGAIN, NORMALLY THAT WOULD BE A BIG TURN-ON FOR ME, BUT NOW... I MIGHT BE A CHANGED MAN.
I DON'T WANT TO SAY MATURED, BUT...
...OKAY, NICE TALKING TO YOU.
I TRY NOT TO JUDGE.
IT'S THE NATURAL ORDER OF THINGS.
I GET IT.
SOME OF MY OLD PLATOON ON EARTH USED TO BLOW OFF STEAM BY--
--UH...
DO...
...DO YOU GUYS SEE THAT?

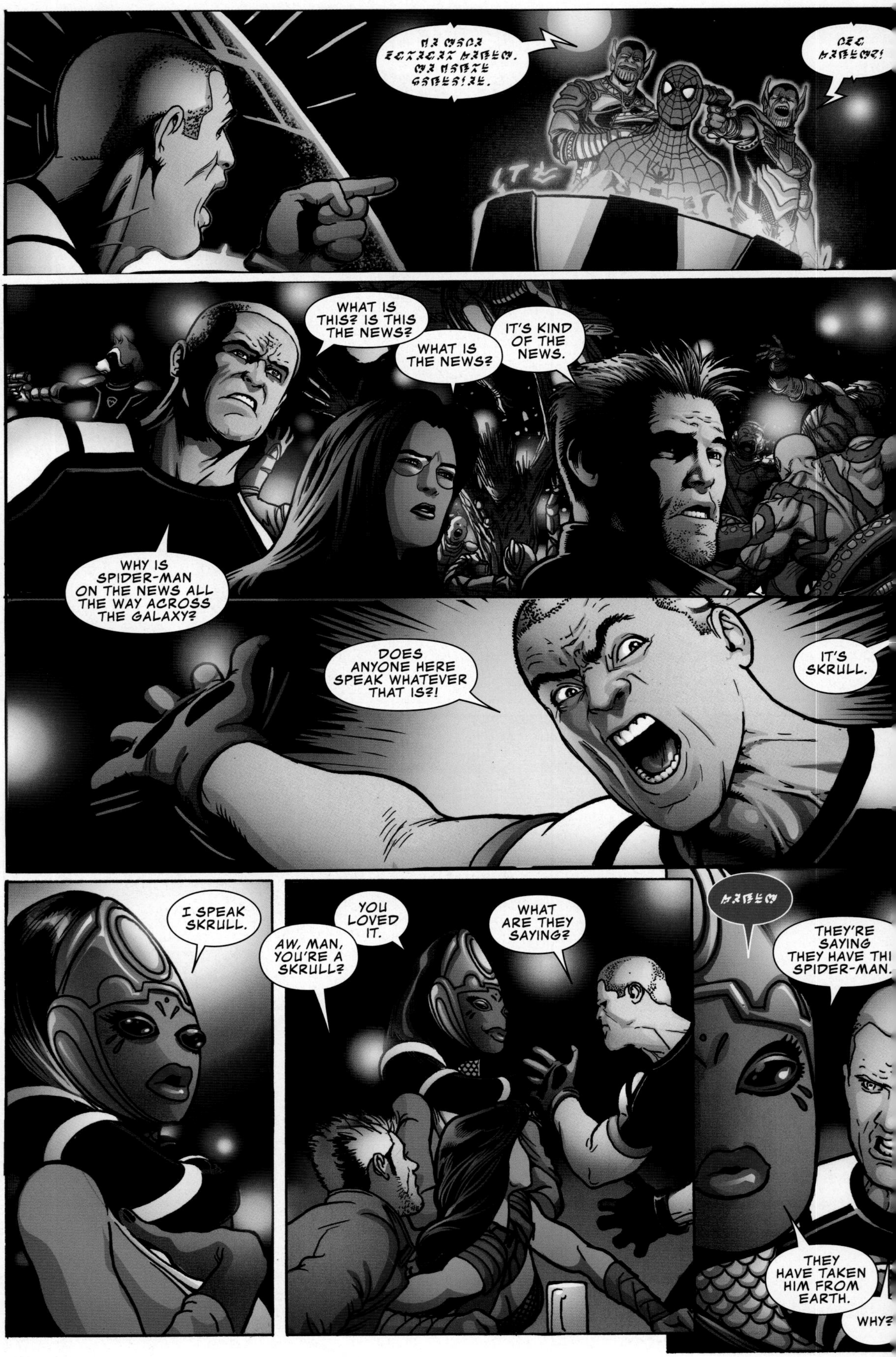
WHAT IS THIS? IS THIS THE NEWS?
WHAT IS THE NEWS?
IT'S KIND OF THE NEWS.
WHY IS SPIDER-MAN ON THE NEWS ALL THE WAY ACROSS THE GALAXY?
DOES ANYONE HERE SPEAK WHATEVER THAT IS?!
IT'S SKRULL.
I SPEAK SKRULL.
AW, MAN, YOU'RE A SKRULL?
YOU LOVED IT.
WHAT ARE THEY SAYING?
THEY'RE SAYING THEY HAVE THI SPIDER-MAN.
THEY HAVE TAKEN HIM FROM EARTH.
WHY?

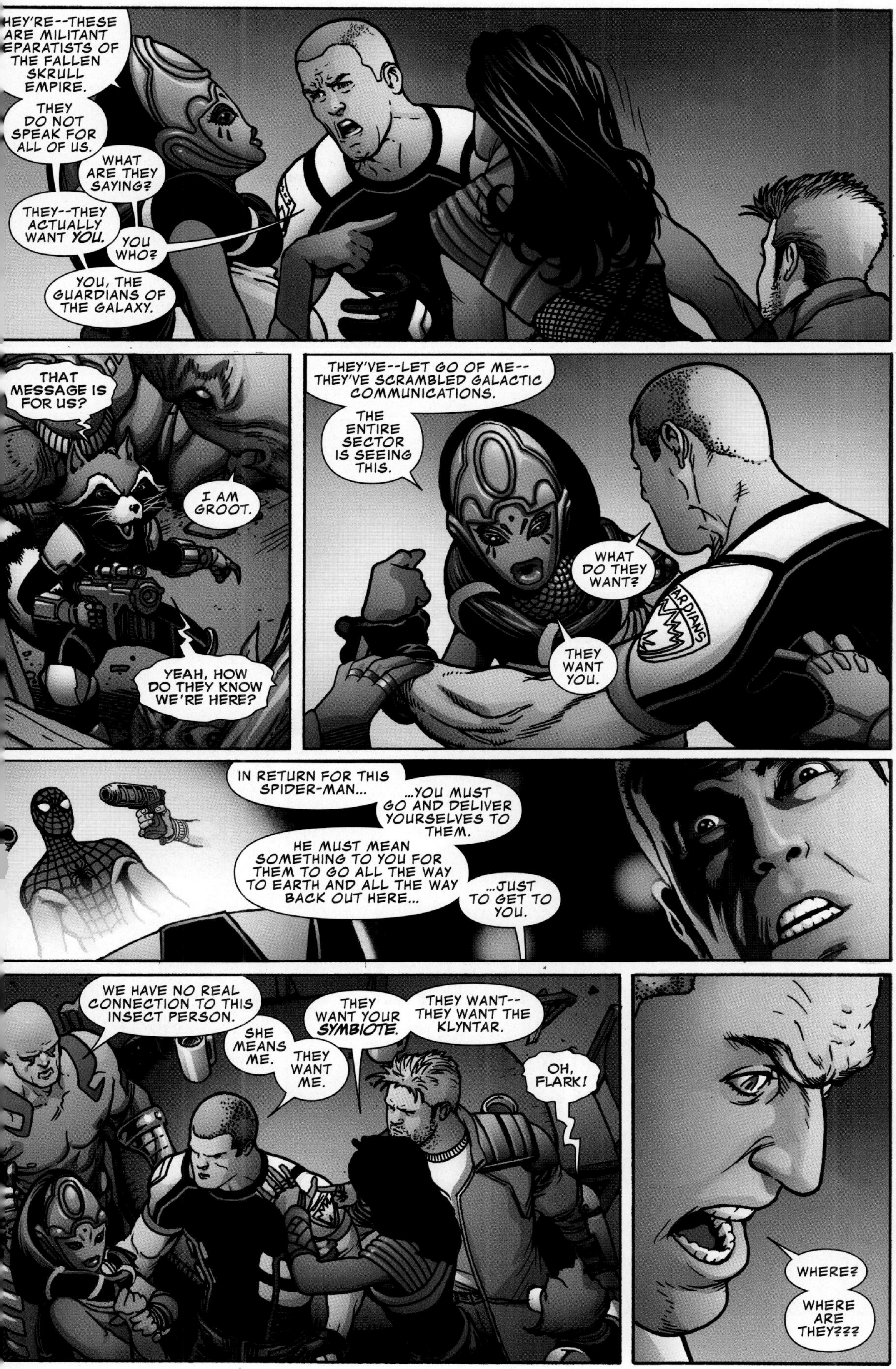
HEY'RE--THESE ARE MILITANT EPARATISTS OF THE FALLEN SKRULL EMPIRE.
THEY DO NOT SPEAK FOR ALL OF US.
WHAT ARE THEY SAYING?
THEY--THEY ACTUALLY WANT YOU.
YOU WHO?
YOU, THE GUARDIANS OF THE GALAXY.
THAT MESSAGE IS FOR US?
I AM GROOT.
YEAH, HOW DO THEY KNOW WE'RE HERE?
THEY'VE--LET GO OF ME--THEY'VE SCRAMBLED GALACTIC COMMUNICATIONS.
THE ENTIRE SECTOR IS SEEING THIS.
WHAT DO THEY WANT?
THEY WANT YOU.
IN RETURN FOR THIS SPIDER-MAN...
...YOU MUST GO AND DELIVER YOURSELVES TO THEM.
HE MUST MEAN SOMETHING TO YOU FOR THEM TO GO ALL THE WAY TO EARTH AND ALL THE WAY BACK OUT HERE...
...JUST TO GET TO YOU.
WE HAVE NO REAL CONNECTION TO THIS INSECT PERSON.
SHE MEANS ME.
THEY WANT ME.
THEY WANT YOUR SYMBIOTE.
THEY WANT--THEY WANT THE KLYNTAR.
OH, FLARK!
WHERE?
WHERE ARE THEY???

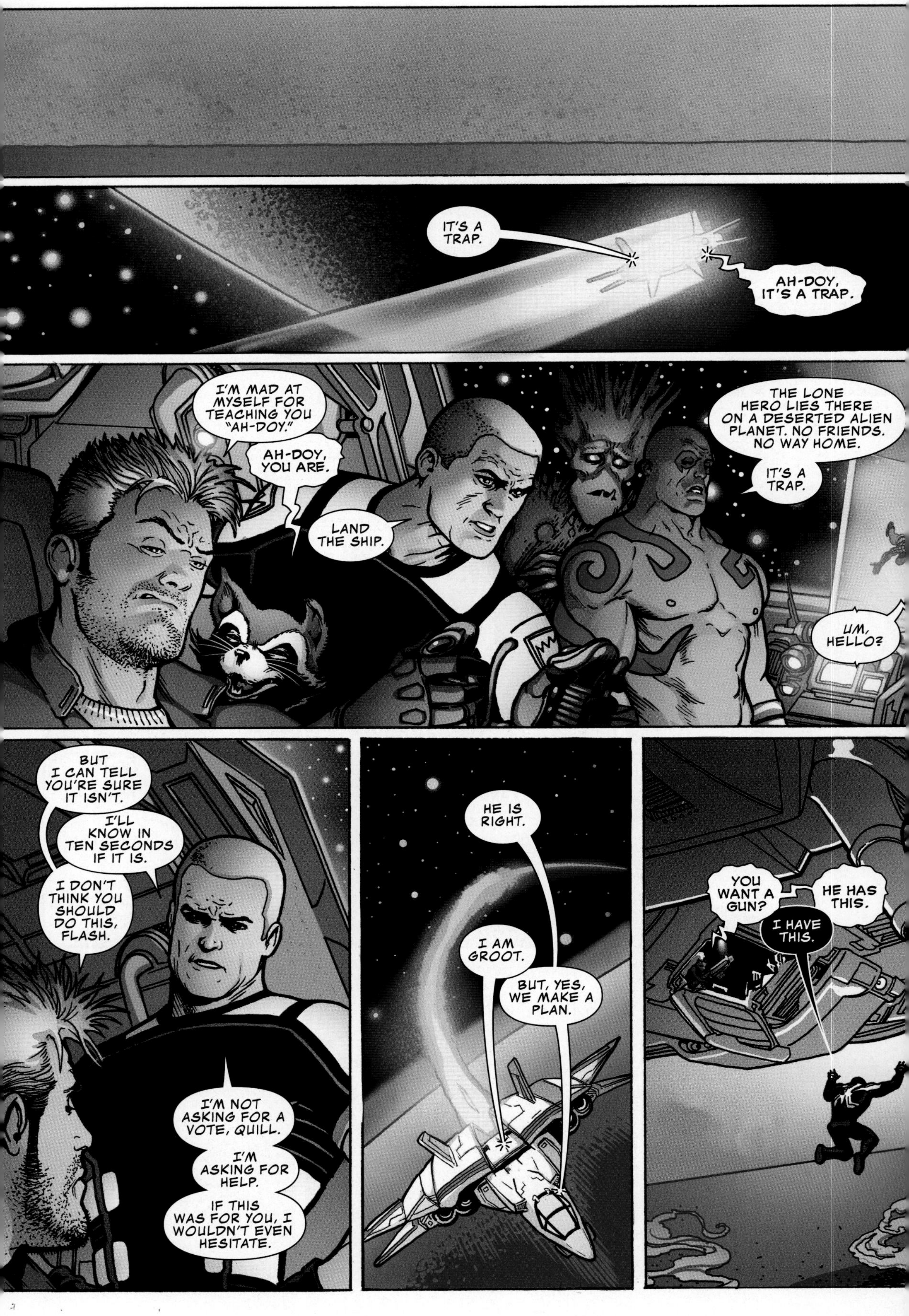
IT'S A TRAP.
AH-DOY, IT'S A TRAP.
I'M MAD AT MYSELF FOR TEACHING YOU "AH-DOY."
AH-DOY, YOU ARE.
LAND THE SHIP.
THE LONE HERO LIES THERE ON A DESERTED ALIEN PLANET. NO FRIENDS. NO WAY HOME.
IT'S A TRAP.
UM, HELLO?
BUT I CAN TELL YOU'RE SURE IT ISN'T.
I'LL KNOW IN TEN SECONDS IF IT IS.
I DON'T THINK YOU SHOULD DO THIS, FLASH.
I'M NOT ASKING FOR A VOTE, QUILL.
I'M ASKING FOR HELP.
IF THIS WAS FOR YOU, I WOULDN'T EVEN HESITATE.
HE IS RIGHT.
I AM GROOT.
BUT, YES, WE MAKE A PLAN.
YOU WANT A GUN?
HE HAS THIS.
I HAVE THIS.

WE CANNOT LET THE SKRULLS HAVE A SYMBIOTE. ESPECIALLY YOURS.

YOURS IS PURE NOW. IT IS TOO POWERFUL A WEAPON TO HAND OVER TO THEM.

I KNOW THAT! DON'T YOU THINK I KNOW THAT?

IT'S PROBABLY NOT EVEN REALLY SPIDER-MAN.

THE SKRULL ARE SHAPE-SHIFTING LITTLE TROLLS.

THIS IS EXACTLY THE KIND OF THING THEY WOULD TRY.

FINE! IF IT IS A SKRULL, I'LL PULL THEM ALL APART.

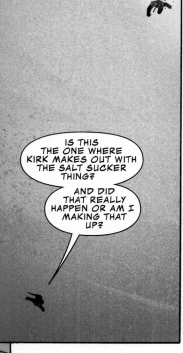

IS THIS THE ONE WHERE KIRK MAKES OUT WITH THE SALT SUCKER THING?

AND DID THAT REALLY HAPPEN OR AM I MAKING THAT UP?

ALL I'M ASKING FOR IS A--OH.

TAKE OFF YOUR MASK.

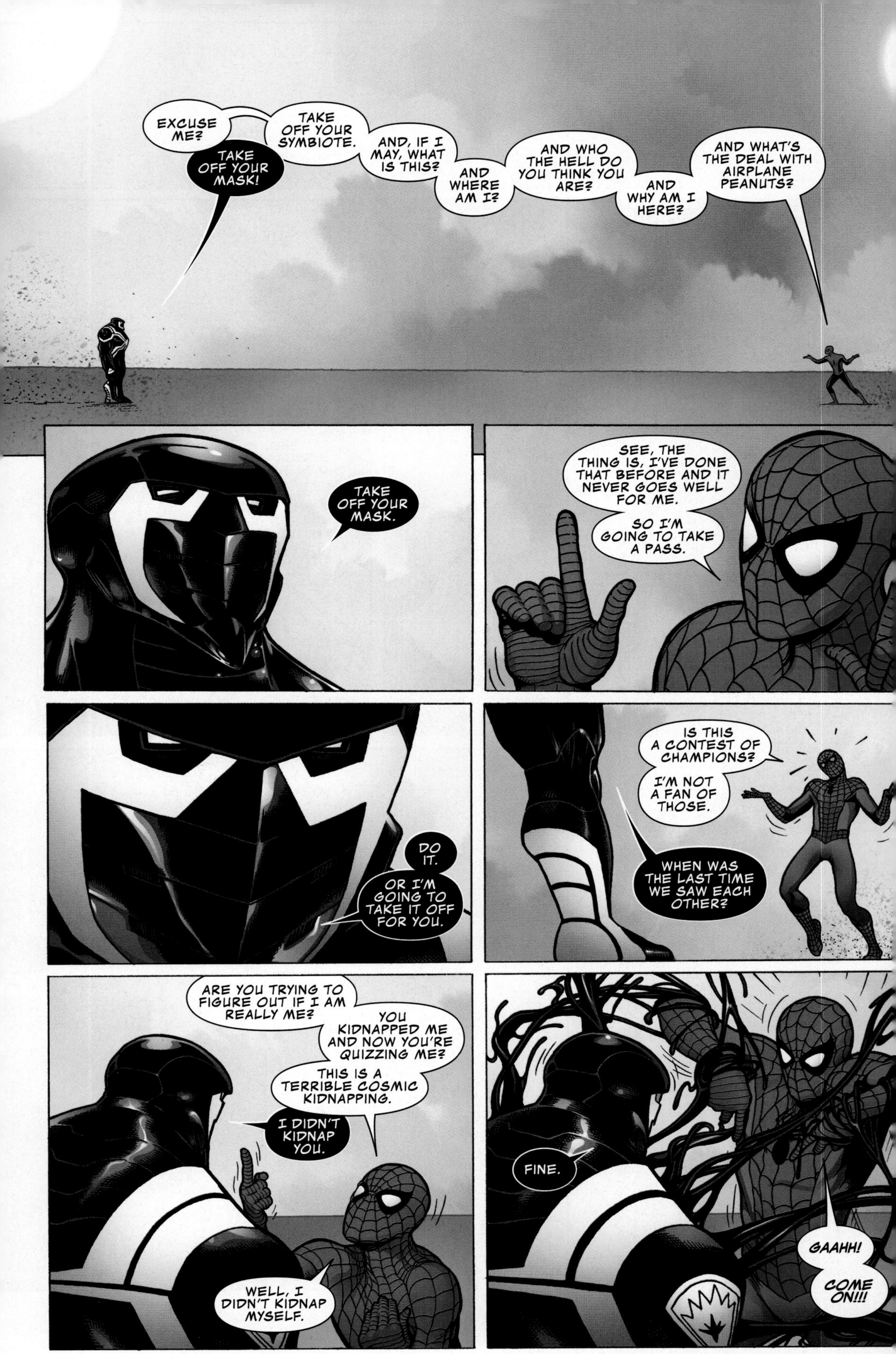
EXCUSE ME?
TAKE OFF YOUR MASK!
TAKE OFF YOUR SYMBIOTE.
AND, IF I MAY, WHAT IS THIS?
AND WHERE AM I?
AND WHO THE HELL DO YOU THINK YOU ARE?
AND WHY AM I HERE?
AND WHAT'S THE DEAL WITH AIRPLANE PEANUTS?
TAKE OFF YOUR MASK.
SEE, THE THING IS, I'VE DONE THAT BEFORE AND IT NEVER GOES WELL FOR ME.
SO I'M GOING TO TAKE A PASS.
DO IT.
OR I'M GOING TO TAKE IT OFF FOR YOU.
IS THIS A CONTEST OF CHAMPIONS?
I'M NOT A FAN OF THOSE.
WHEN WAS THE LAST TIME WE SAW EACH OTHER?
ARE YOU TRYING TO FIGURE OUT IF I AM REALLY ME?
YOU KIDNAPPED ME AND NOW YOU'RE QUIZZING ME?
THIS IS A TERRIBLE COSMIC KIDNAPPING.
I DIDN'T KIDNAP YOU.
WELL, I DIDN'T KIDNAP MYSELF.
FINE.
GAAHH!
COME ON!!!

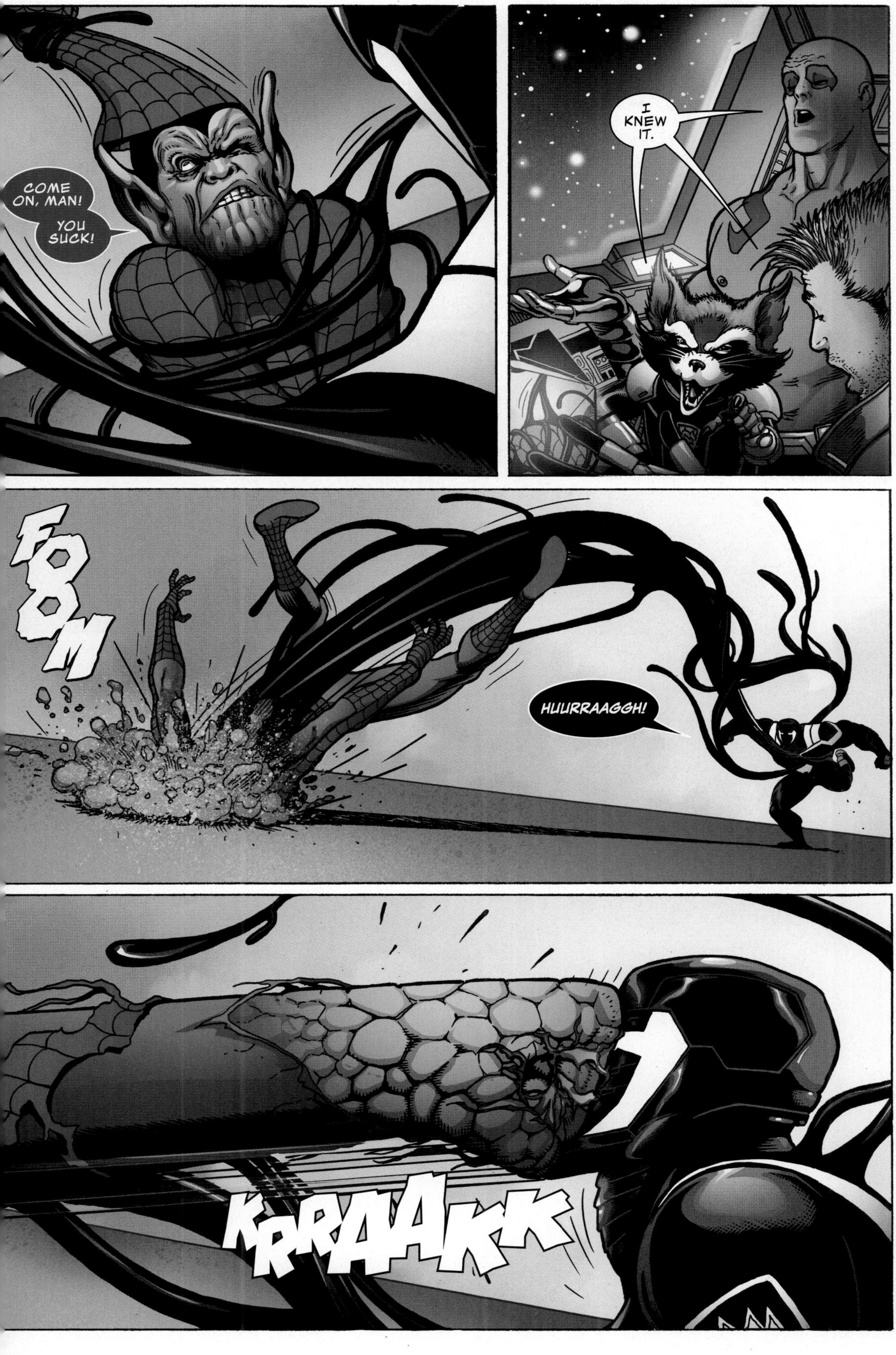
COME ON, MAN!
YOU SUCK!
I KNEW IT.
FOOM
HUURRAAGGH!
KRRAAKK

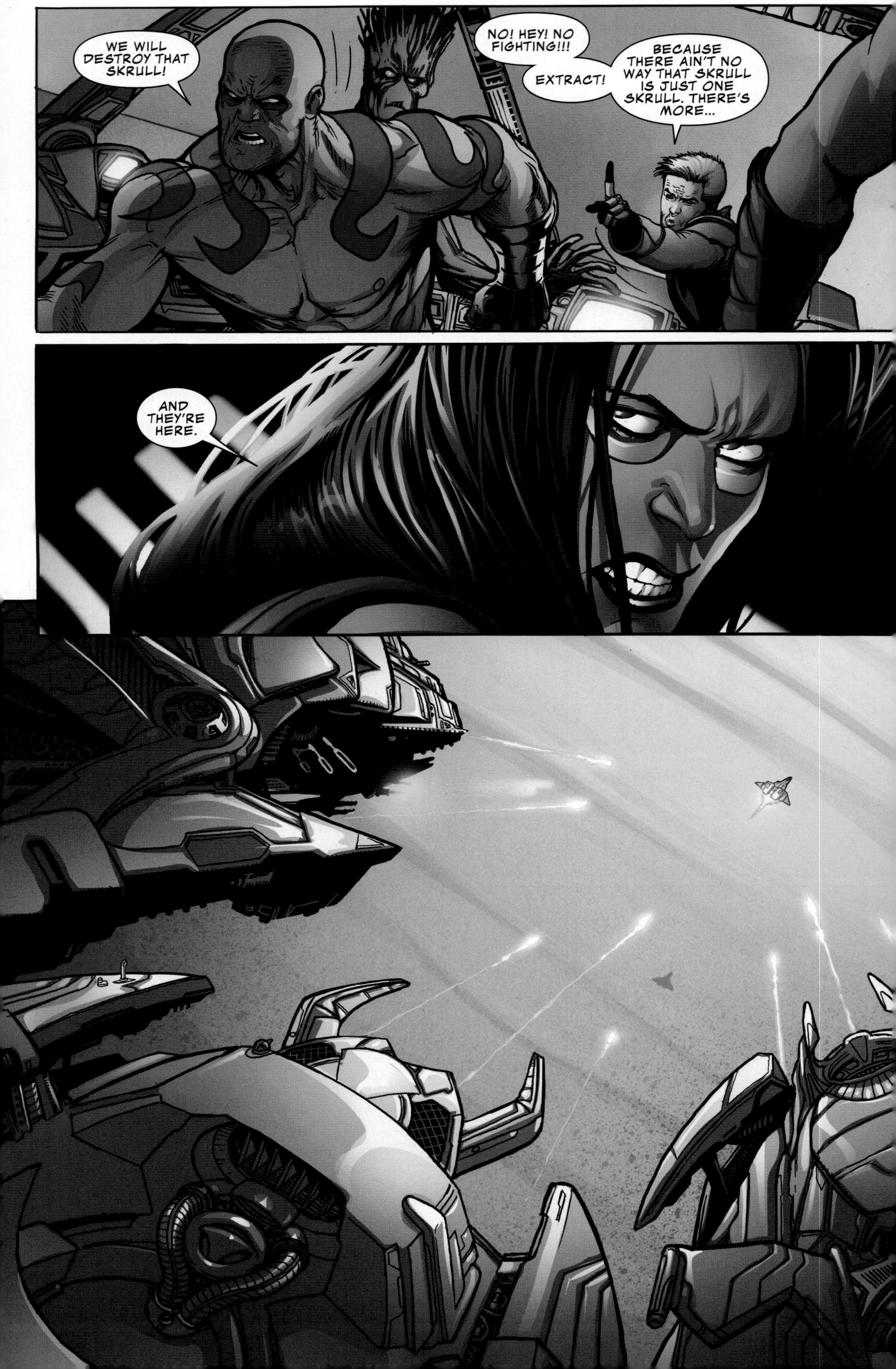
WE WILL DESTROY THAT SKRULL!
NO! HEY! NO FIGHTING!!!
EXTRACT!
BECAUSE THERE AIN'T NO WAY THAT SKRULL IS JUST ONE SKRULL. THERE'S MORE...
AND THEY'RE HERE.

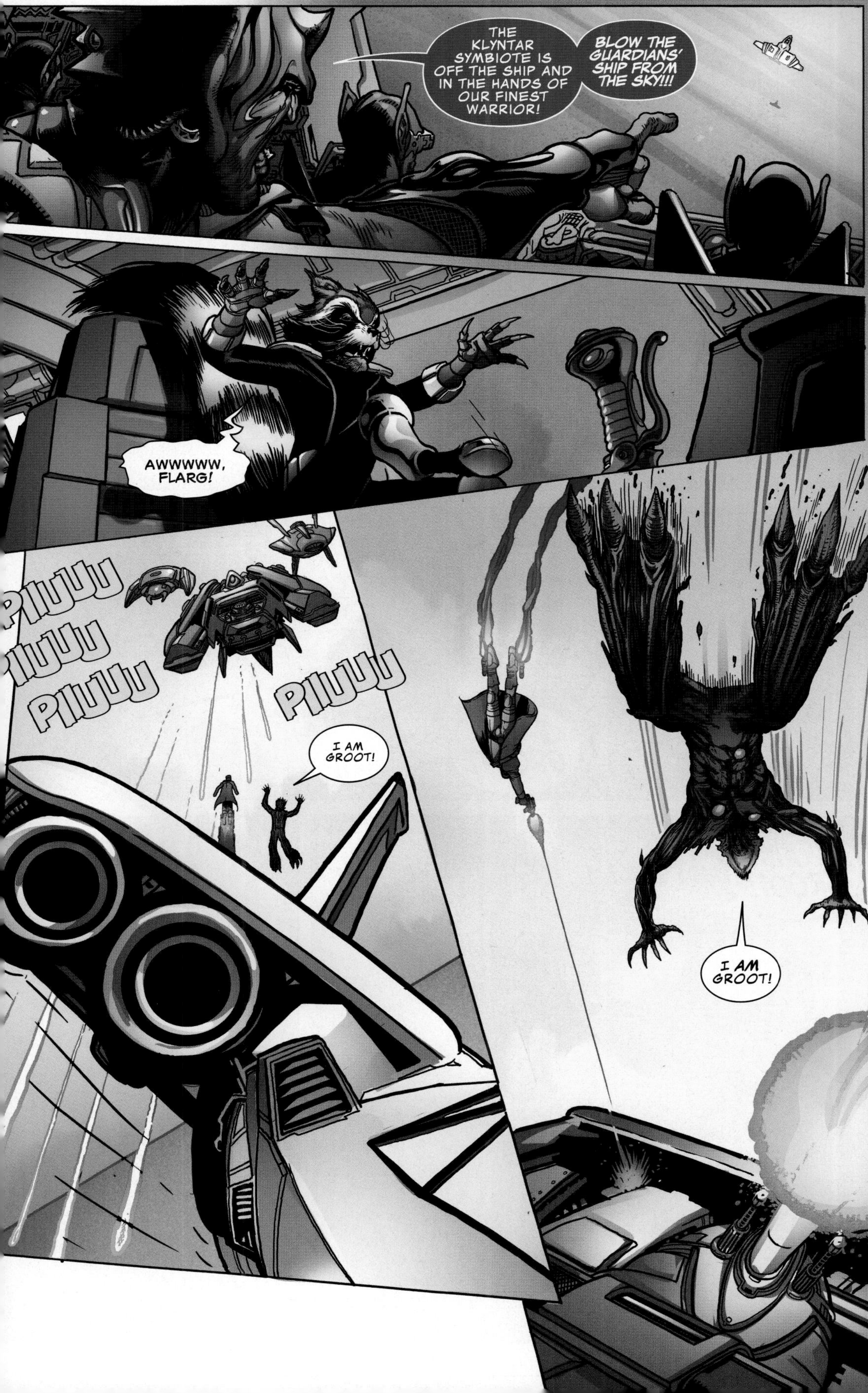
THE KLYNTAR SYMBIOTE IS OFF THE SHIP AND IN THE HANDS OF OUR FINEST WARRIOR!
BLOW THE GUARDIANS' SHIP FROM THE SKY!!!
AWWWWW, FLARG!
PIIUUU
PIIUUU
PIIUUU
PIIUUU
I AM GROOT!
I AM GROOT!

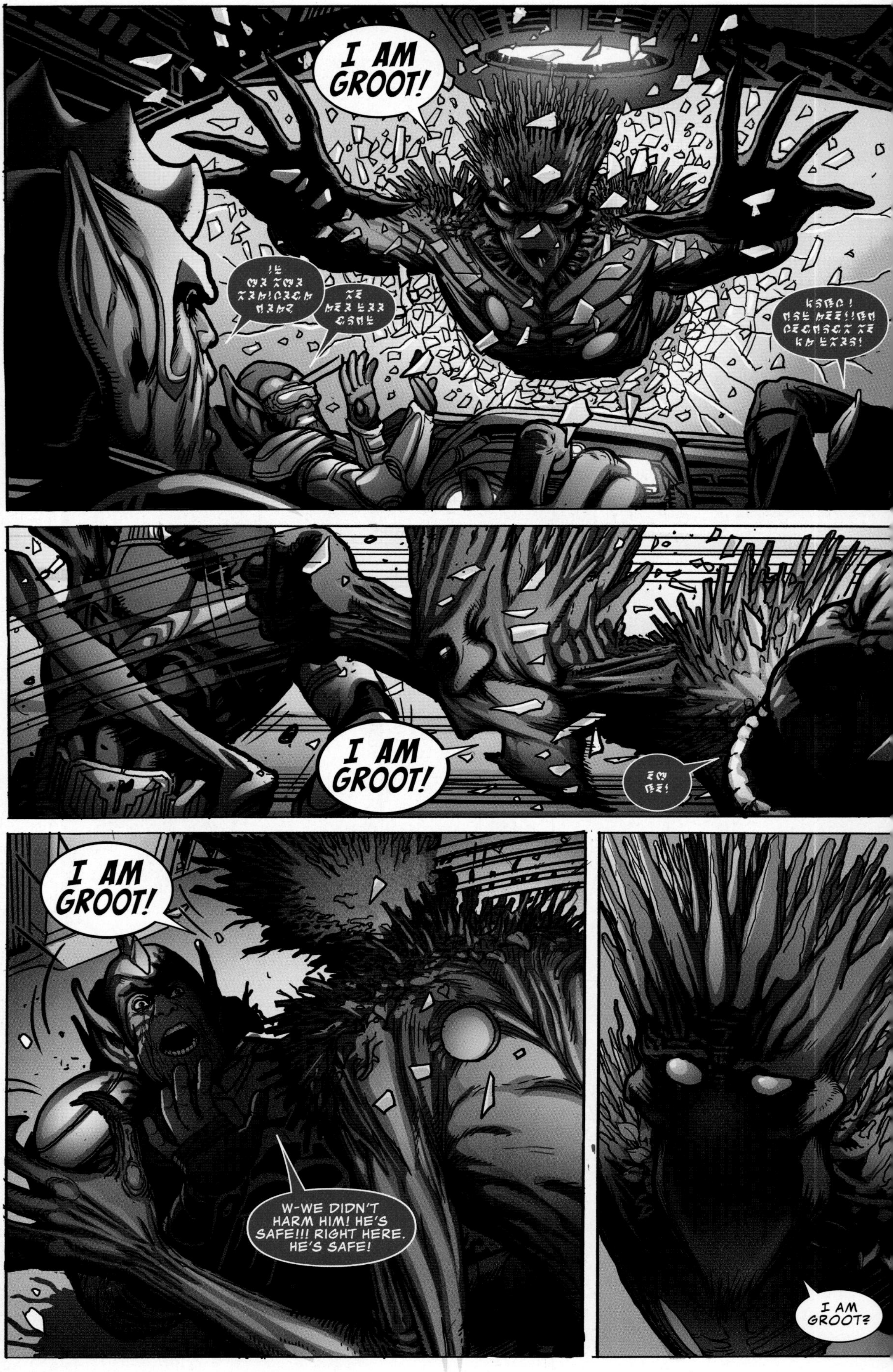
I AM GROOT!
I AM GROOT!
I AM GROOT!
W-WE DIDN'T HARM HIM! HE'S SAFE!!! RIGHT HERE. HE'S SAFE!
I AM GROOT?

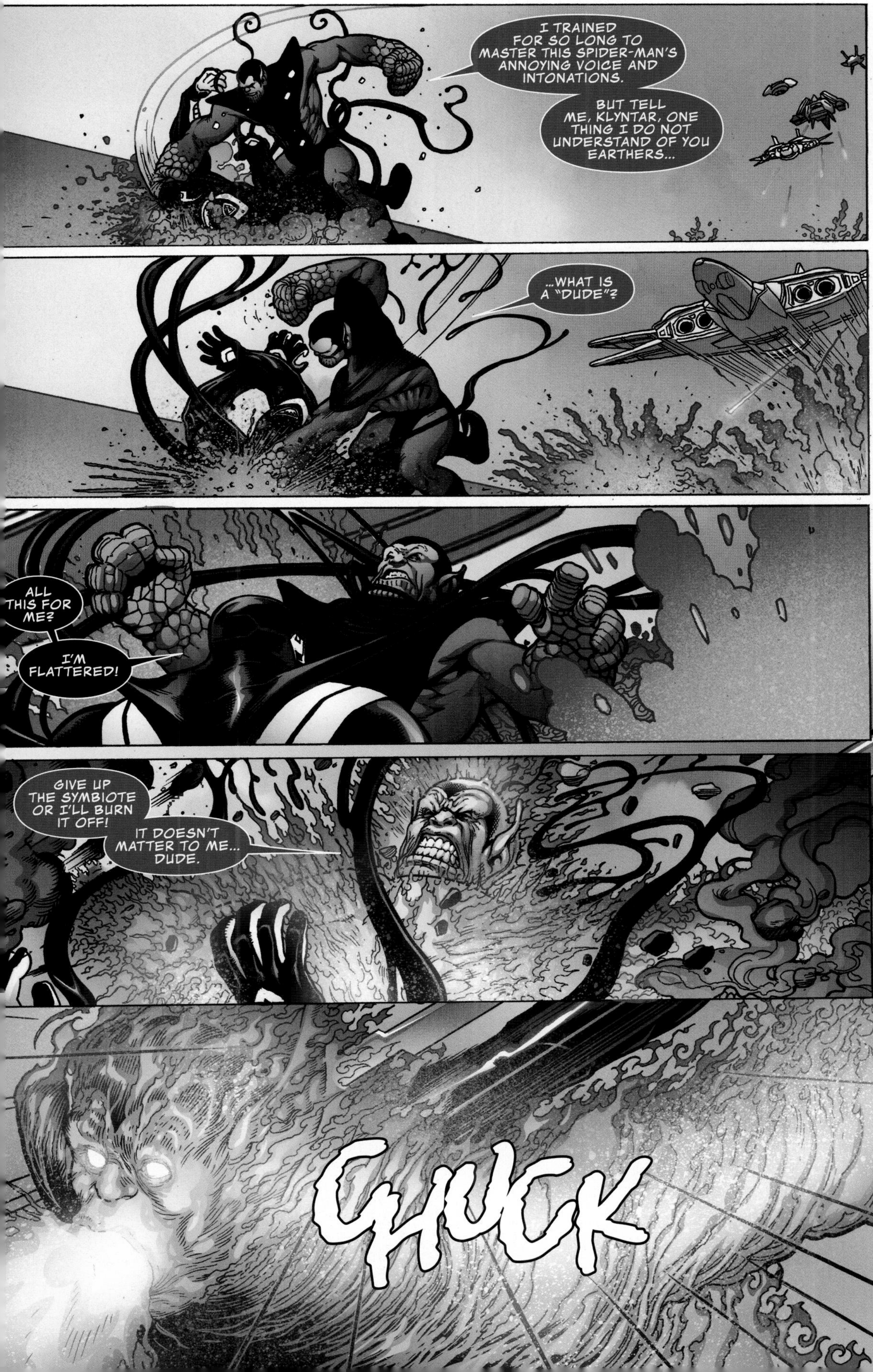
I TRAINED FOR SO LONG TO MASTER THIS SPIDER-MAN'S ANNOYING VOICE AND INTONATIONS.
BUT TELL ME, KLYNTAR, ONE THING I DO NOT UNDERSTAND OF YOU EARTHERS...
...WHAT IS A "DUDE"?
ALL THIS FOR ME?
I'M FLATTERED!
GIVE UP THE SYMBIOTE OR I'LL BURN IT OFF!
IT DOESN'T MATTER TO ME... DUDE.
GLUCK

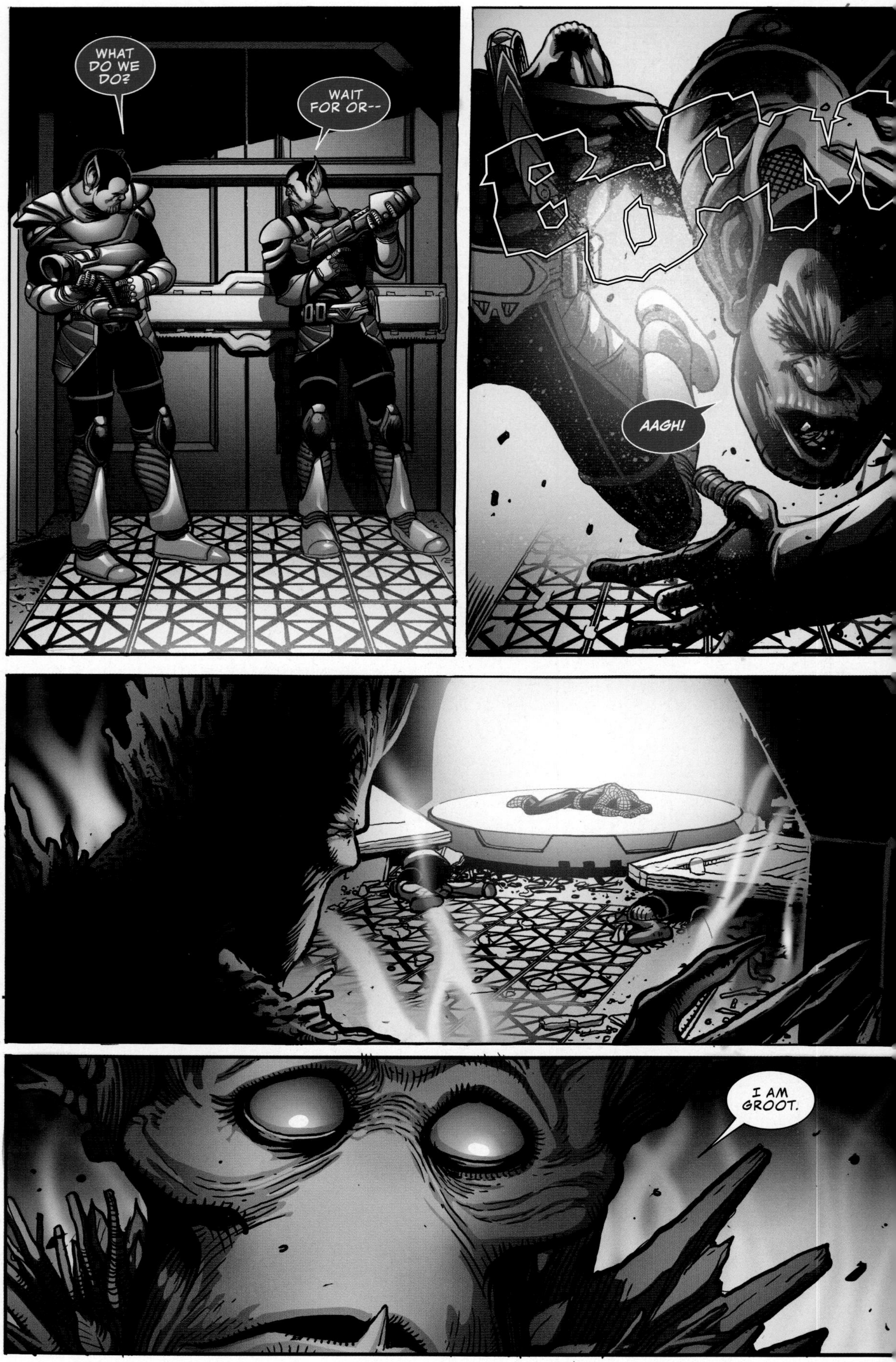
WHAT DO WE DO?
WAIT FOR OR--
BOOM
AAGH!
I AM GROOT.

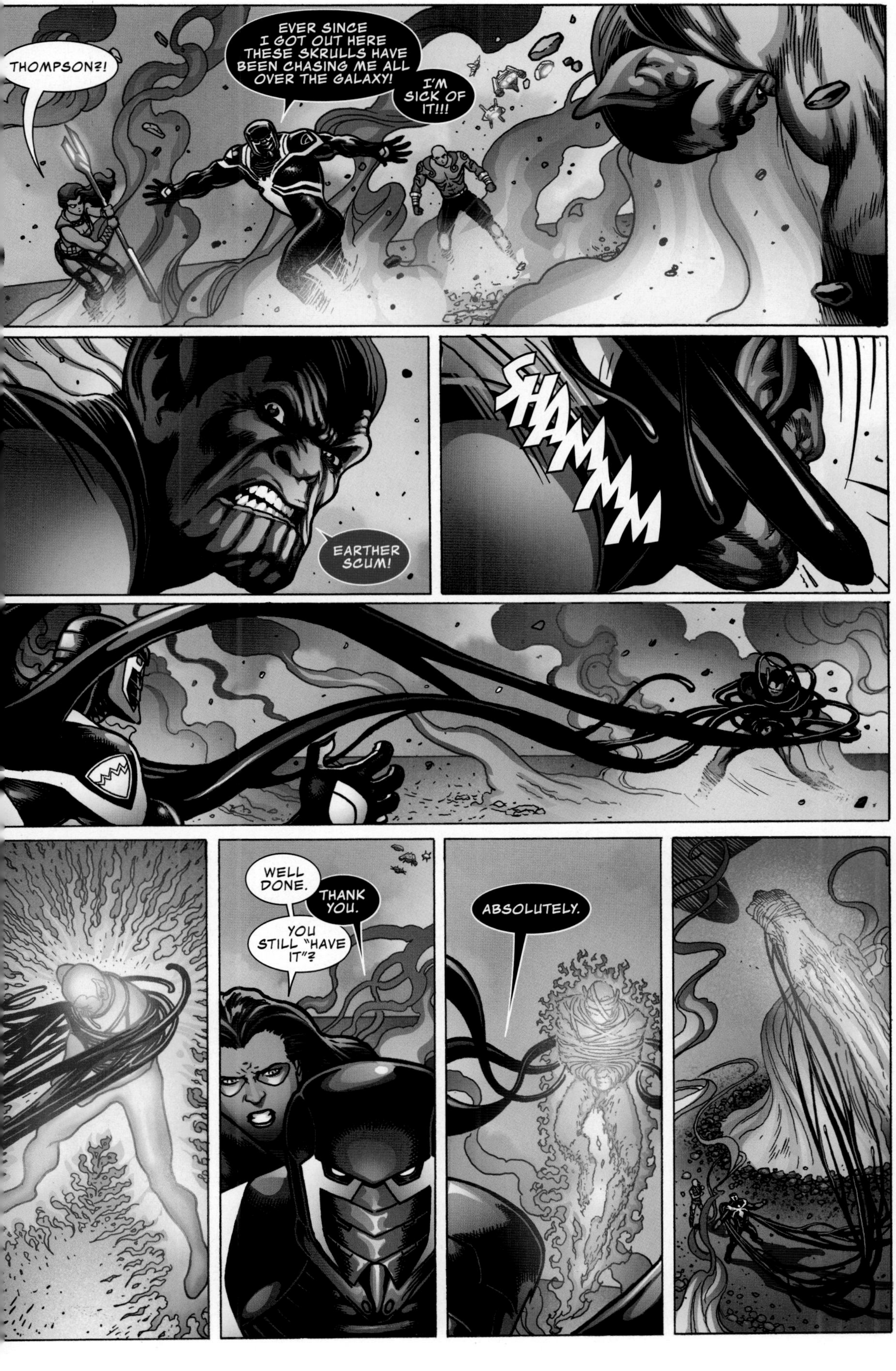
THOMPSON?!
EVER SINCE I GOT OUT HERE THESE SKRULLS HAVE BEEN CHASING ME ALL OVER THE GALAXY!
I'M SICK OF IT!!!
EARTHER SCUM!
SHHAMMMM
WELL DONE.
THANK YOU.
YOU STILL "HAVE IT"?
ABSOLUTELY.

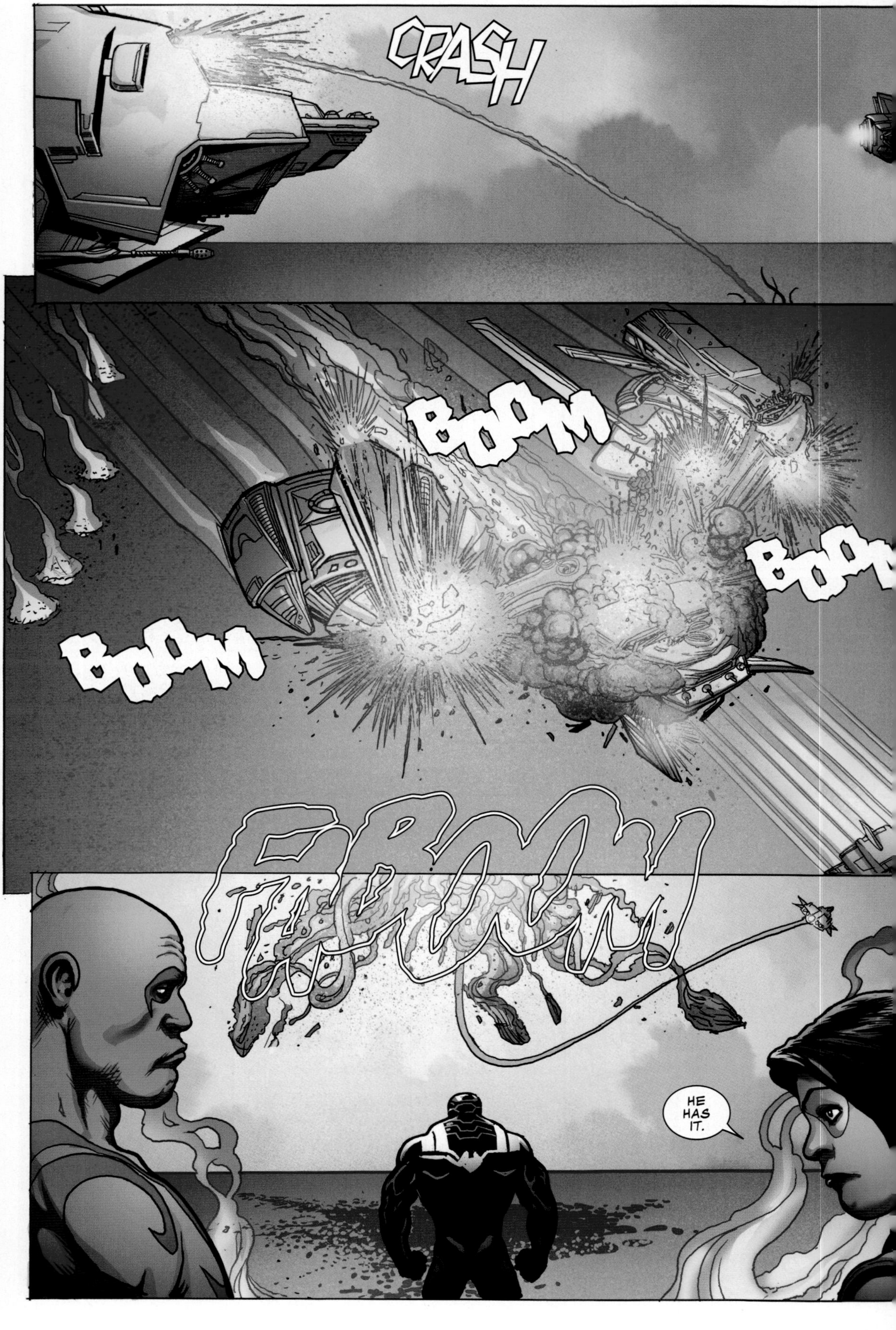
CRASH
BOOM
BOOM
HE HAS IT.

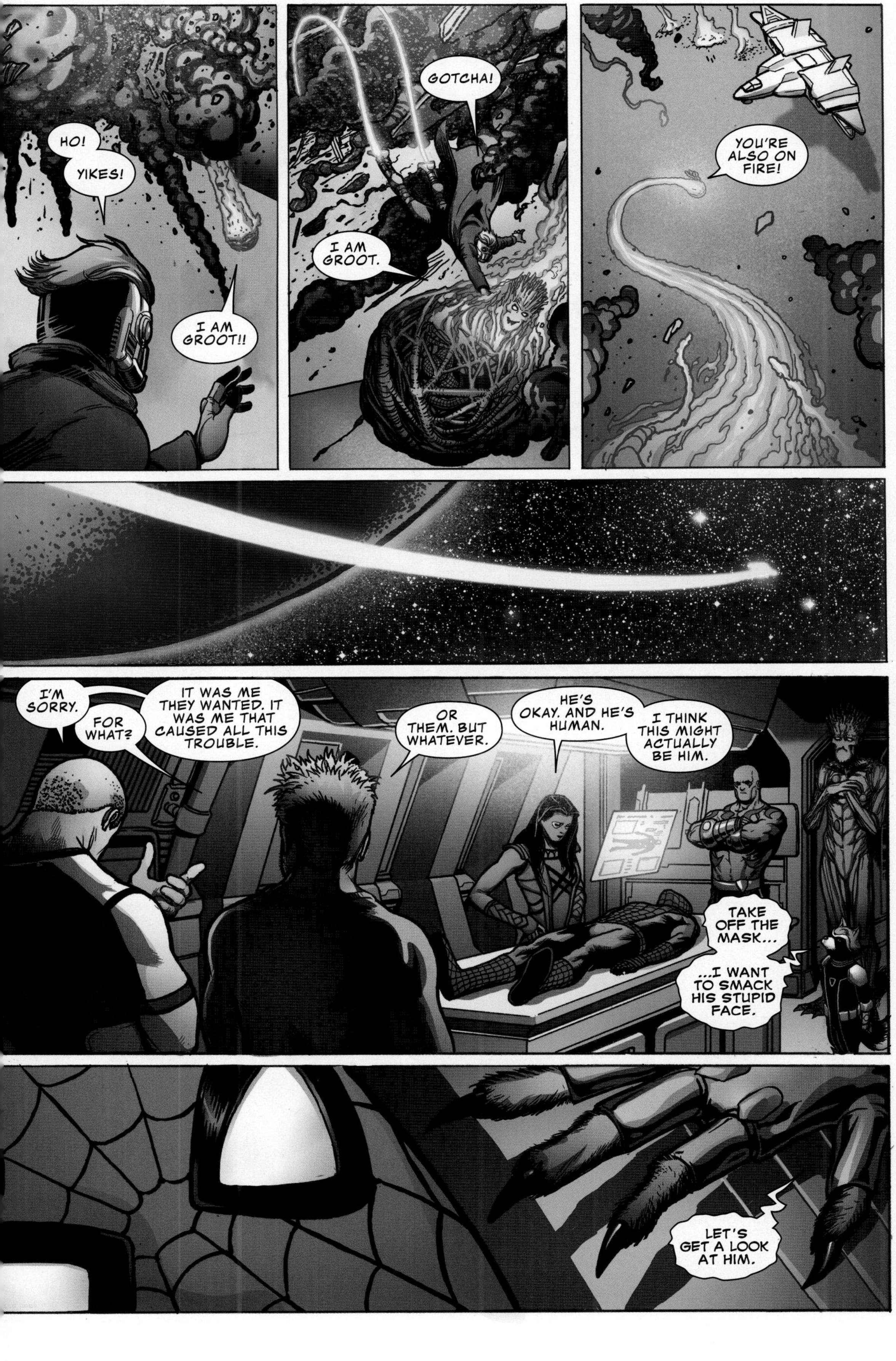
HO!
YIKES!
I AM GROOT!!
GOTCHA!
I AM GROOT.
YOU'RE ALSO ON FIRE!
I'M SORRY.
FOR WHAT?
IT WAS ME THEY WANTED. IT WAS ME THAT CAUSED ALL THIS TROUBLE.
OR THEM. BUT WHATEVER.
HE'S OKAY. AND HE'S HUMAN.
I THINK THIS MIGHT ACTUALLY BE HIM.
TAKE OFF THE MASK...
...I WANT TO SMACK HIS STUPID FACE.
LET'S GET A LOOK AT HIM.

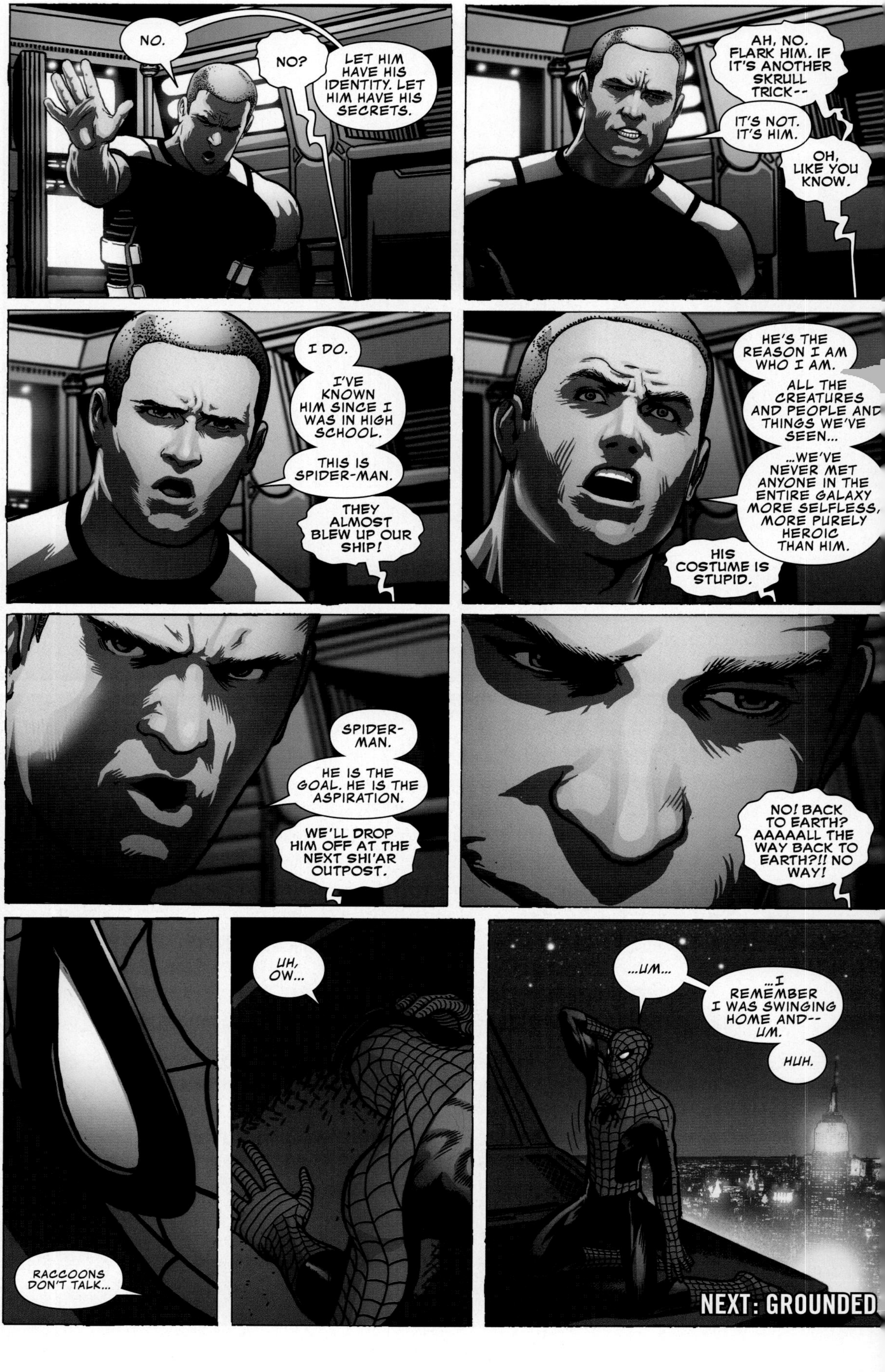
NO.
NO?
LET HIM HAVE HIS IDENTITY. LET HIM HAVE HIS SECRETS.
AH, NO. FLARK HIM. IF IT'S ANOTHER SKRULL TRICK--
IT'S NOT. IT'S HIM.
OH, LIKE YOU KNOW.
I DO.
I'VE KNOWN HIM SINCE I WAS IN HIGH SCHOOL.
THIS IS SPIDER-MAN.
THEY ALMOST BLEW UP OUR SHIP!
HE'S THE REASON I AM WHO I AM.
ALL THE CREATURES AND PEOPLE AND THINGS WE'VE SEEN...
...WE'VE NEVER MET ANYONE IN THE ENTIRE GALAXY MORE SELFLESS, MORE PURELY HEROIC THAN HIM.
HIS COSTUME IS STUPID.
SPIDER-MAN.
HE IS THE GOAL. HE IS THE ASPIRATION.
WE'LL DROP HIM OFF AT THE NEXT SHI'AR OUTPOST.
NO! BACK TO EARTH? AAAAALL THE WAY BACK TO EARTH?!! NO WAY!
RACCOONS DON'T TALK...
UH, OW...
...UM...
...I REMEMBER I WAS SWINGING HOME AND-- UM.
HUH.
NEXT: GROUNDED

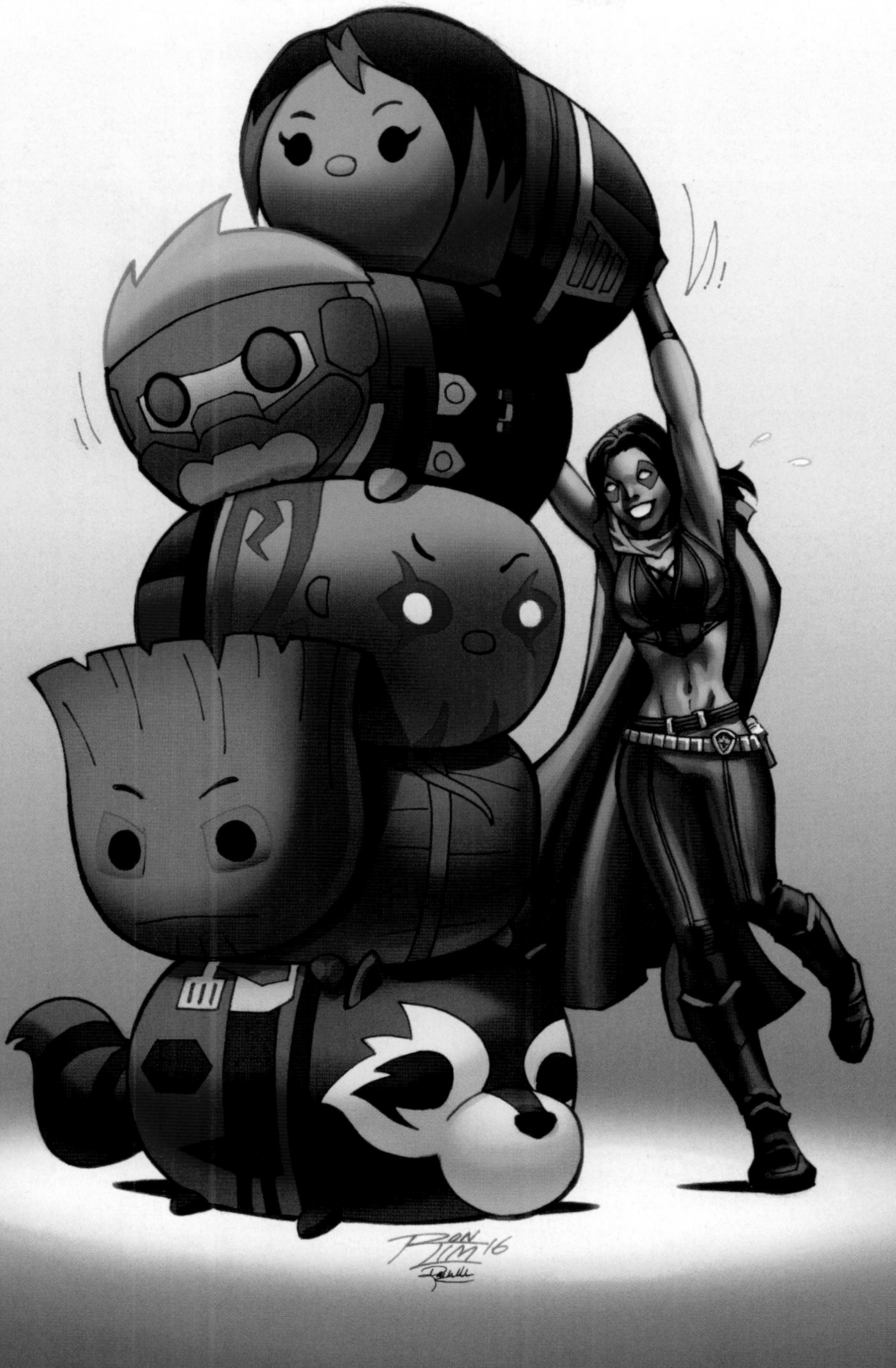

#11 MARVEL TSUM

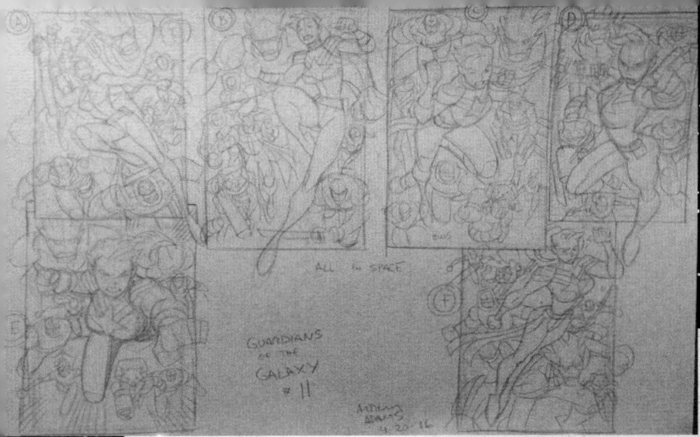
ALL IN SPACE
GUARDIANS OF THE GALAXY #11

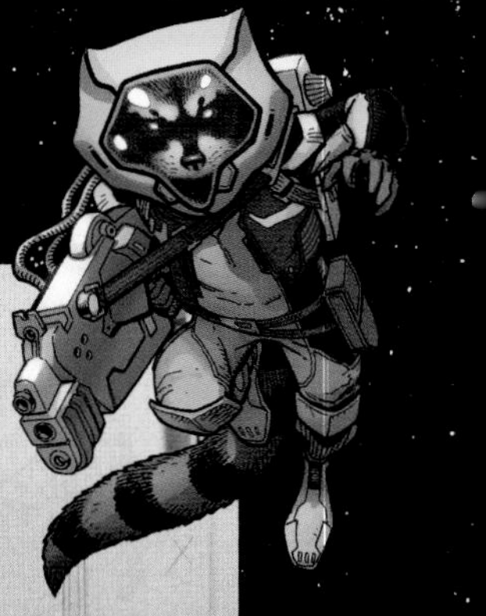

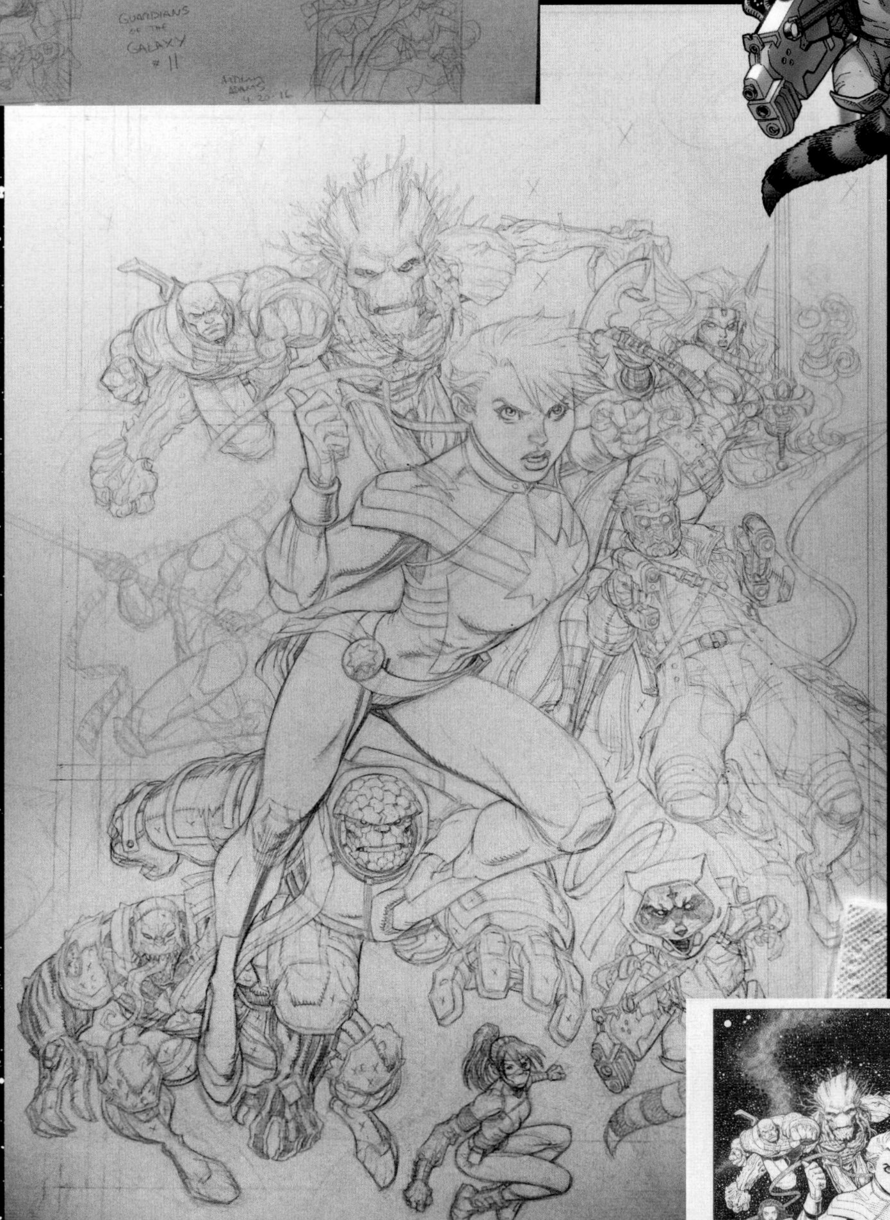

COVER PROCESS BY

ARTHUR ADAMS

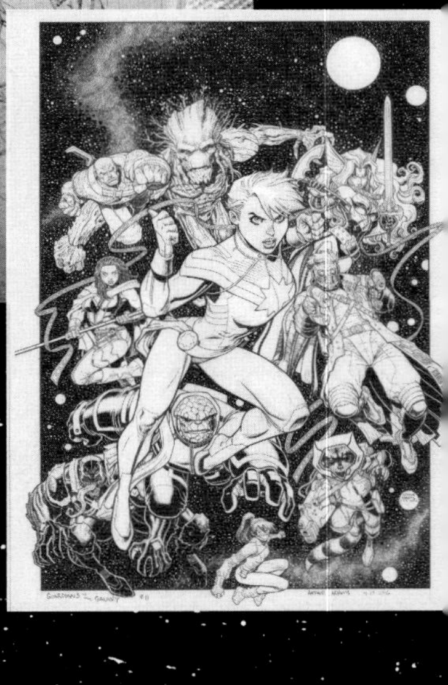

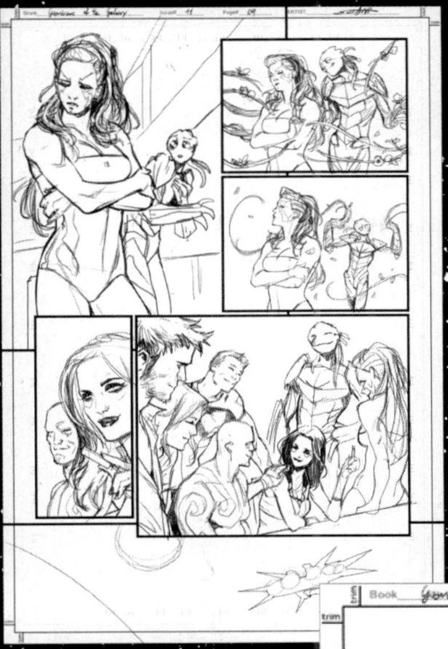

#11, PAGE 8 ART PROCESS BY
VALERIO SCHITI

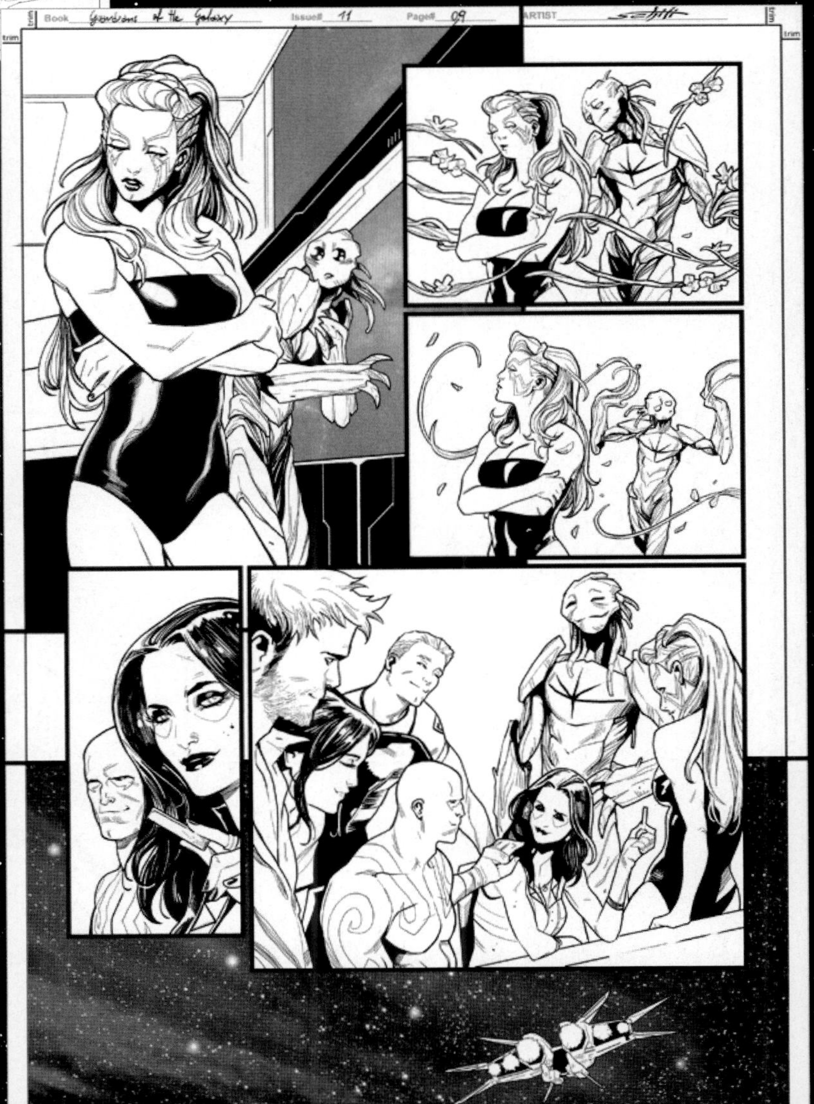
Book Guardians of the Galaxy
Issue# 11
Page# 09
ARTIST
trim

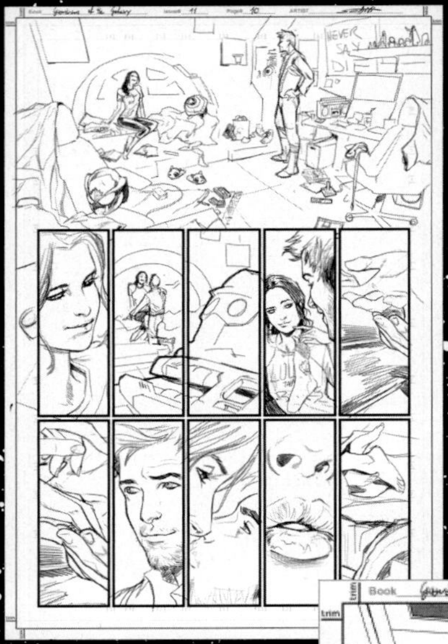

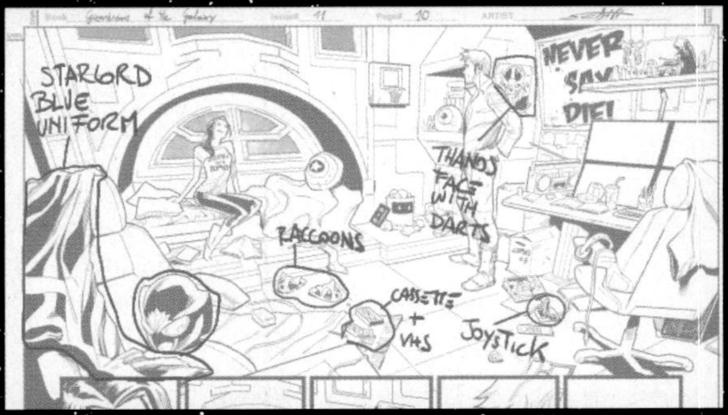
STARLORD BLUE UNIFORM
NEVER SAY DIE!
THANOS FACE WITH DARTS
RACCOONS
CASETTE + VHS
JOYSTICK

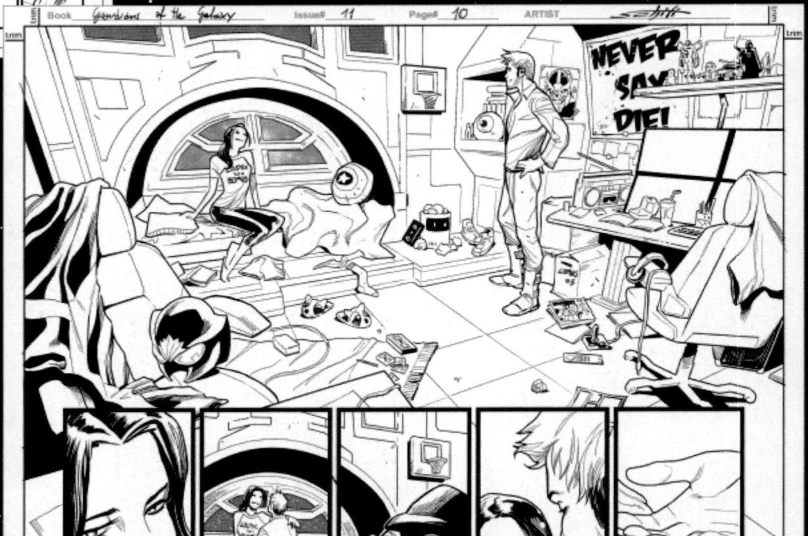
Book Guardians of the Galaxy Issue# 11 Page# 10 ARTIST
NEVER SAY DIE!

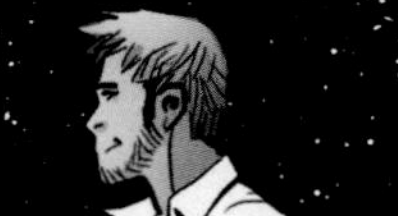

#11, PAGE 11 ART PROCESS BY
VALERIO SCHITI

#11, PAGE 12 ART PROCESS BY
VALERIO SCHITI

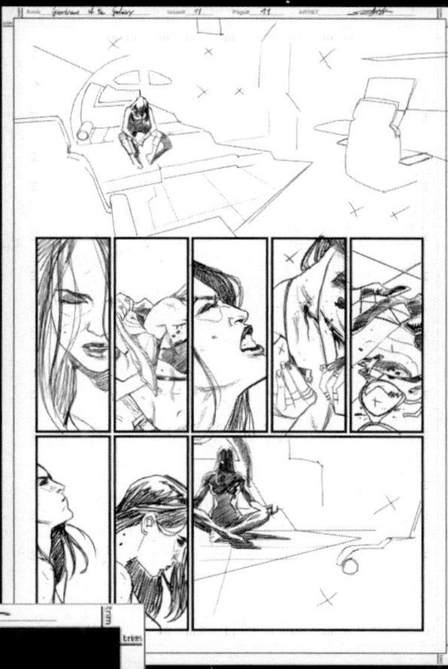

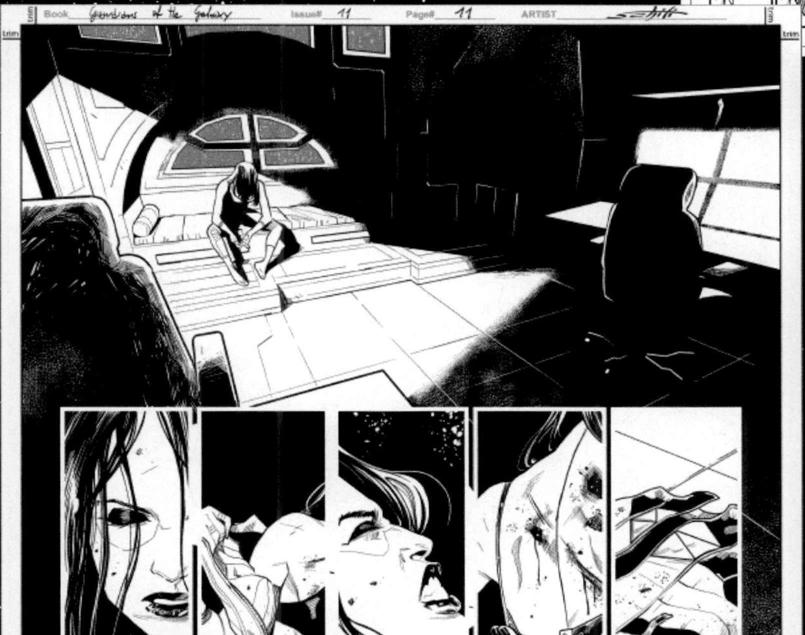

Book Guardians of the Galaxy Issue# 11 Page# 11 ARTIST

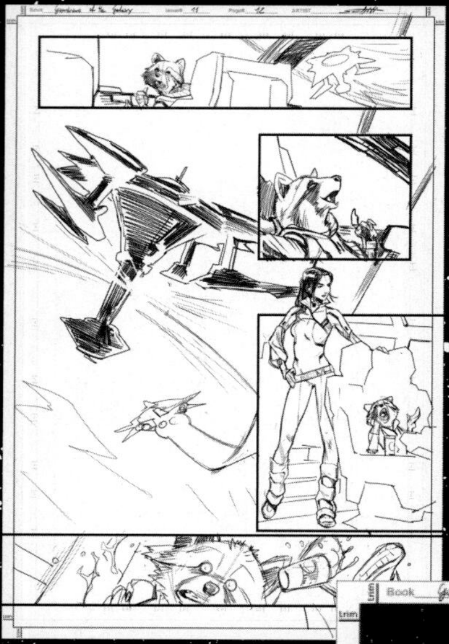

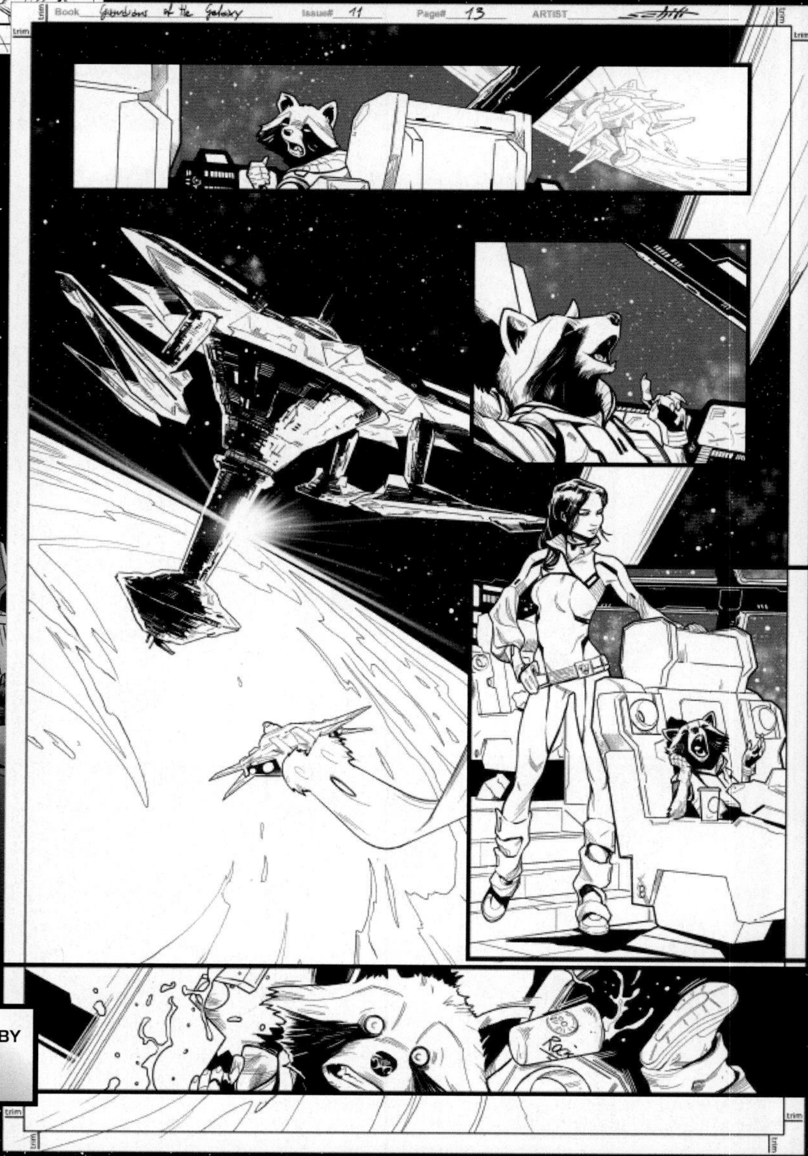
Book Guardians of the Galaxy Issue# 11 Page# 13 ARTIST

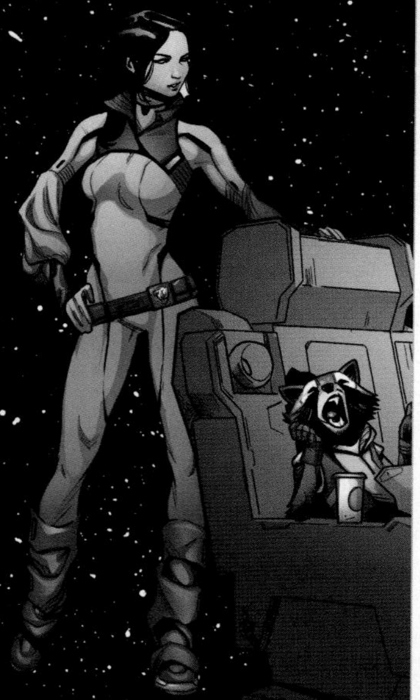

#11, PAGE 13 ART PROCESS BY
VALERIO SCHITI

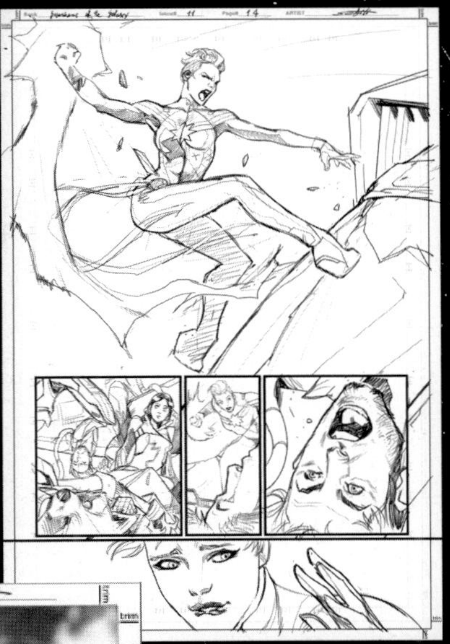

#11, PAGE 14 ART PROCESS BY

VALERIO SCHITI

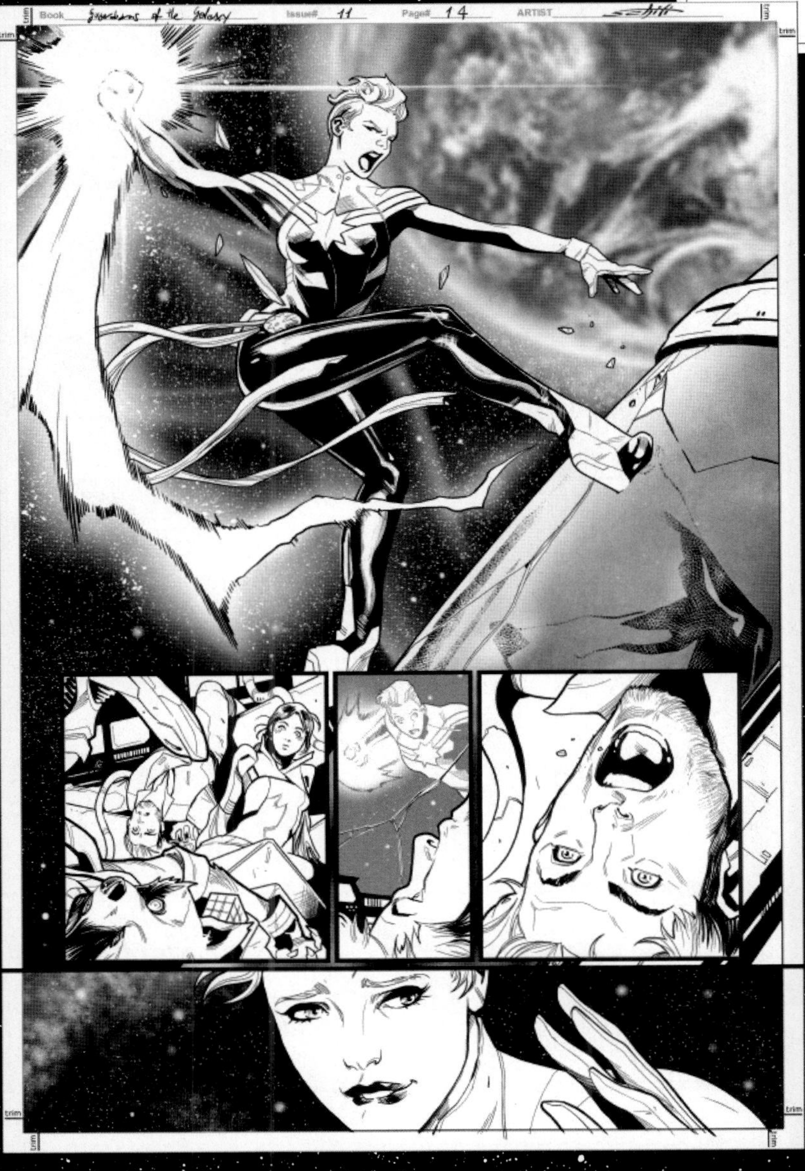
Book Guardians of the Galaxy Issue# 11 Page# 14 ARTIST

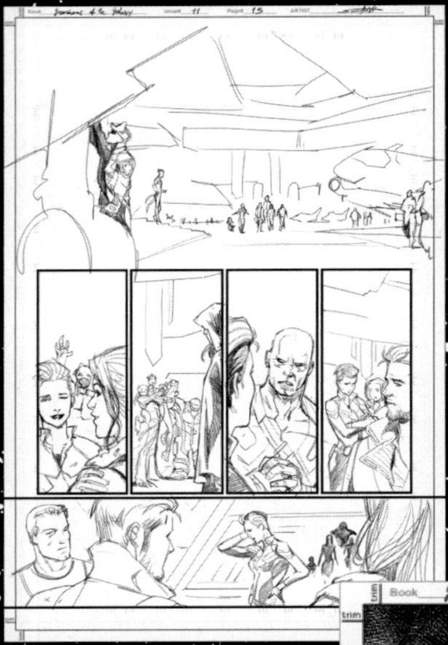

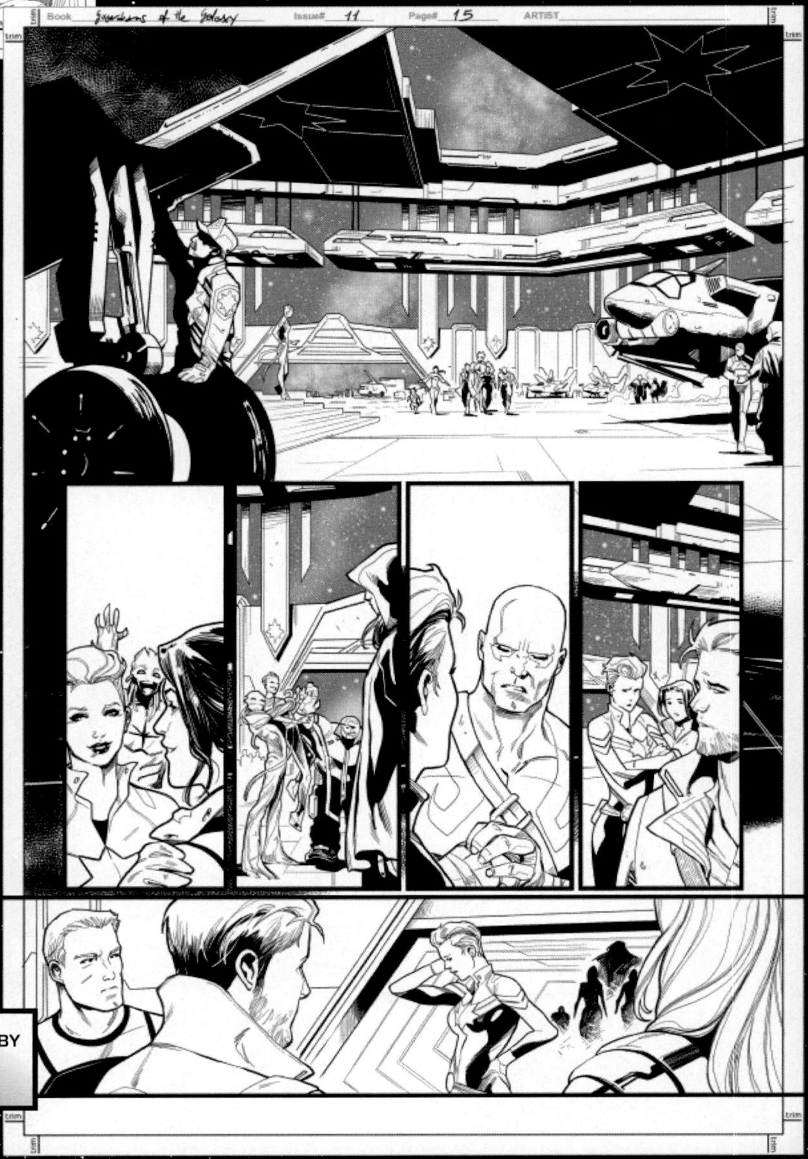
Book Guardians of the Galaxy
Issue# 11
Page# 15
ARTIST

#11, PAGE 15 ART PROCESS BY
VALERIO SCHITI

#11, PAGE 16-17 ART PROCESS

VALERIO SCHITI

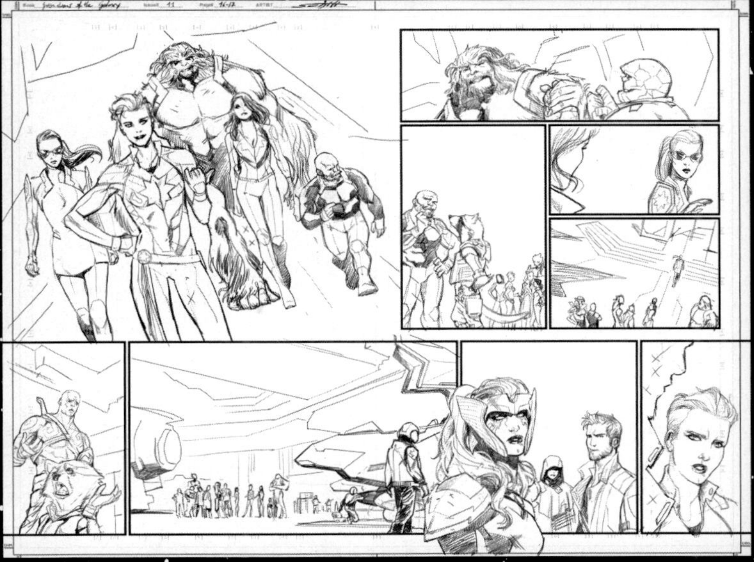

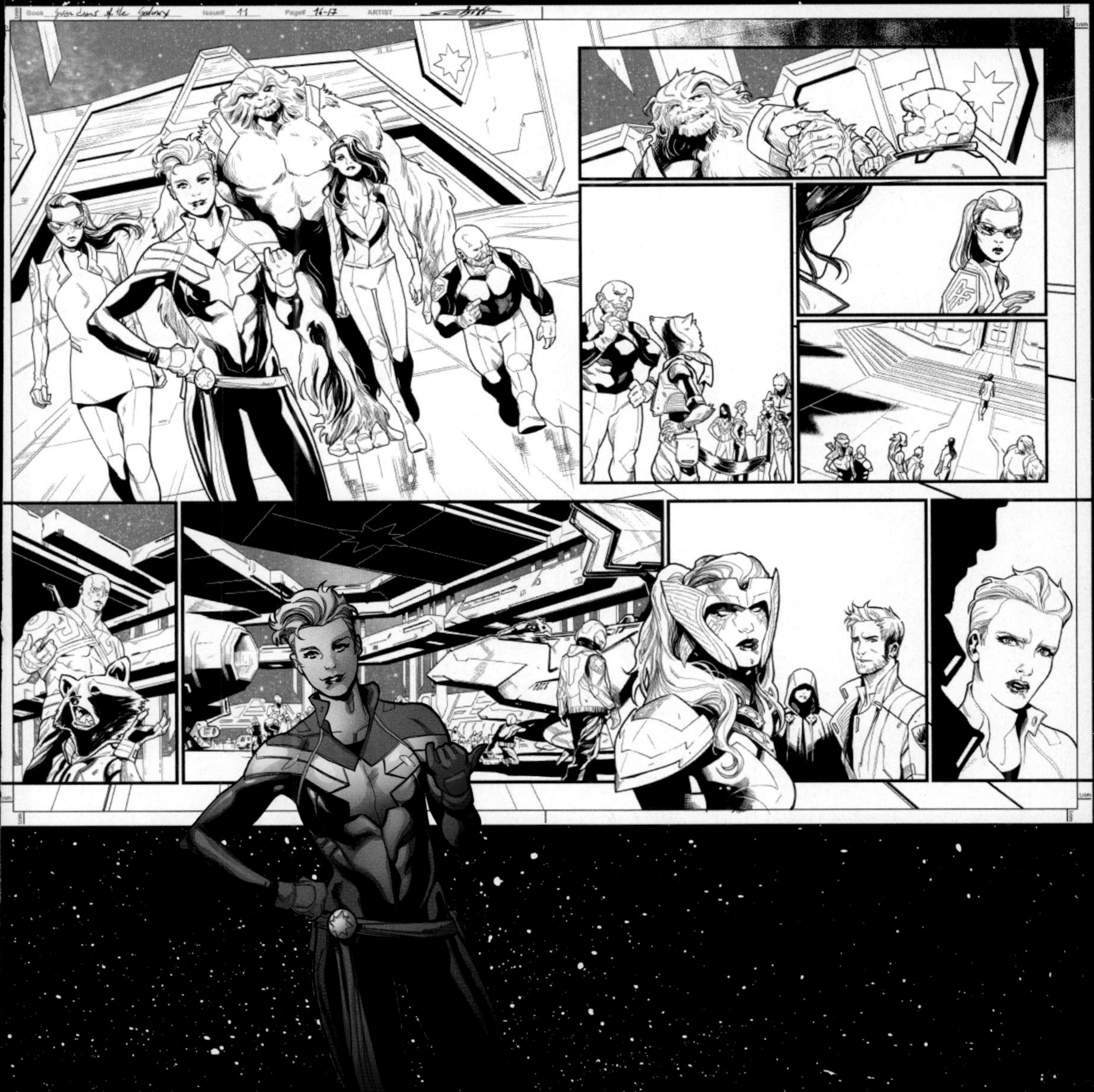

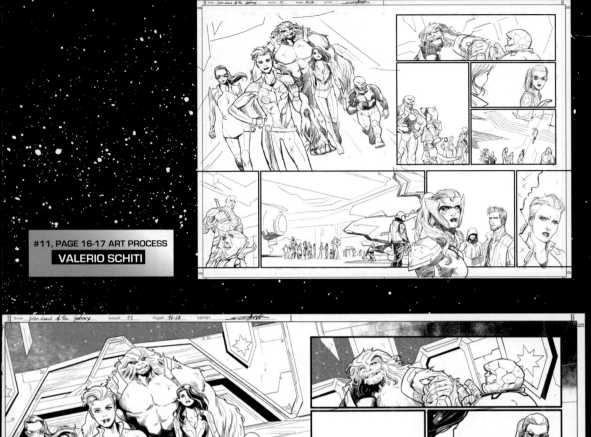

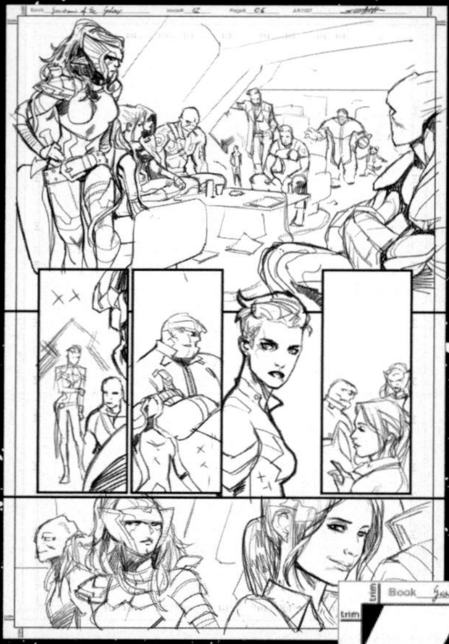

#12, PAGE 5 ART PROCESS BY

VALERIO SCHITI

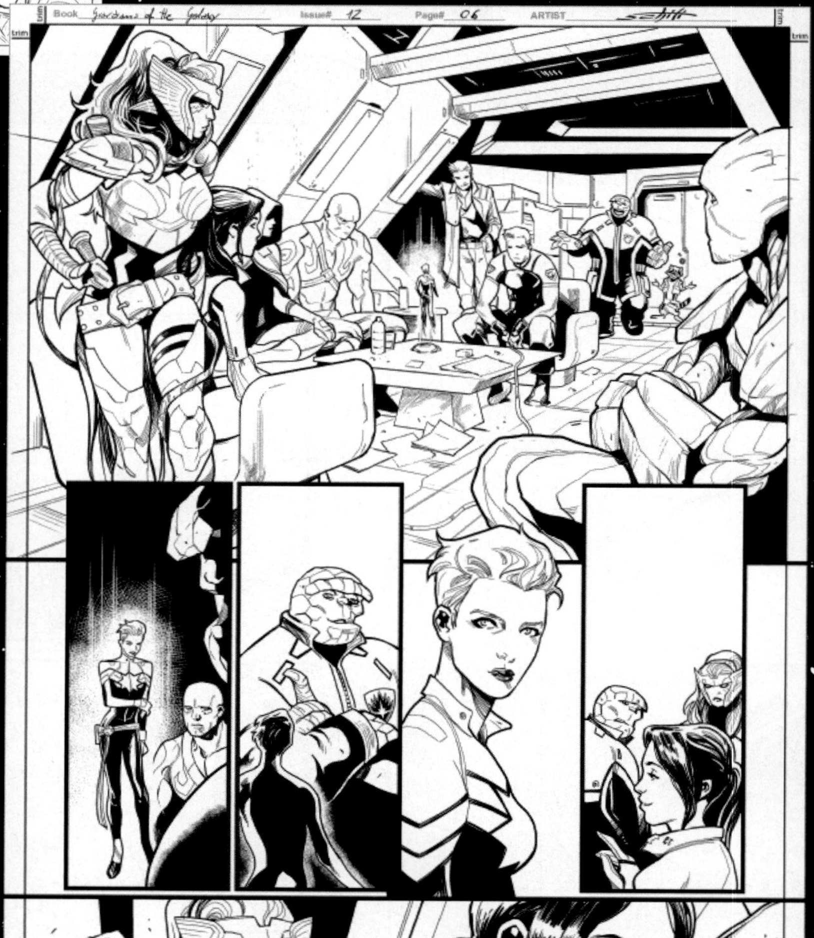
Book
Issue# 12
Page# 06
ARTIST
trim

#12, PAGE 6 ART PROCESS BY

VALERIO SCHITI

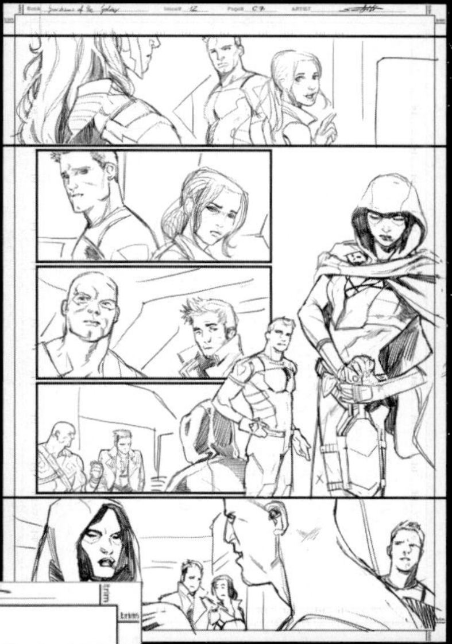

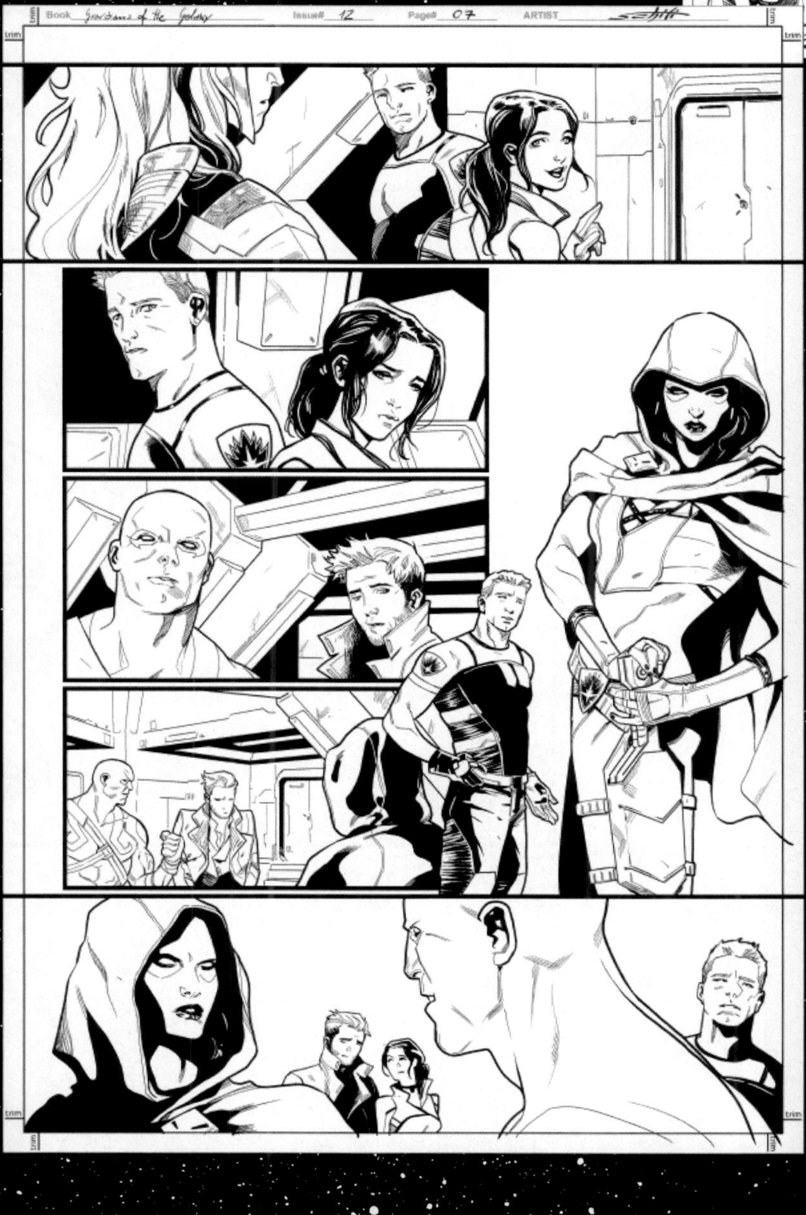
Book Guardians of the Galaxy
Issue# 12
Page# 07
ARTIST

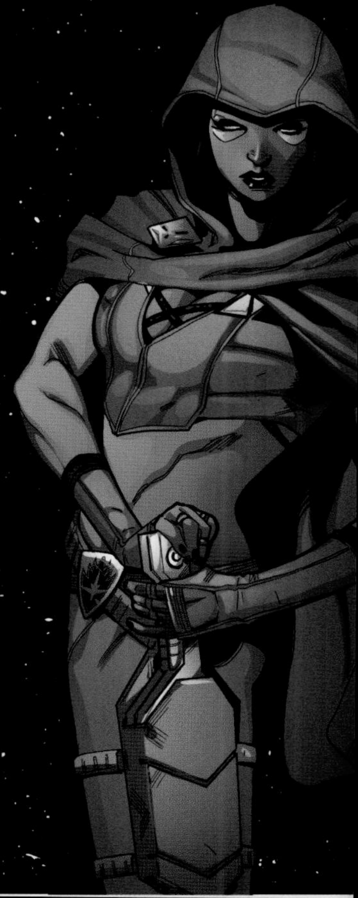

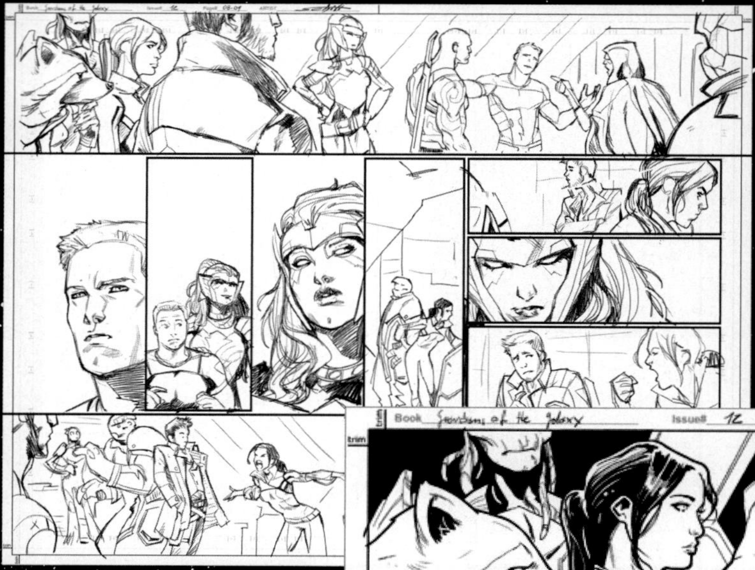

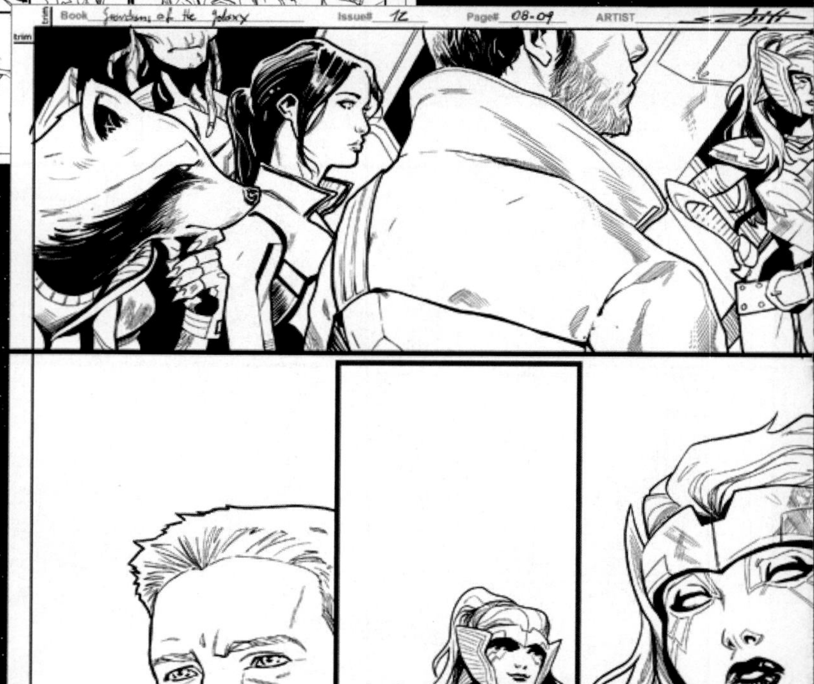

trim
Book
Issue# 12
Page# 08-09
ARTIST

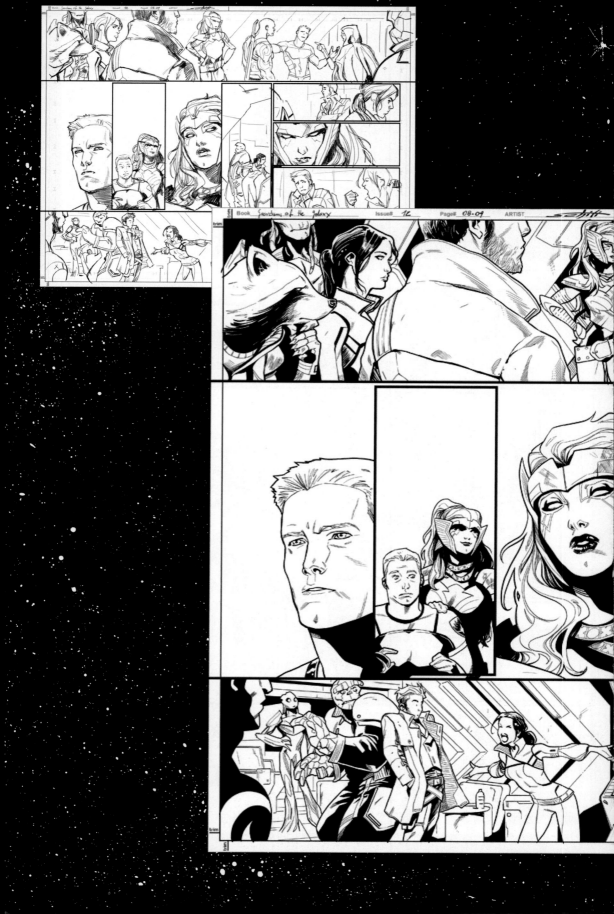

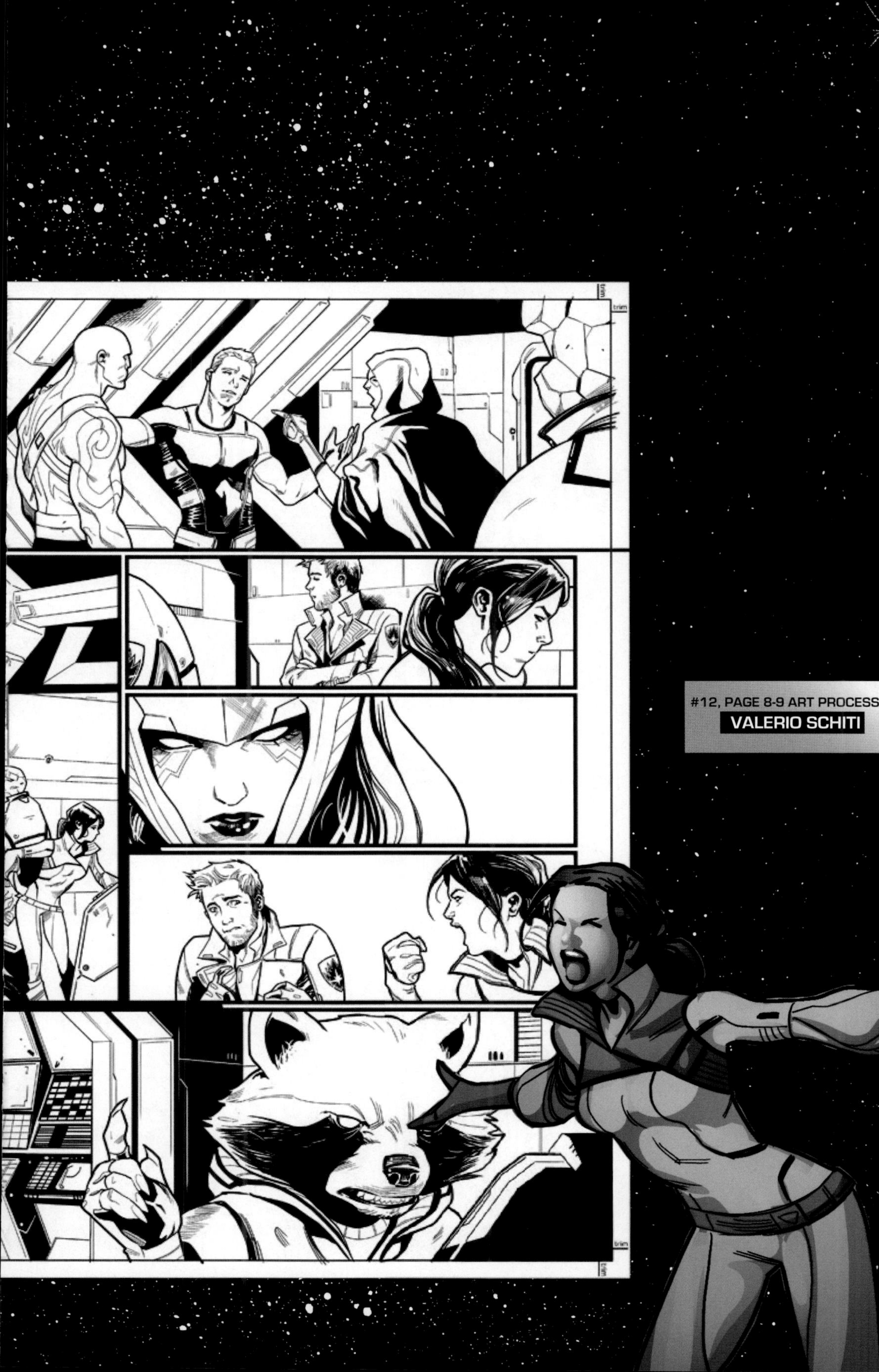

#12, PAGE 8-9 ART PROCESS
VALERIO SCHITI

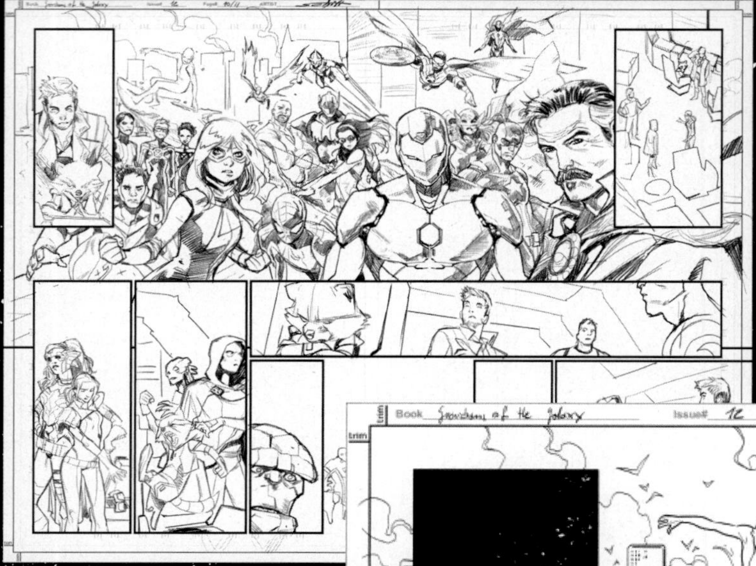

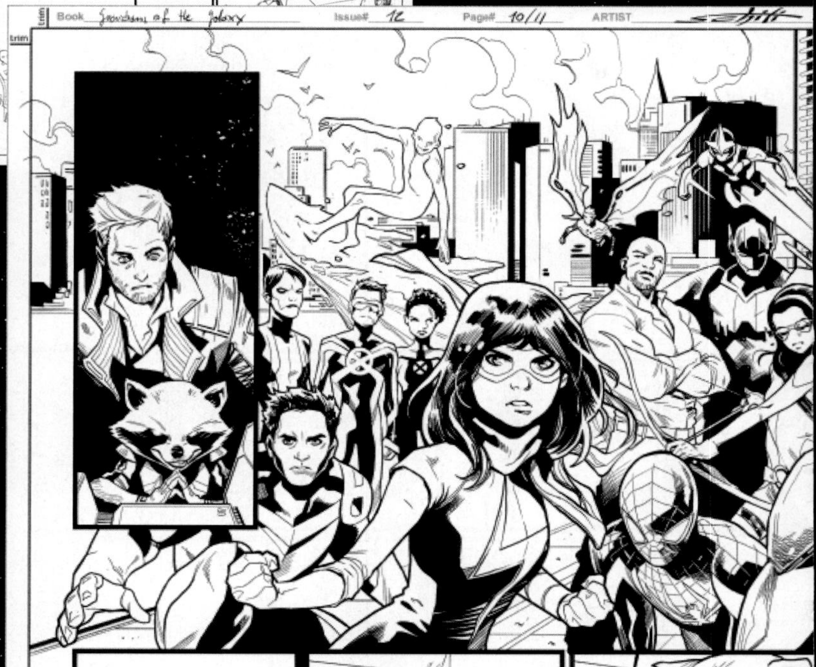

Book
Issue# 12
Page# 10/11
ARTIST
trim

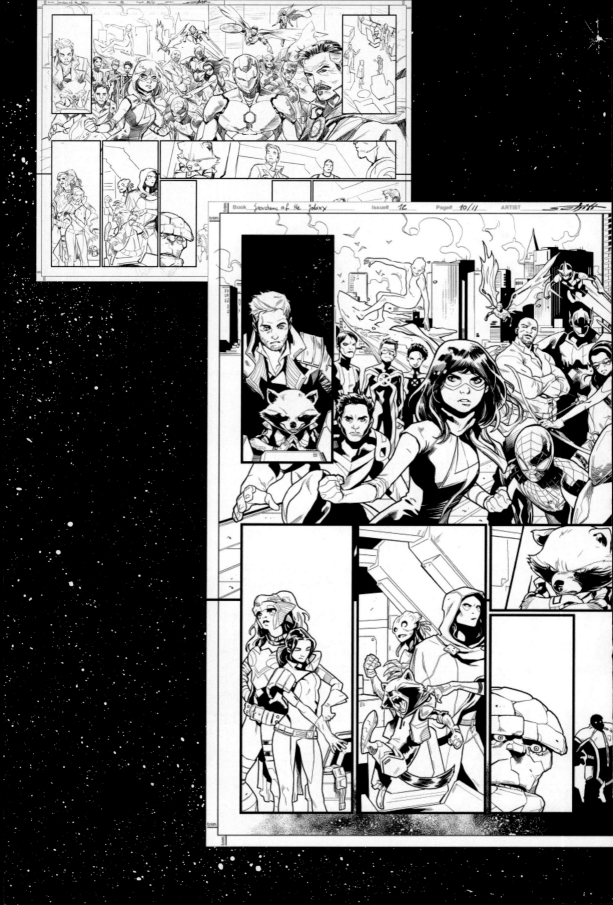

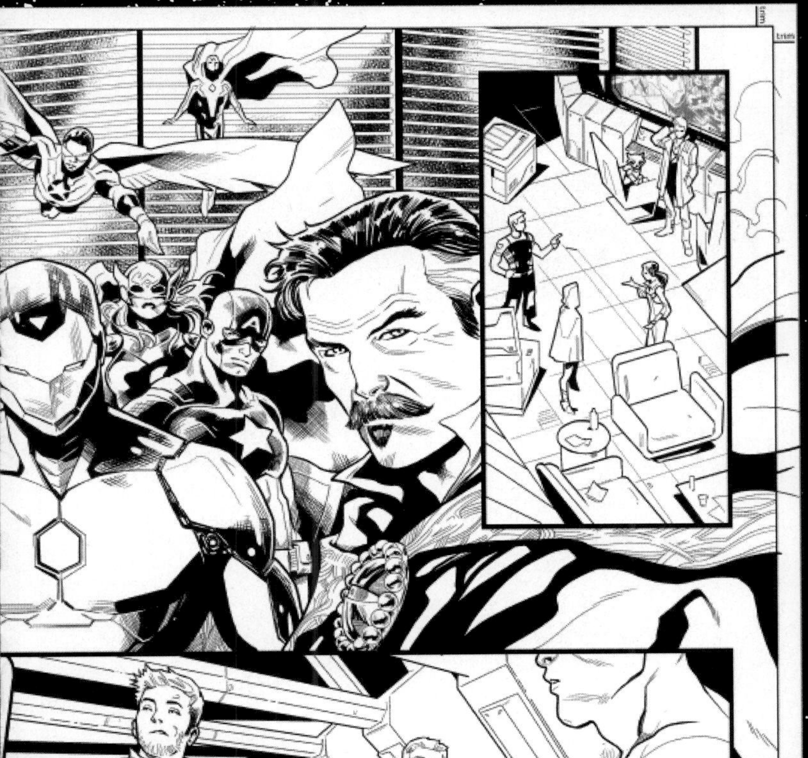

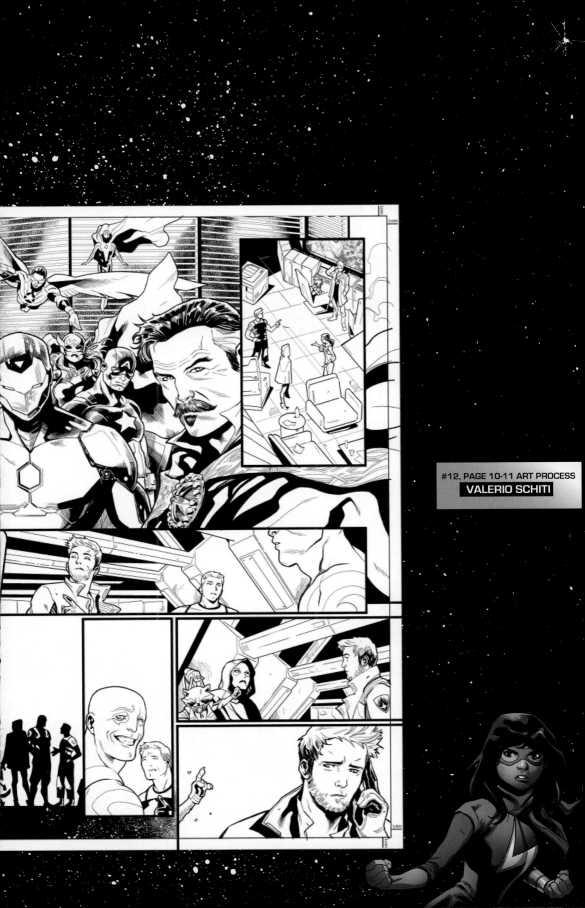

#12, PAGE 10-11 ART PROCESS

VALERIO SCHITI

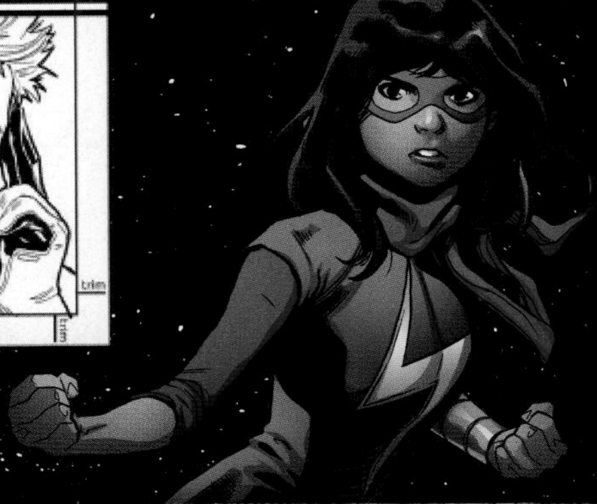

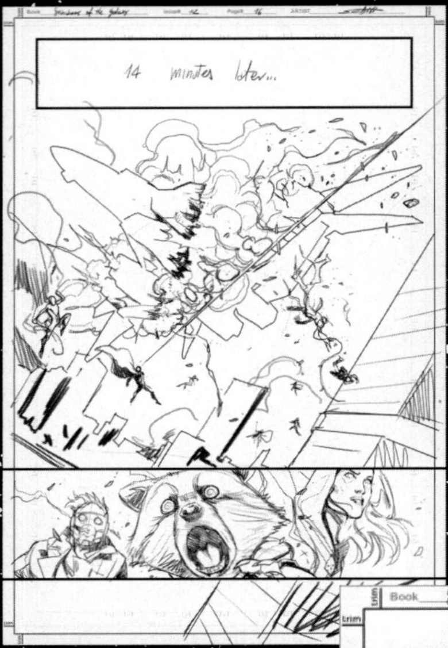
14 minutes later...

#12, PAGE 16 ART PROCESS BY
VALERIO SCHITI

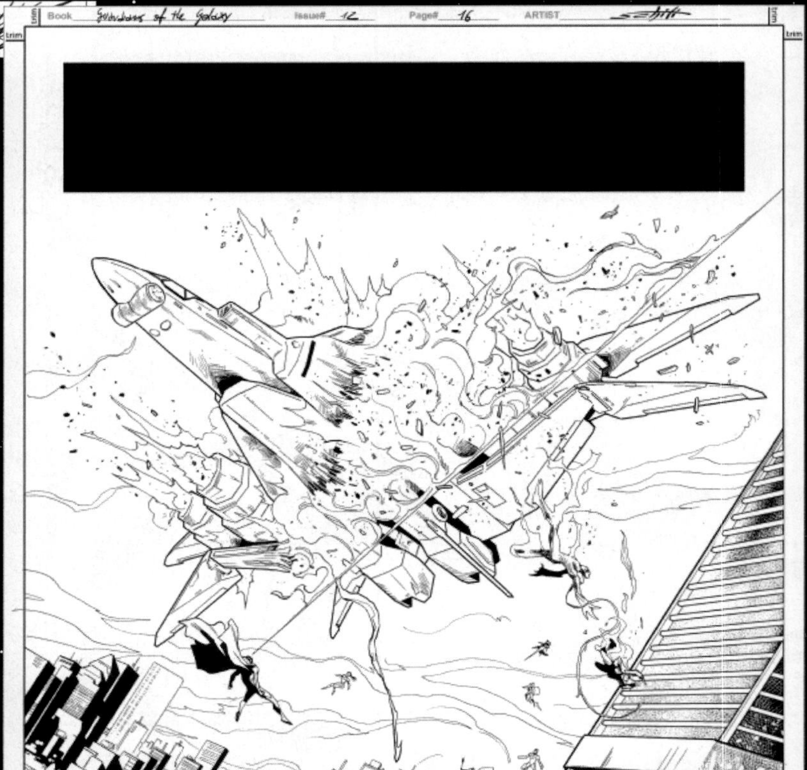
Book Guardians of the Galaxy
Issue# 12
Page# 16
ARTIST

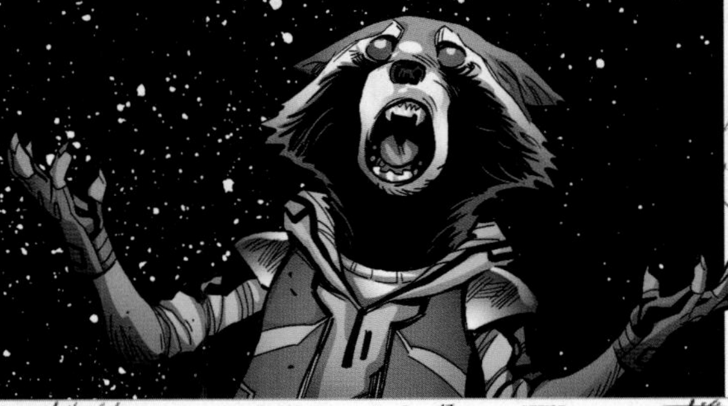

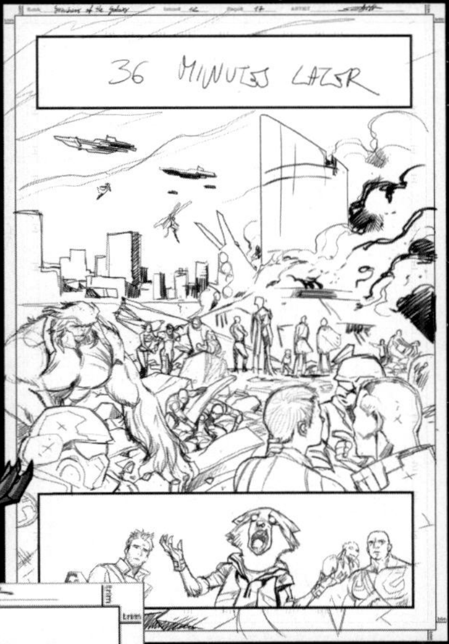
36 MINUTES LATER

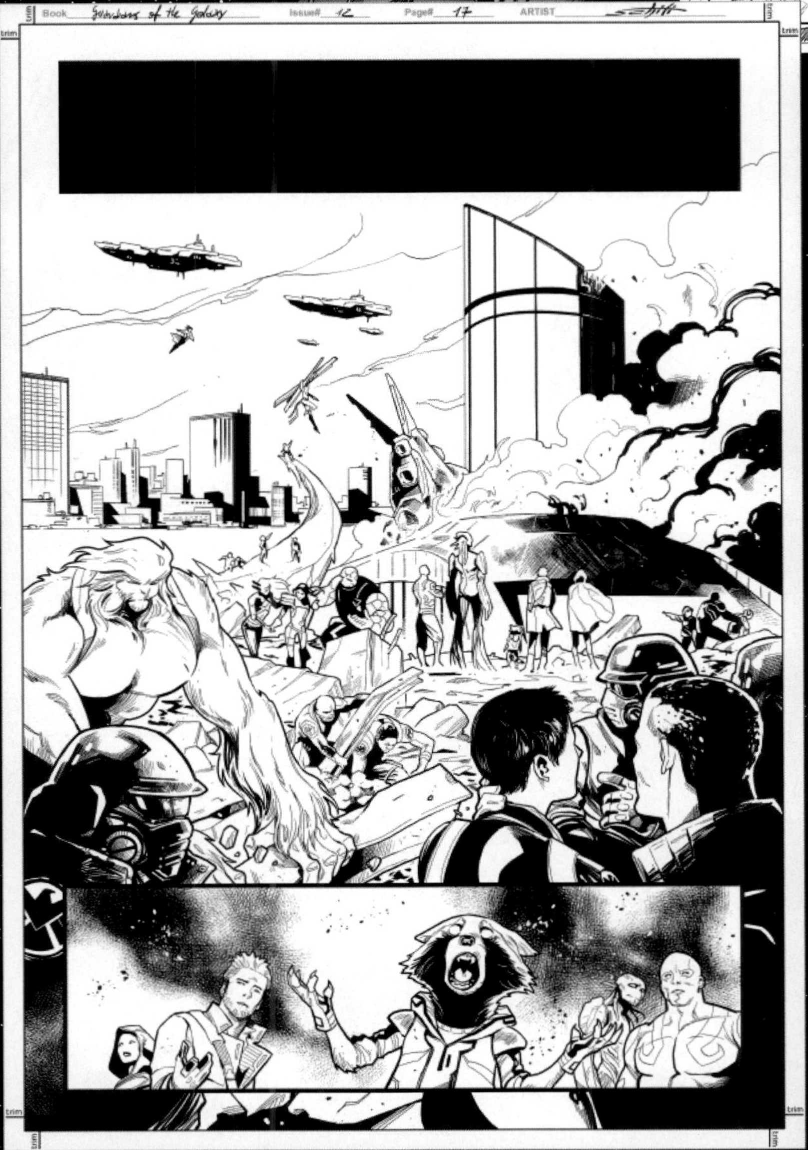
Book Guardians of the Galaxy
Issue# 12
Page# 17
ARTIST

#12, PAGE 17 ART PROCESS BY
VALERIO SCHITI

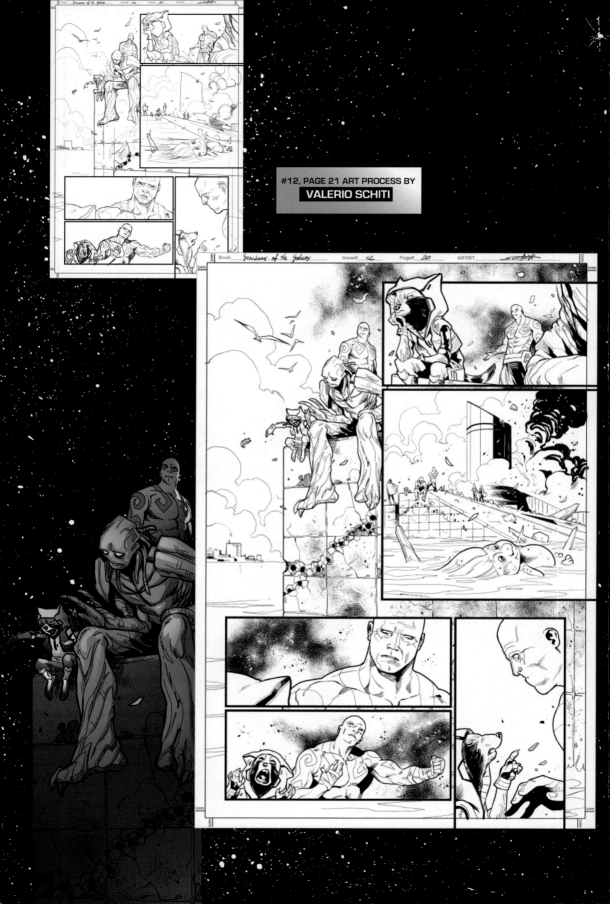

#12, PAGE 21 ART PROCESS BY
VALERIO SCHITI

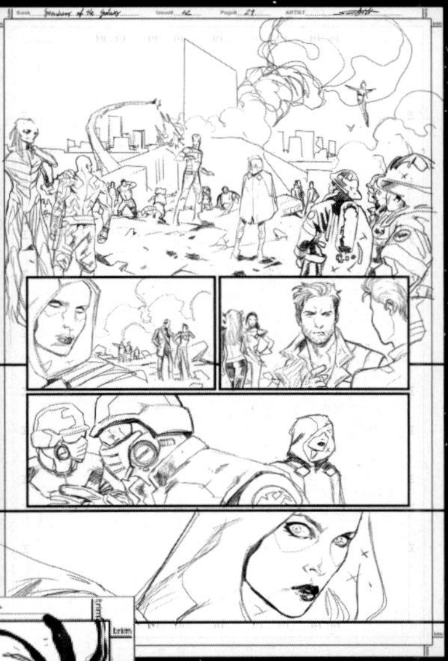

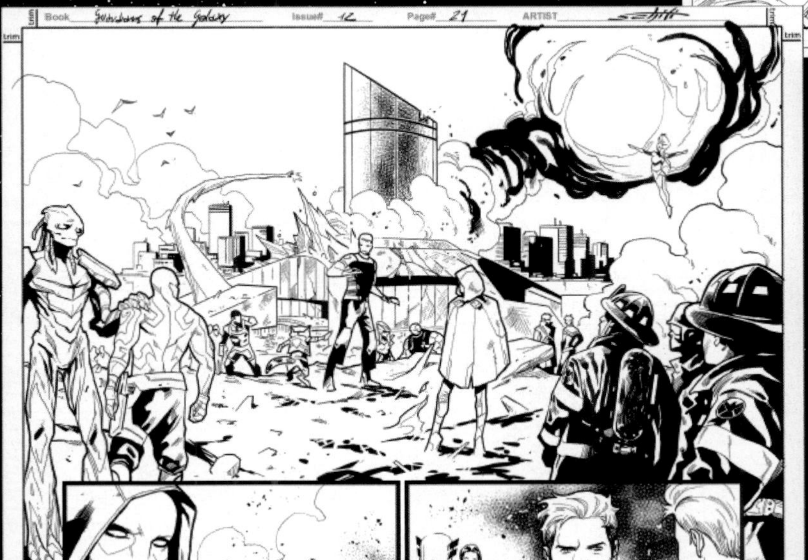
Book
Issue# 12
Page# 21
ARTIST
trim

#12, PAGE 22 ART PROCESS BY
VALERIO SCHITI

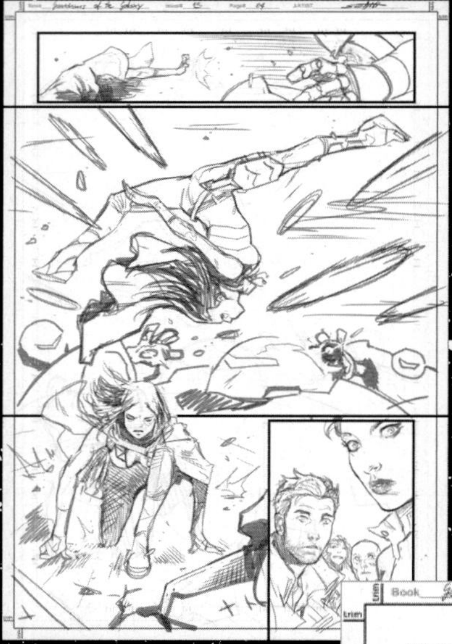

#13, PAGE 3 ART PROCESS BY
VALERIO SCHITI

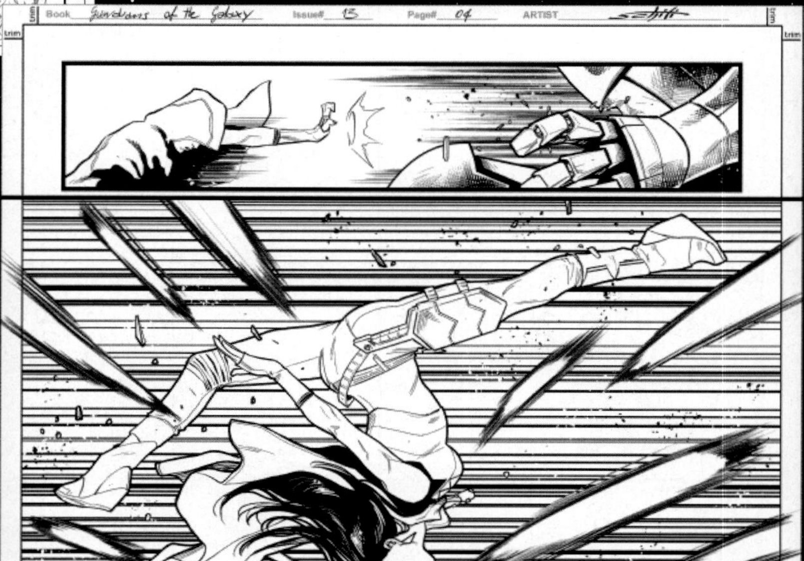
Book Guardians of the Galaxy Issue# 13 Page# 04 ARTIST

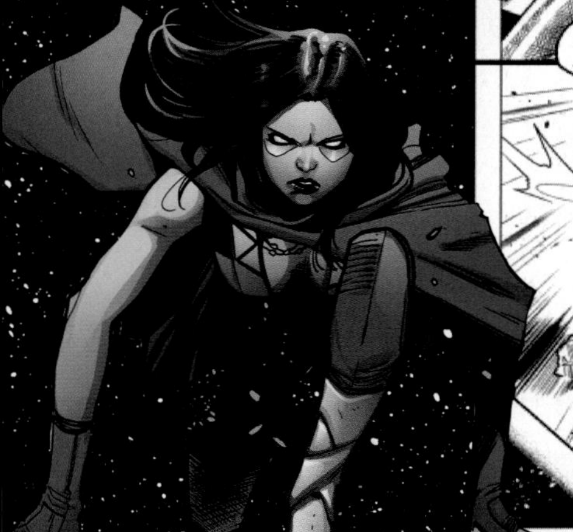

#13, PAGE 4 ART PROCESS BY

VALERIO SCHITI

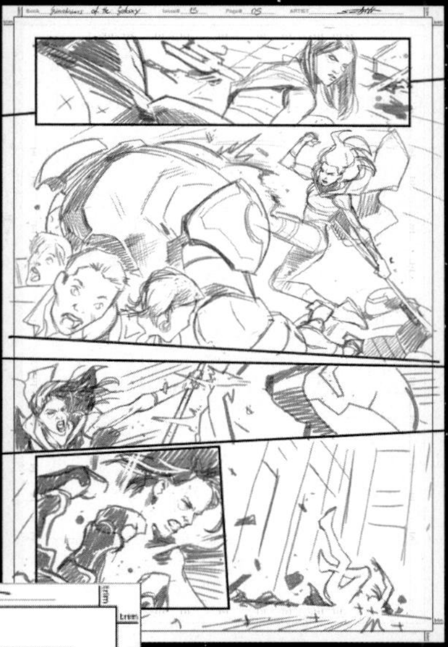

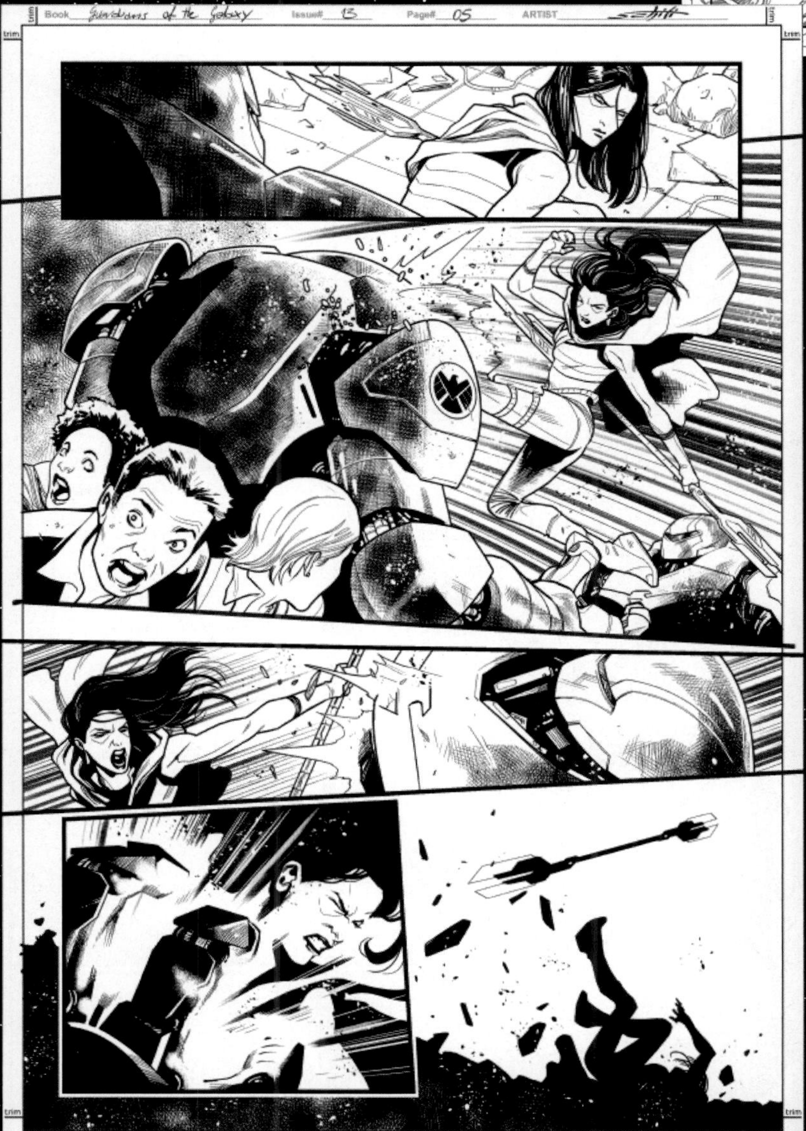
Book Guardians of the Galaxy
Issue# 13
Page# 05
ARTIST
trim

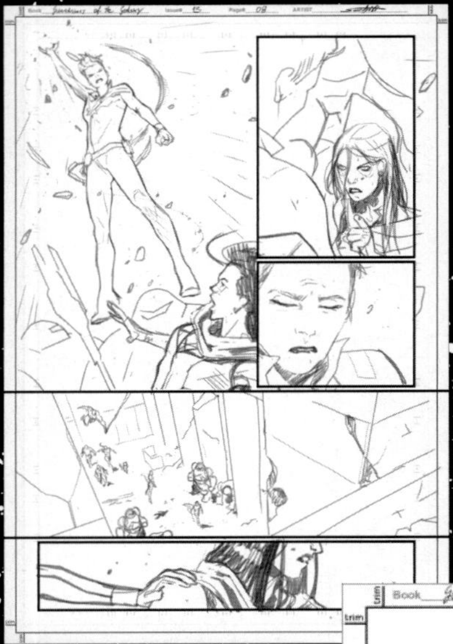

#13, PAGE 7 ART PROCESS BY

VALERIO SCHITI

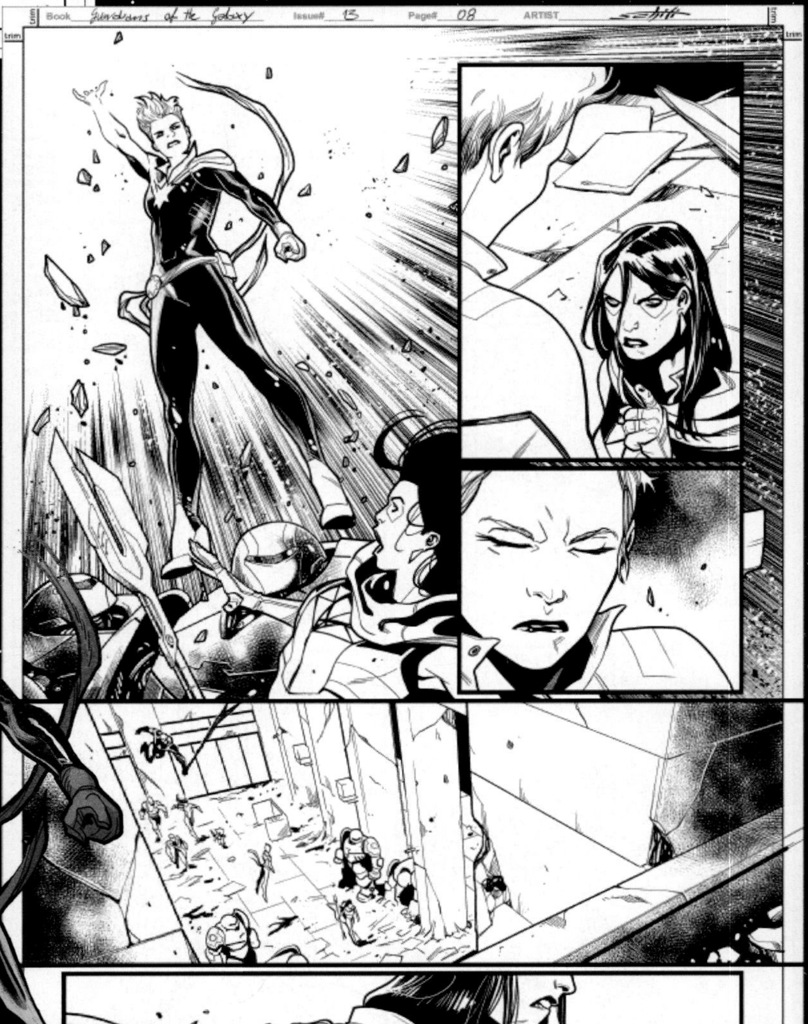
Book Guardians of the Galaxy
Issue# 13
Page# 08
ARTIST

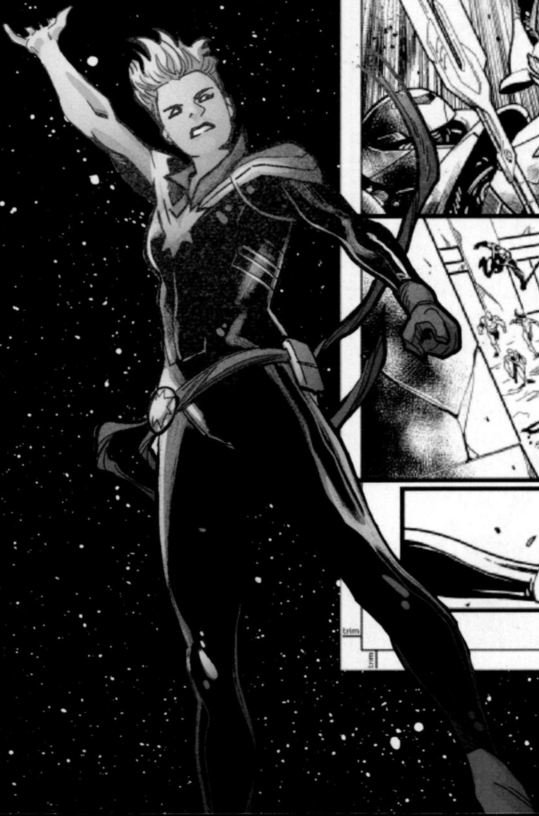

#13, PAGE 8 ART PROCESS BY
VALERIO SCHITI

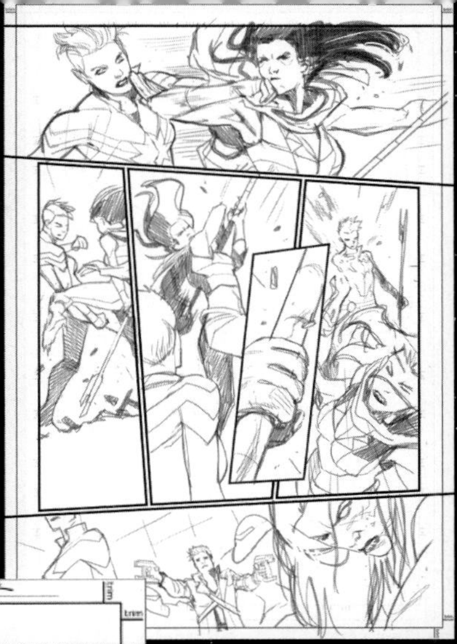

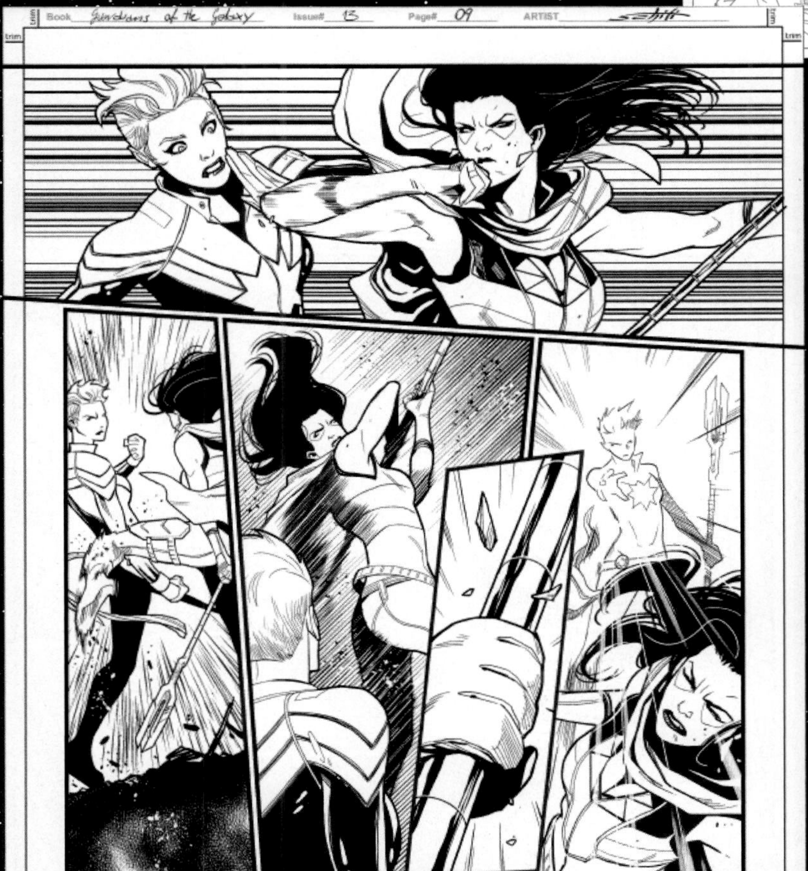
Book Guardians of the Galaxy Issue# 13 Page# 09 ARTIST

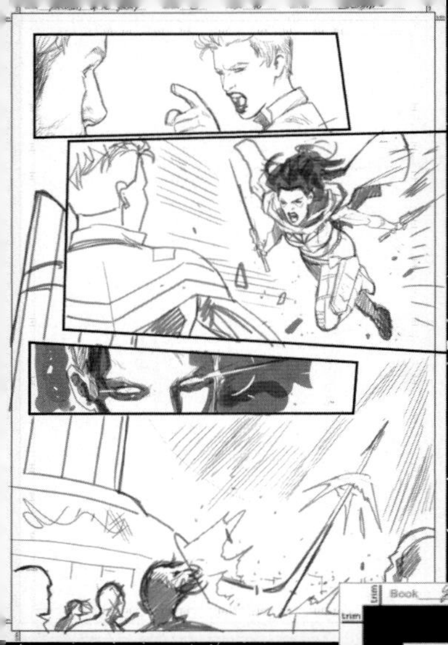

#13, PAGE 9 ART PROCESS BY
VALERIO SCHITI

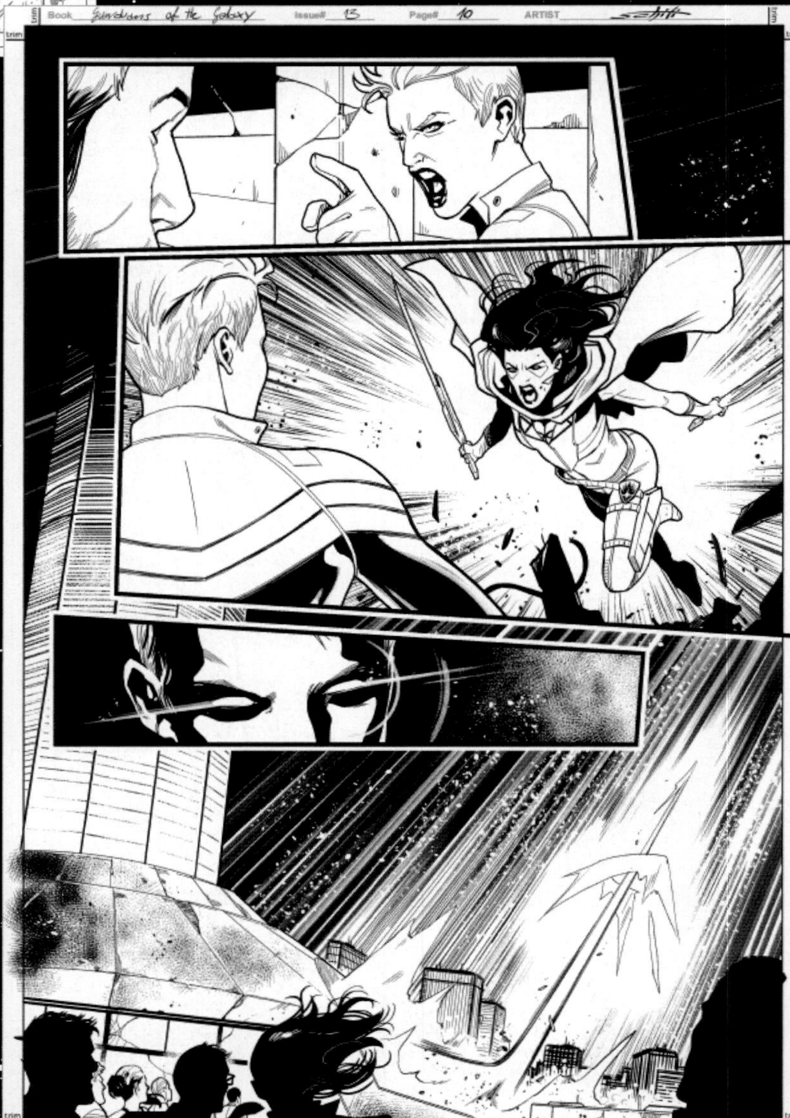
Book
Issue# 13
Page# 10
ARTIST

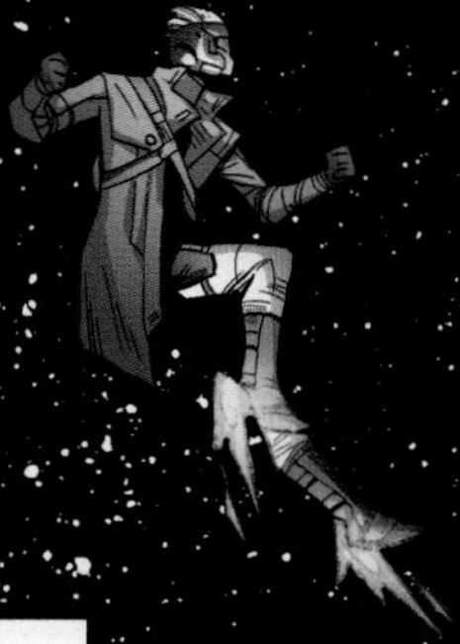

#13, PAGE 10 ART PROCESS BY
VALERIO SCHITI

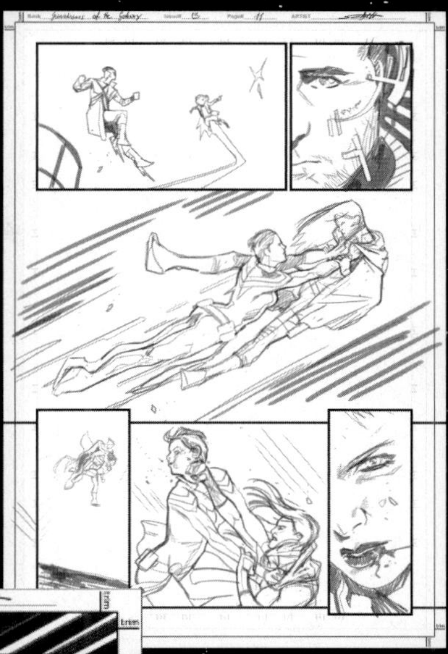

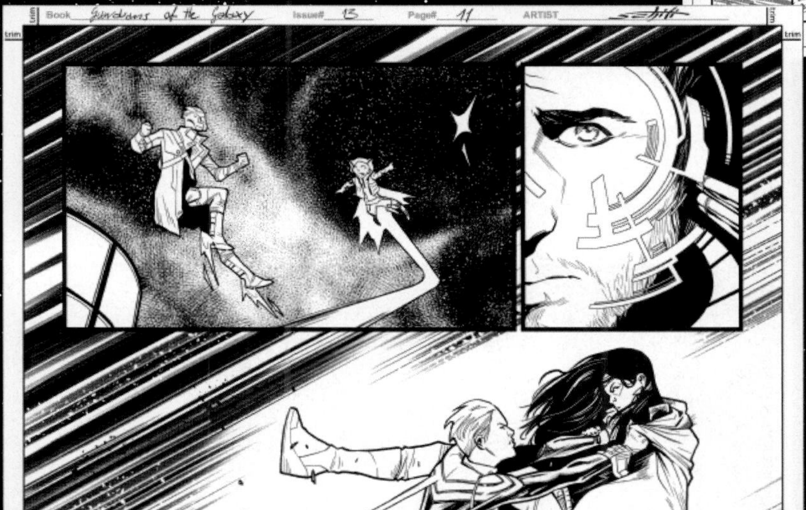
Book Guardians of the Galaxy Issue# 13 Page# 11 ARTIST
trim

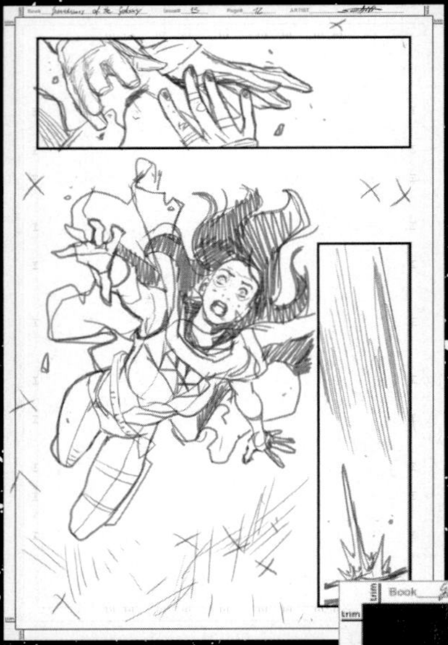

#13, PAGE 11 ART PROCESS BY
VALERIO SCHITI

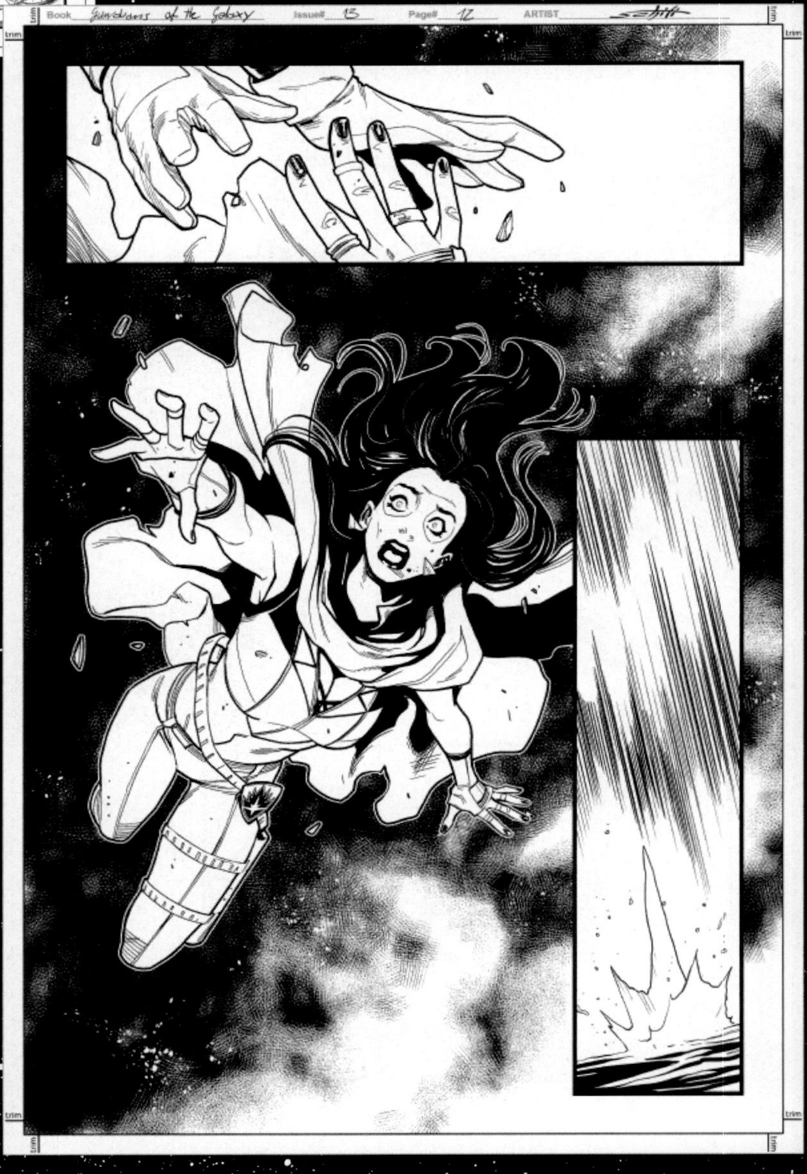
Book Guardians of the Galaxy
Issue# 13
Page# 12
ARTIST
trim

#13, PAGE 12 ART PROCESS BY

VALERIO SCHITI

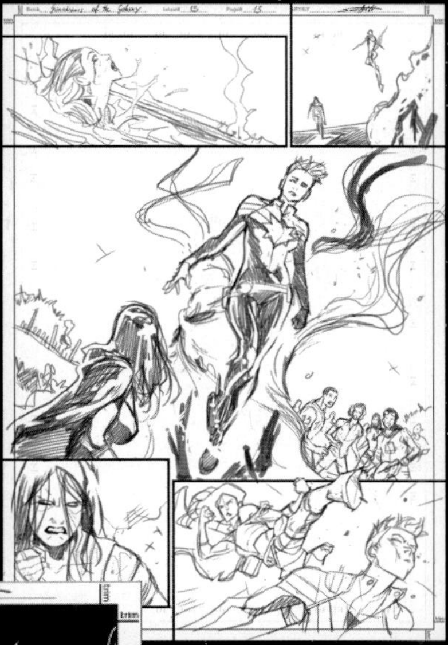

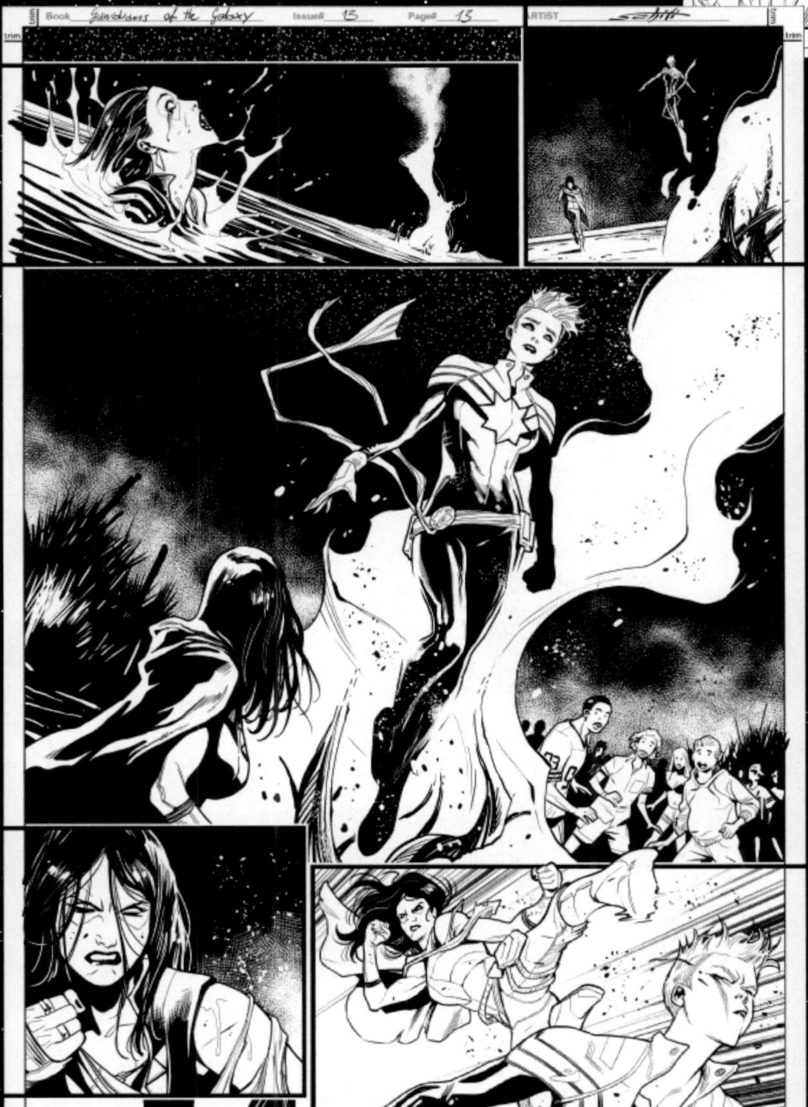
Book
Issue# 13
Page# 13
ARTIST
trim

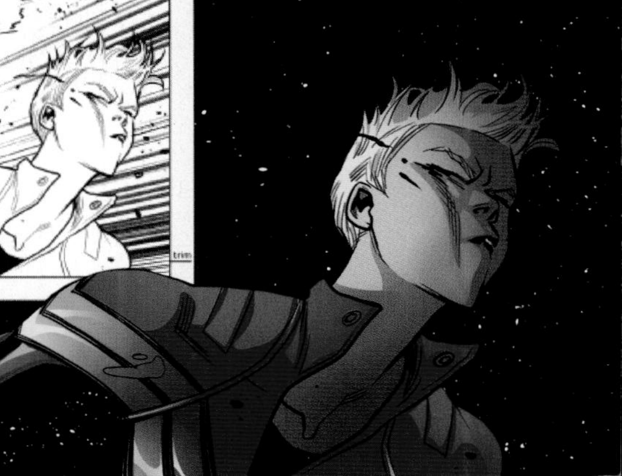

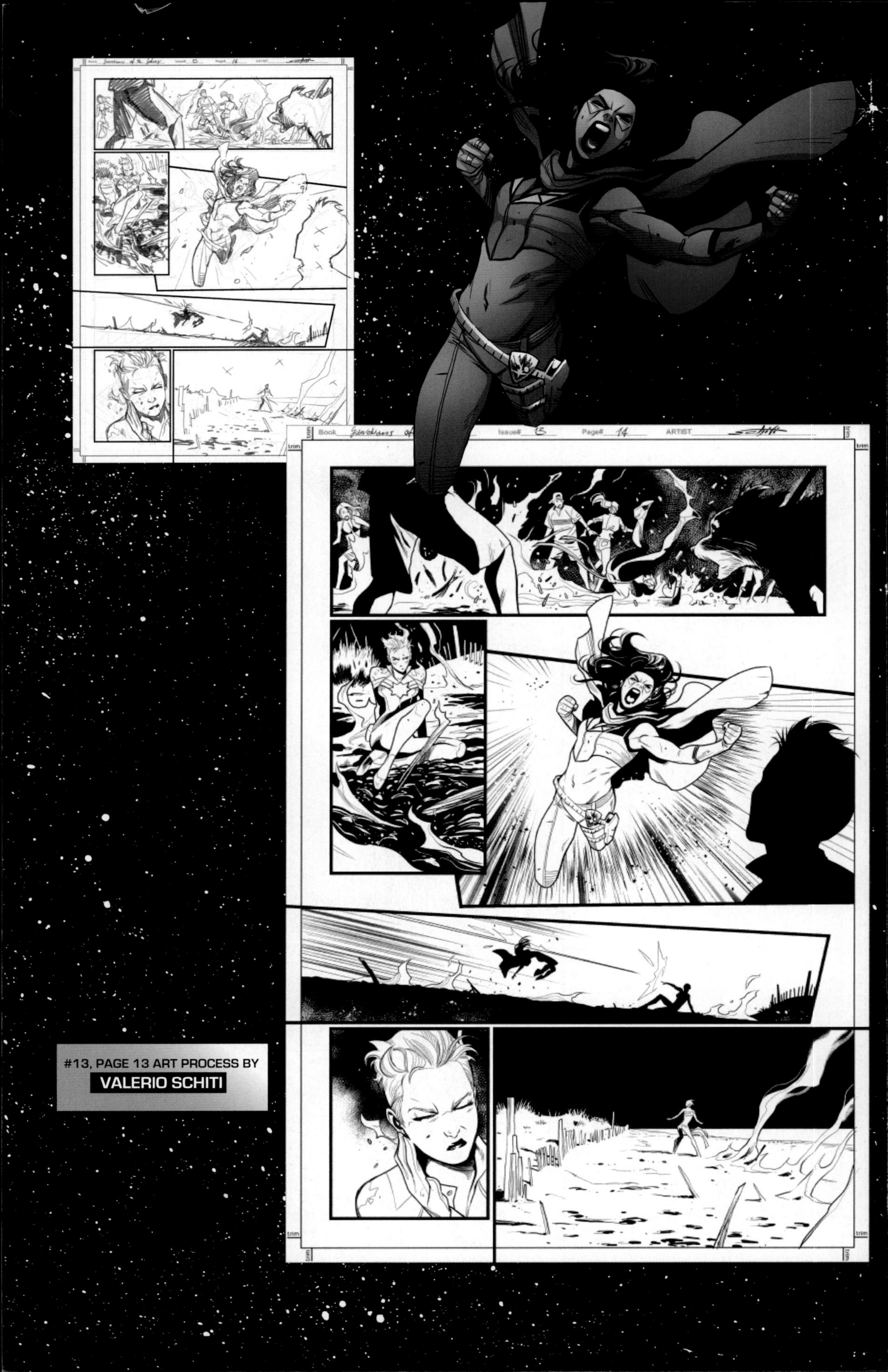
Book Issue# 13 Page# 14 ARTIST

#13, PAGE 13 ART PROCESS BY
VALERIO SCHITI

#13, PAGE 14 ART PROCESS BY
VALERIO SCHITI

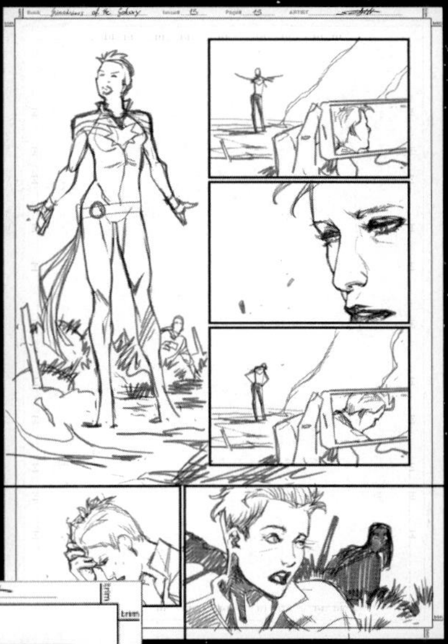

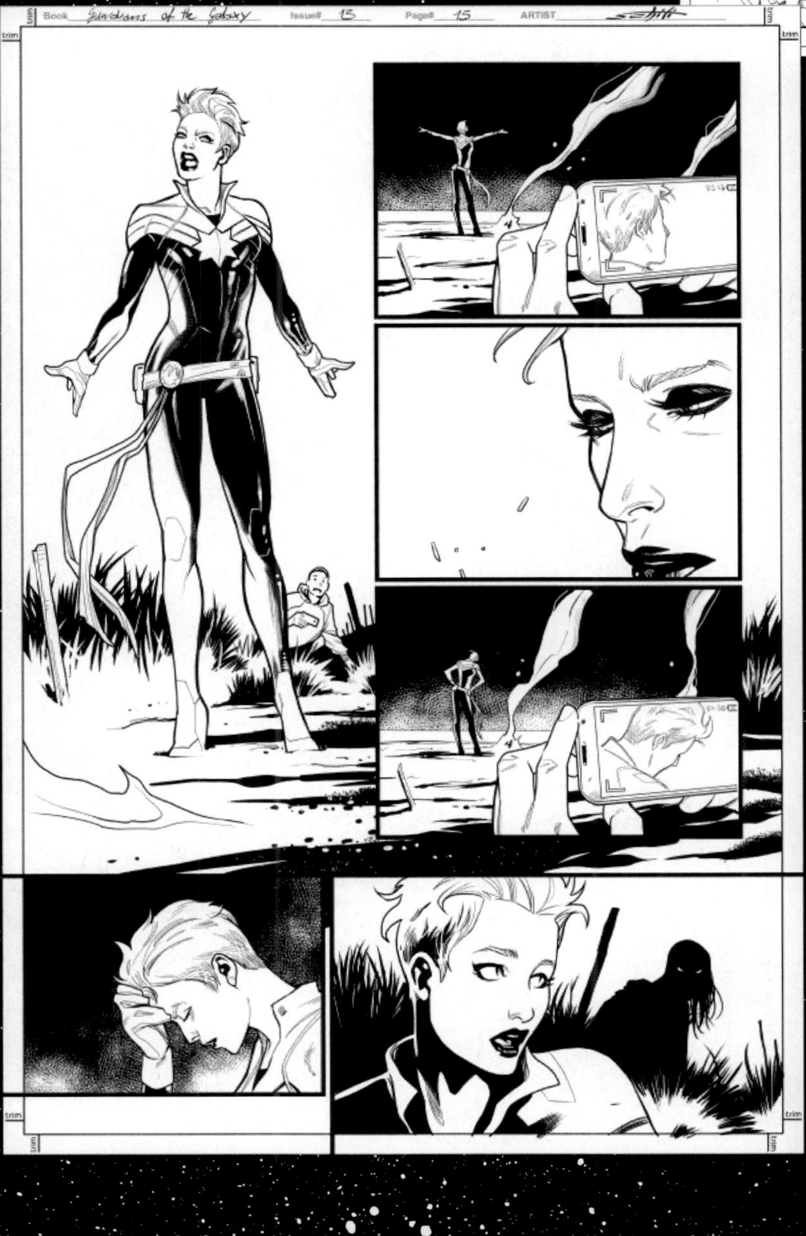

Book Guardians of the Galaxy Issue# 13 Page# 15 ARTIST

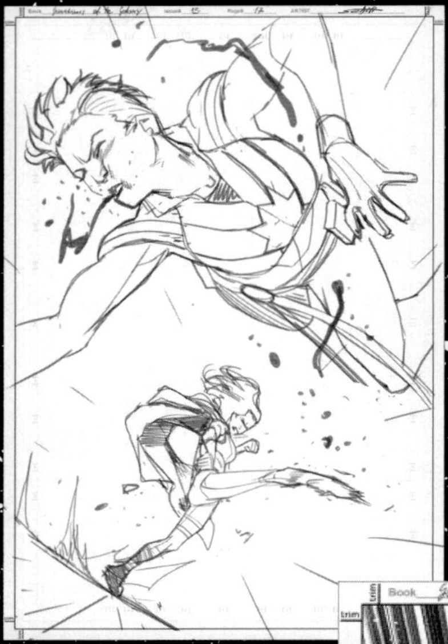

#13, PAGE 16 ART PROCESS BY
VALERIO SCHITI

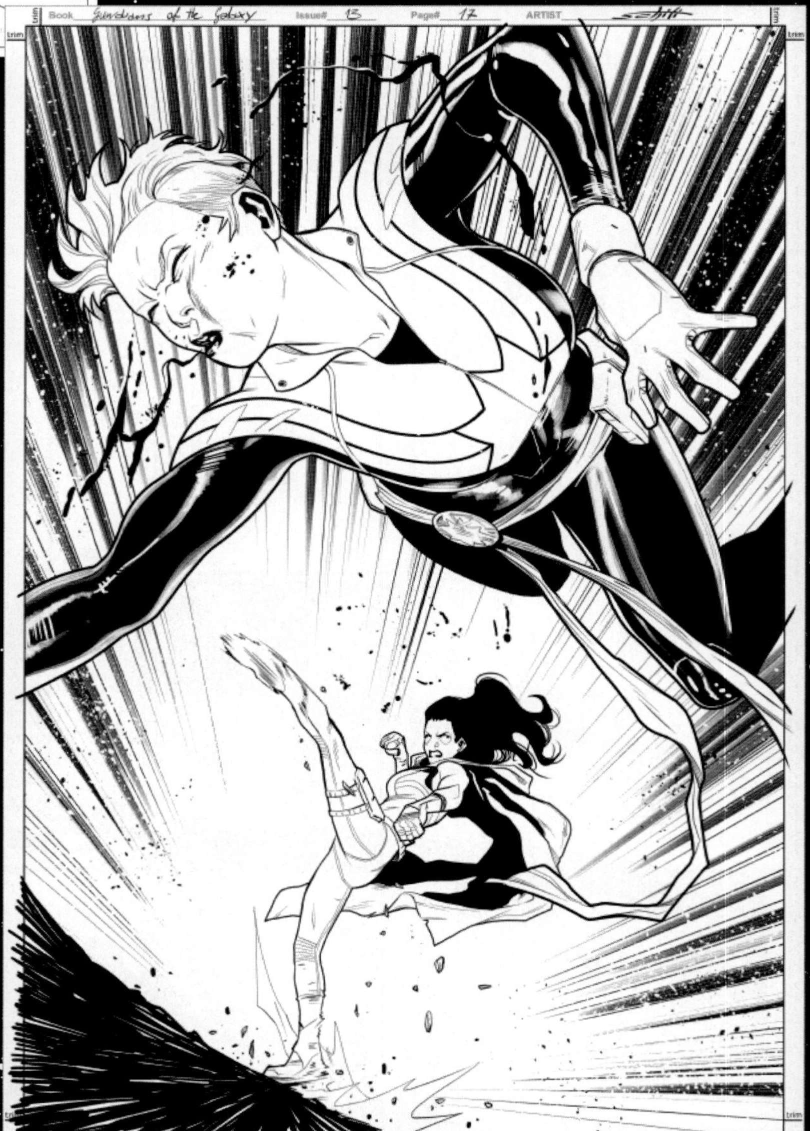
Book Guardians of the Galaxy Issue# 13 Page# 17 ARTIST

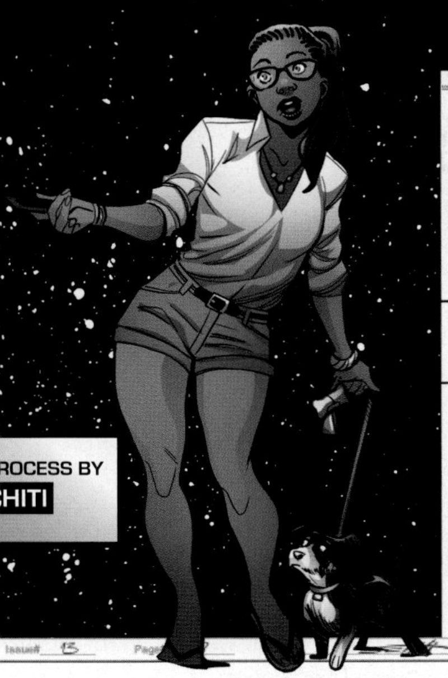

#13, PAGE 17 ART PROCESS BY
VALERIO SCHITI

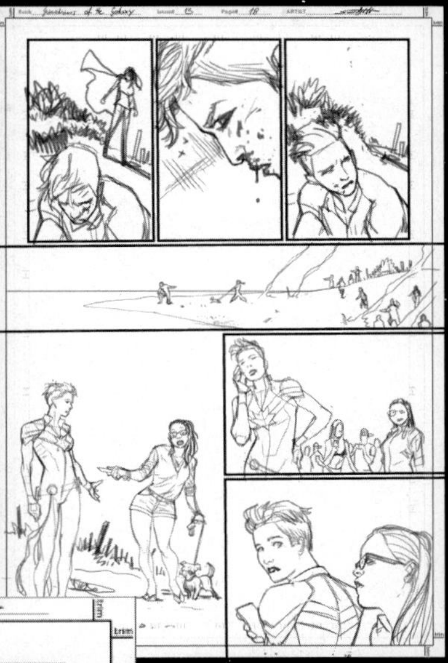

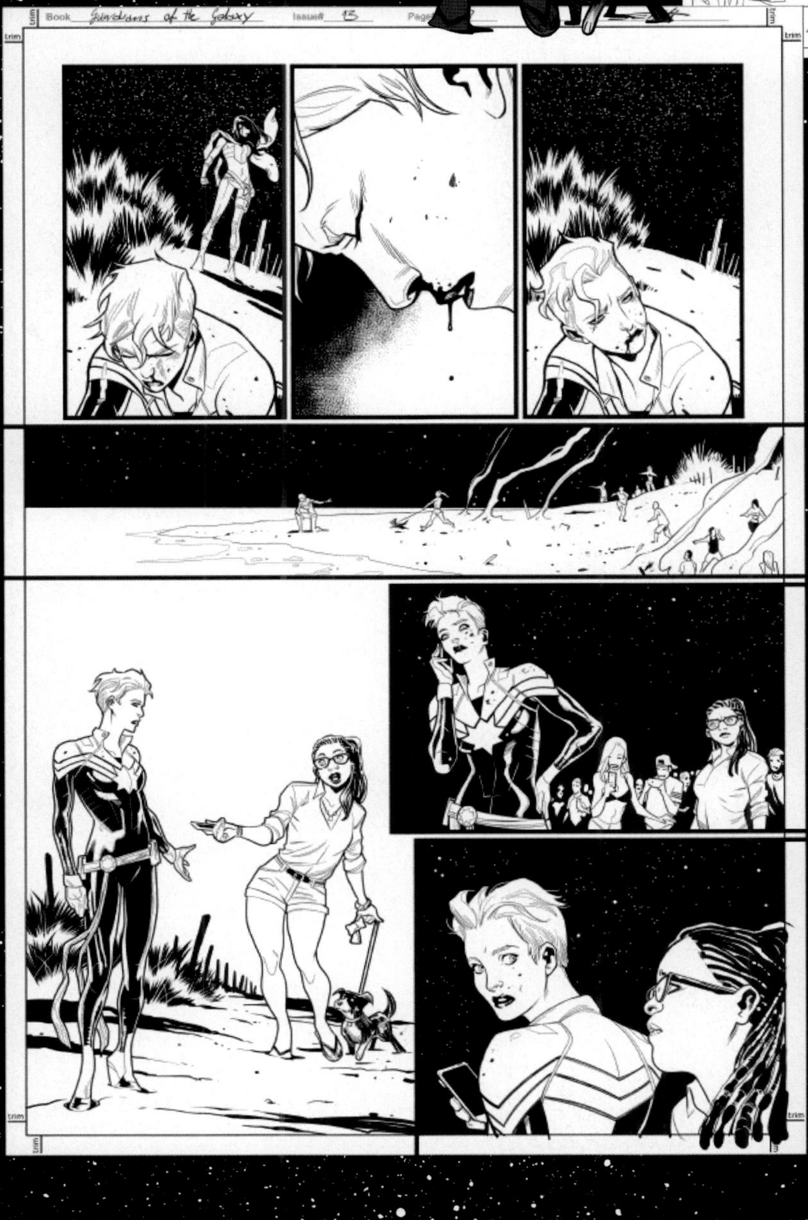

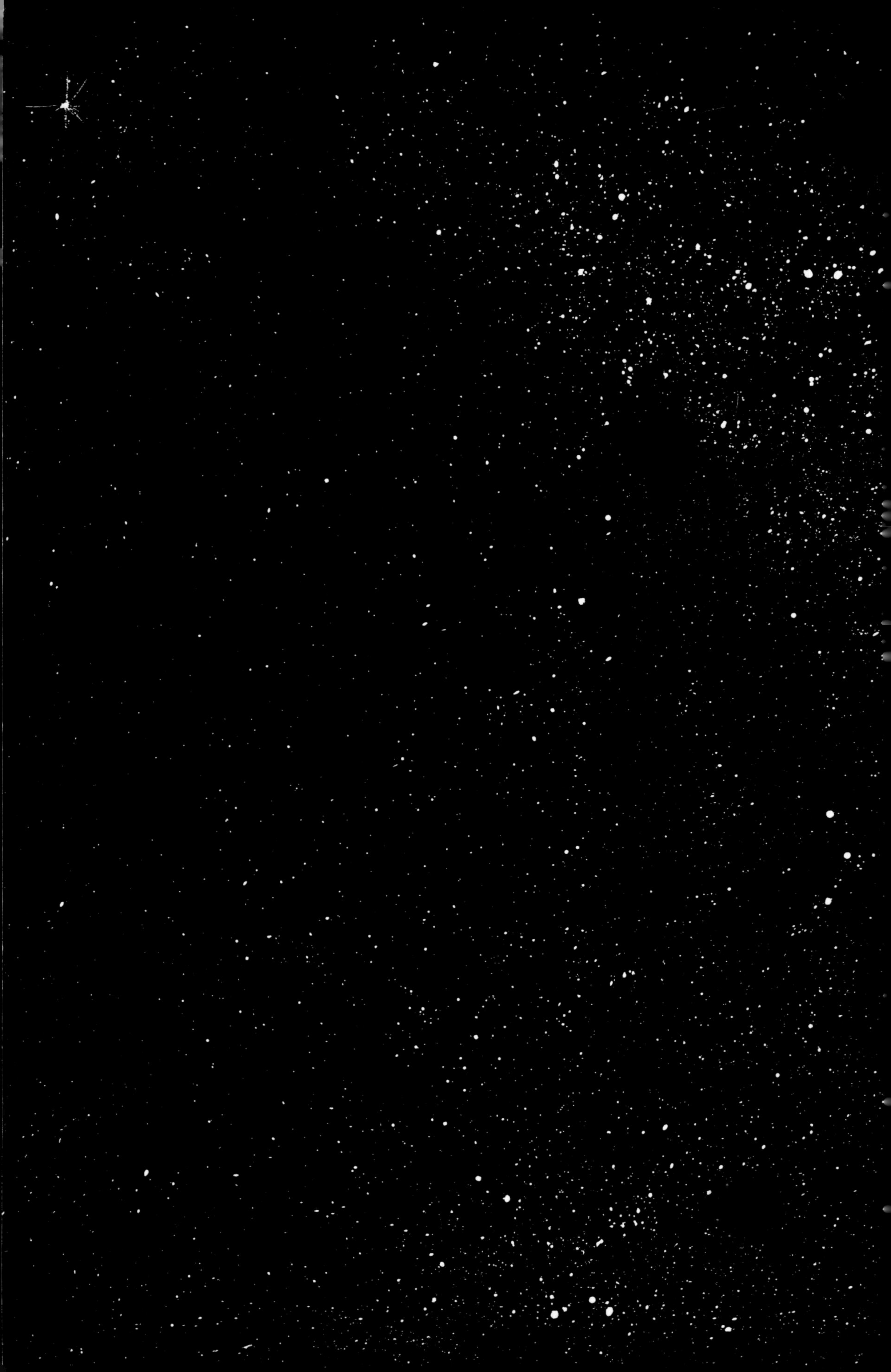